North America
in
Colonial Times

An Encyclopedia
for Students

EDITORS

JACOB ERNEST COOKE
John Henry MacCracken Professor of History Emeritus
Lafayette College
Lafayette, Pennsylvania

MILTON M. KLEIN
Alumni Distinguished Service Professor Emeritus
University of Tennessee
Knoxville, Tennessee

CONSULTANTS

BEVERLEY ACKERT
Teacher of Government, retired
Mount Vernon High School
Mount Vernon, New York

ELEANOR J. BROWN
Library Media Specialist and Head, Information Center
Mount Vernon High School
Mount Vernon, New York

NEAL SALISBURY
Professor of History
Smith College
Northampton, Massachusetts

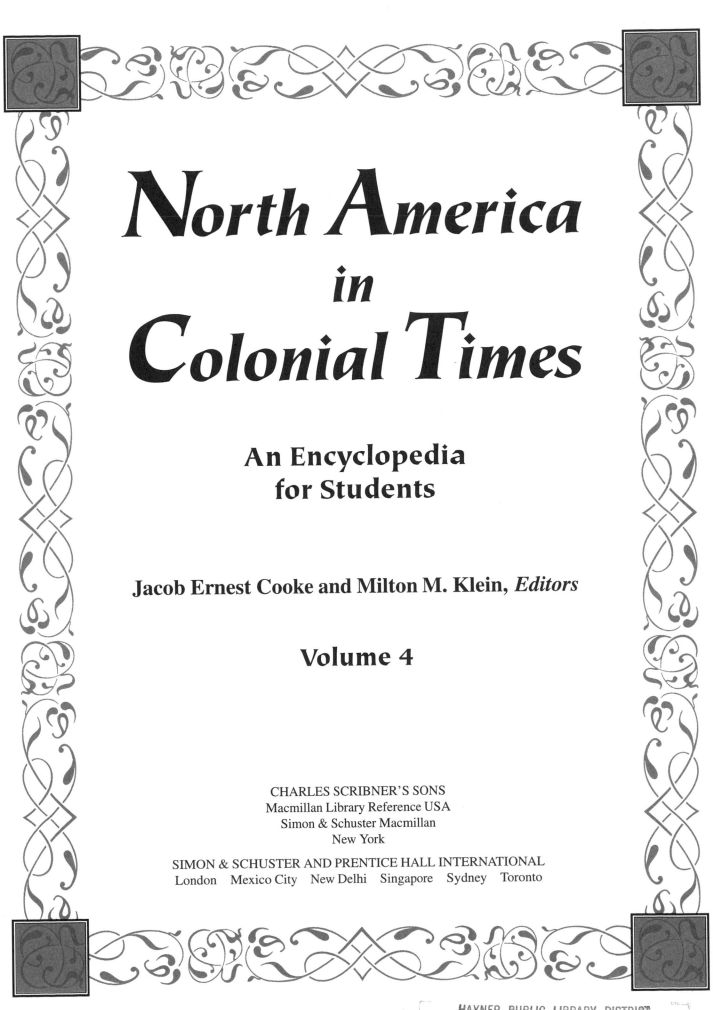

North America
in
Colonial Times

An Encyclopedia
for Students

Jacob Ernest Cooke and Milton M. Klein, *Editors*

Volume 4

CHARLES SCRIBNER'S SONS
Macmillan Library Reference USA
Simon & Schuster Macmillan
New York

SIMON & SCHUSTER AND PRENTICE HALL INTERNATIONAL
London   Mexico City   New Delhi   Singapore   Sydney   Toronto

Developed for Scribners by Visual Education Corporation, Princeton, N.J.

Library of Congress Cataloging-in-Publication Data

North America in colonial times : an encyclopedia for students / Jacob Ernest Cooke and Milton M. Klein, editors.

    p.   cm.

    Adaptation and revision of Encyclopedia of the North American colonies for young readers.
Includes bibliographical references and index.

    Summary: An encyclopedia of the history of the American colonies and Canada, including Native Americans, Spanish missions, English and Dutch exploration, the slave trade, and the French and Indian War.

    ISBN 0-684-80538-3 (set : alk. paper).— ISBN 0-684-80534-0 (v.1 : alk. paper).— ISBN 0-684-80535-9 (v.2 : alk. paper).— ISBN 0-684-80536-7 (v.3 : alk. paper).— ISBN 0-684-80537-5 (v.4: alk. paper)

    1. Europe—Colonies—America—History—Encyclopedias, Juvenile.   2. North America—History—Encyclopedias, Juvenile. [1. North America—History—Colonial period, ca. 1600–1775—Encyclopedias.] I. Cooke, Jacob Ernest, 1924– . II. Klein, Milton M. (Milton Martin), 1917– . III. Encyclopedia of the North American colonies.
E45.N65 1998
970.02—dc21
                        98-29862
                        CIP
                        AC

1 2 3 4 5 6 7 8 9 10

PRINTED IN THE UNITED STATES OF AMERICA

Time Line of North America in Colonial Times

ca. 20,000 B.C.	*The first human inhabitants of the Americas cross from Siberia into Alaska.*
A.D. 985	*Erik the Red establishes a Norse colony in Greenland.*
ca. 1000	*Leif Eriksson lands on the coast of North America.*
ca. 1420	*Prince Henry of Portugal establishes a school of navigation at Sagres, from which seamen set out and discover the Canary, Madeira, and Azores islands.*
1492	*Christopher Columbus, attempting to sail west to Asia, finds the "New World."*
1494	*The Treaty of Tordesillas divides the world between the Spanish and Portuguese empires.*
ca. 1500	*The French begin fishing off the coast of Newfoundland.*
	The Mohawk, Oneida, Onondaga, Cayuga, and Seneca peoples unite to form the Iroquois Confederacy.
1507	*Martin Waldseemüller calls the land explored by Columbus "America" in honor of Amerigo Vespucci, an Italian navigator who was the first to use the term "New World."*
1513	*Juan Ponce de León claims Florida for Spain.*
1518	*African slaves are brought to Hispaniola (Haiti and Dominican Republic) to work in gold mines.*
1518–1521	*Hernando Cortés conquers the Aztecs in Mexico.*
1519–1522	*Ships under the command of Ferdinand Magellan sail around the world.*
1524	*Giovanni da Verrazano explores the North American coast.*
1534–1536	*Jacques Cartier explores the Gulf of St. Lawrence and the St. Lawrence River as far as Montreal.*
1539–1543	*Hernando de Soto explores North America from Florida to the Mississippi River.*
1540–1542	*Francisco Vásquez de Coronado explores the Southwest as far as the Grand Canyon.*
1562–1568	*John Hawkins makes slave-trading voyages from Africa to the West Indies.*
1564	*France establishes Fort Caroline in Florida but quickly loses it to the Spanish.*
1565	*Pedro Menéndez de Avilés founds St. Augustine in Florida.*
1565–1574	*Spain sets up missions and forts between Florida and Virginia.*
1572	*Chief Powhatan unites Algonquian-speaking tribes in the Chesapeake region to form the Powhatan Confederacy.*
1578	*Francis Drake sails around South America and lands in present-day California.*
1583	*Sir Humphrey Gilbert leads an expedition to Newfoundland.*
1585–1590	*The English attempt twice to establish a colony at Roanoke Island. The second settlement mysteriously disappears.*
1598	*Juan de Oñate founds the colony of New Mexico.*
1602	*Bartholomew Gosnold explores the Atlantic coast from southern Maine to Narragansett Bay and transmits smallpox to his Indian trading partners.*

1604	Samuel de Champlain and Pierre du Gua de Monts establish a French settlement at Port Royal in Acadia (present-day Nova Scotia).
1606	James I of England grants charters to the Virginia Company and the Plymouth Company to colonize the Atlantic coast of North America.
1606~1608	The Plymouth Company establishes Saghadoc, an unsuccessful colony in present-day Maine.
1607	Colonists found Jamestown, the first permanent English settlement, in Virginia. Massasoit becomes chief of the powerful Wampanoag of New England.
1608	Samuel de Champlain establishes a French settlement at Quebec.
1609	Henry Hudson explores the Hudson River as far north as present-day Albany. Santa Fe is founded in New Mexico.
1612	New varieties of tobacco are planted in Virginia, launching a tobacco boom in the Chesapeake region.
1613	English forces destroy the Acadian town of Port Royal.
1614	Captain John Smith explores the New England coast. New Netherland Company gains a monopoly on trade in the Dutch colony.
1616	Africans arrive in Bermuda, the first slaves in the English colonies.
1619	The Dutch bring the first blacks to Virginia.
1620	The Pilgrims establish Plymouth colony.
1622	Powhatan Indians fight the English in Virginia.
1624	Thirty families arrive in the Dutch colony of New Netherland.
1625	Jesuits arrive in Quebec.
1626	Peter Minuit becomes director general of New Netherland and buys Manhattan Island from the Indians.
1628	The English take over Acadia and Quebec, which are returned to France in 1632.
1630	The Massachusetts Bay Company establishes a new colony at Boston.
1630~1642	The Great Migration brings 16,000 settlers from England to the Massachusetts Bay colony.
1632	George Calvert, Lord Baltimore, receives a grant to found the colony of Maryland.
1633	French Jesuits establish Quebec College.
1633~1638	English colonists begin settling along the Connecticut River.
1636	Roger Williams founds the colony of Rhode Island. Harvard College is established at Cambridge, Massachusetts.
1636~1637	In the Pequot War, English colonists in Connecticut destroy most of the Pequot tribe.
1636~1638	Anne Hutchinson challenges the authority of religious leaders in Massachusetts, is exiled, and settles in Rhode Island.
1638	Peter Minuit founds New Sweden on the Delaware River.
1639	North America's first hospital, the Hôtel-Dieu, is established in Quebec.
1641	The Bay Psalm Book, the first book printed in the English colonies, appears in Boston.

1642   *French fur traders establish a base at Montreal.*

1642~1649   *The English Civil War pits supporters of the monarch against Parliamentarians (mostly Puritans). King Charles I is executed in 1649, and England becomes a commonwealth.*

1643   *Massachusetts Bay, Plymouth, Connecticut, and New Haven colonies form the New England Confederation.*

1646~1665   *Iroquois Indians raid the Algonquin, Huron, and other neighboring tribes, driving refugees into Quebec and the Great Lakes region.*

1647   *Peter Stuyvesant becomes director general of New Netherland.*

1649   *Maryland passes the Act of Toleration establishing religious freedom for Christians; the act is repealed in 1654.*

1650   *Poems by Anne Bradstreet, the first published American poet, are printed in London.*

1652~1654   *First war between English and Dutch colonists.*

1653~1660   *England is ruled by Oliver Cromwell, Lord Protector of the Commonwealth.*

1654   *The first Jews arrive in New Amsterdam.*

1655   *Peter Stuyvesant conquers New Sweden, ending Swedish colonization in North America.*

1660   *The first Navigation Act requires all goods going into or out of the English colonies to be carried on English ships. The English monarchy is restored under Charles II.*

1663   *Louis XIV of France declares New France a royal province. Charles II of England gives eight proprietors a grant for the colony of Carolina.*

1664   *English naval forces capture New Netherland, which is renamed New York.*

1665~1667   *Second war between the English and the Dutch.*

1666~1667   *French colonial forces attack the Iroquois Confederacy and force it to accept French terms for peace.*

1668   *The English establish Charles Fort at the mouth of the Rupert River in present-day Canada.*

1669   *John Locke draws up the Fundamental Constitutions, a proposed plan of government for the Carolinas.*

1670   *The Hudson's Bay Company gains control of the fur trade in the Hudson Bay region.*

1672   *Royal African Company gains a monopoly on the English slave trade to America and the West Indies.*

1672~1674   *In the third war between the English and the Dutch, the Dutch temporarily regain control of New York.*

1673   *Louis Jolliet and Father Jacques Marquette explore the Mississippi River.*

1675~1676   *King Philip's War: Wampanoag leader Metacom, called King Philip, leads Indians of southern New England in an unsuccessful uprising against the English.*

1676   *Bacon's Rebellion: Virginia settlers, led by Nathaniel Bacon, seize control of the colony.*

1680   *Pueblo Revolt: Pueblo Indians drive Spanish from New Mexico.*

1681   *William Penn receives a charter to establish Pennsylvania from King Charles II of England.*

1682   *English colonists attack Quebec.*
            René-Robert Cavelier, Sieur de La Salle, claims Mississippi River valley for France, calling it Louisiana.

1686–1689	King James II of England creates the Dominion of New England, which includes the colonies of New Hampshire, Massachusetts, Rhode Island, Connecticut, New York, and New Jersey. Sir Edmund Andros is renamed governor of the new province.
1687	Father Eusebio Francisco Kino establishes mission settlements in Pimería Alta (modern Arizona).
1688	Protestant monarchs William II and Mary ascend the throne in England in what is called the Glorious Revolution.
1689–1691	Glorious Revolution in America: Colonists revolt against the Dominion of New England and receive new charters from William and Mary. Leisler's Rebellion: Jacob Leisler seizes control in New York and is executed in 1691.
1689–1697	King William's War brings French and English colonies and their Indian allies into conflict.
1692–1693	Salem witchcraft trials: Nineteen people are hanged as witches in Massachusetts.
1693	The College of William and Mary is founded in Virginia.
1696	Carolina adopts the first slave laws in the British mainland colonies. Spain reconquers New Mexico from the Pueblo Indians.
1699	Pierre Le Moyne d'Iberville founds the first French settlement in Louisiana.
1701	Anglicans create the Society for the Propagation of the Gospel (SPG) to convert Indians and Africans. Yale College is established in New Haven. Antoine de la Mothe Cadillac founds Detroit.
1702–1713	Queen Anne's War brings new conflict between French and English colonists and their Indian allies.
1707	The Act of Union unites England and Scotland into the United Kingdom of Great Britain.
1709	African and Indian slavery is legalized in New France.
1710	British forces conquer Port Royal in Acadia and rename it Annapolis Royal.
1711–1713	Tuscarora War: Carolina colonists join the Yamassee to defeat the Tuscarora Indians.
1713	Treaty of Utrecht: France gives up Acadia, Newfoundland, and Hudson Bay to Great Britain.
1715–1728	Yamassee War: Yamassee attack South Carolina towns and plantations and are defeated by British and Cherokee forces.
1718	Jean Baptiste Le Moyne de Bienville founds New Orleans.
1729	North and South Carolina become separate royal colonies.
1729–1731	Natchez Revolt in Louisiana.
1730	The Great Wagon Road is begun. It eventually stretches from Philadelphia to Georgia.
1731	Benjamin Franklin establishes a circulating library in Philadelphia.
1732	Franklin publishes Poor Richard's Almanack.
1733	James Oglethorpe founds Georgia as a refuge for British debtors. British Parliament passes the Molasses Act, taxing sugar and molasses from the French West Indies.

1734~1735	Clergyman Jonathan Edwards leads a religious revival in Massachusetts.
1735 ·	The trial of publisher John Peter Zenger in New York promotes the principle of freedom of the press.
1737	"Walking Purchase": Delaware Indians sell the colony of Pennsylvania the entire Lehigh Valley.
1738~1745	Great Awakening: English preacher George Whitefield sparks religious revivals throughout the British colonies.
1739	Stono Rebellion: Slaves in South Carolina revolt and are stopped by the militia.
1740s	Eliza Pinckney begins indigo cultivation in South Carolina.
1741	Rumors of plots by slaves to revolt lead to arrests and executions in New York. Russian explorer Vitus Bering lands in Alaska.
1743	Benjamin Franklin establishes the American Philosophical Society in Philadelphia.
1744~1748	King George's War: European war between Britain, France, and Spain spreads to North America.
1746	College of New Jersey (later Princeton University) is founded.
1754	French and Indian War begins when Virginia sends its militia, led by George Washington, to challenge the French in the Ohio Valley. France and Britain officially declare war in 1756.
1755	Britain expels French colonists from Acadia. Many Acadians migrate to Louisiana.
1759~1760	British forces under General James Wolfe capture Quebec. A year later, the French surrender at Montreal.
1762	Spain declares war on Great Britain.
1763	Treaty of Paris: Great Britain wins Florida from Spain and Canada and Cape Breton from France. Spain gains Louisiana. Britain issues proclamation forbidding colonists to settle west of the Appalachian Mountains. Touro Synagogue opens in Newport, Rhode Island.
1763~1766	Chief Pontiac of the Ottawa leads an alliance of Indians against the British in the Great Lakes region.
1764	The Sugar Act imposes high import taxes on non-British sugar, leading to colonial protests.
1765	The Stamp Act provokes outrage and widespread protest in the colonies and is repealed.
1766	British Parliament passes the Declaratory Act to emphasize its "full power and authority" over the colonies.
1767	Jesuits are expelled from Spanish territories. Franciscans take over the western missions. In the British colonies, the Townshend Acts impose new taxes on certain imported items.
1769	Junípero Serra founds the first Spanish mission in California at San Diego.
1770	Boston Massacre: British troops fire into a crowd, killing five colonists.
1773	Boston Tea Party: Colonists protest the tea tax by dumping a shipload of tea into Boston harbor. Publication of Poems on Various Subjects, Religious and Moral by Phillis Wheatley, a slave in Boston.

1774   *Parliament passes the Intolerable Acts to strengthen British authority in Massachusetts.*

In the Quebec Act, Parliament extends the borders of Quebec province southward and grants religious freedom to Catholics, angering American colonists.

The First Continental Congress meets in Philadelphia.

1775   *Battles are fought at Lexington and Concord.*

The Second Continental Congress assembles in Philadelphia.

George Washington takes command of the Continental Army.

1776   *Thomas Paine's* Common Sense *is published in Philadelphia.*

American colonists issue the Declaration of Independence to explain their separation from Great Britain.

1777   *Under military pressure, Cherokee Indians yield their lands to North and South Carolina.*

Vermont declares its independence from New York and New Hampshire.

1778   *Captain James Cook explores the northern Pacific coast.*

1779   *Spain declares war on Britain and enters the American War of Independence.*

1781   *American troops under George Washington and French forces under General Rochambeau defeat British troops led by General Charles Cornwallis at Yorktown, Virginia, winning independence for the United States.*

1783   *Treaty of Versailles: Great Britain recognizes the independence of the United States of America. Florida is returned to Spain.*

1784   *New Brunswick province is established in Canada as a refuge for American Loyalists.*

1789–1793   *Alexander Mackenzie reaches the Pacific coast by traveling overland across Canada.*

1791   *Constitution Act: Britain divides the province of Quebec into Lower Canada (Quebec) and Upper Canada (Ontario).*

1792   *Captain George Vancouver explores the west coast of Canada.*

1794   *Slavery is abolished in French colonies.*

1799   *The Russian-American Company is chartered and given a monopoly to conduct trade in Alaska.*

1800   *Spain returns Louisiana to France.*

1803   *Louisiana Purchase: France sells Louisiana to the United States for $15 million.*

1812–1841   *The Russian-American Company maintains a base at Fort Ross, in northern California.*

1819   *The United States acquires Florida from Spain.*

1821   *Mexico declares independence from Spain.*

1825–1832   *Stephen F. Austin brings American colonists to Texas.*

1833   *Great Britain declares an end to slavery in all its possessions, beginning in 1834.*

1840   *The Act of Union reunites Upper and Lower Canada and grants them self-rule.*

1867   *The British North America Act establishes the Dominion of Canada.*

Russia sells Alaska to the United States.

Race Relations

discrimination unfair treatment of a group

he North American colonies included a mix of Native American, white, and black inhabitants. In no colony did the races live together in equality. Even in peaceful and friendly interactions, nearly all Europeans saw themselves as different from—and superior to—the other races.

In the 1500s and 1600s, Europeans believed themselves to be set apart from Indians and blacks as much by religion and class as by race. As Christians they felt superior to non-Christians, whom they sometimes compared to children or animals. Over the years, racial differences—which everyone could see and recognize—became the primary basis for discrimination*. At the same time, interracial relationships were producing a growing population of mixed-race Americans. The idea of "racial purity" became important to the European governments, which passed laws to control relationships between people of different races.

Conflicts between Indians and white settlers were common in the British colonies. In this picture, which appeared in William Smith's *Historical Account of the Expedition Against the Ohio Indians* (1766), English colonel Henry Bouquet engages in peace talks with the Indians of the Ohio River region.

Race Relations

* **Enlightenment** European intellectual movement of the 1600s and 1700s, based on faith in the power of reason and the idea that individuals have certain fundamental rights

* **Spanish Borderlands** northern part of New Spain, area now occupied by Florida, Texas, New Mexico, Arizona, and California

* **heathen** not believing in the God of the Bible

* **Moors** North African Muslims

* **heresy** belief that is contrary to church teachings

* **status** social position

In the 1700s, new ideas about race appeared in Europe. Among others, QUAKERS and some Enlightenment* writers rejected the enslavement of Africans, arguing that all people were equal. They declared that education, wealth, and power—not race—made some people seem superior to others. These ideas, however, had little effect on the North American colonies, where racism was a fact of life.

Spanish Borderlands. The Spanish Borderlands* were a melting pot where people of three races merged to form new societies. This racial and cultural blending, called *mestizaje* by the Spanish, shaped both the individual's sense of identity and society's structure. The mixing process passed through three stages. In each of these stages, the most powerful group—the whites—viewed race a little differently.

The first stage lasted from the 1530s to about 1770. During this long period, the Spanish maintained a strong sense of separation from the Native Americans they conquered. The Spanish were Christian, "civilized," victorious—and white. The Indians were heathen*, "primitive," conquered—and darker-skinned. Spaniards living in the Americas often compared the Indians to the Moors*, whom Europeans regarded as enemies.

Even Spanish colonists who tried to protect the Indians from torture or massacre did not regard them as equals. The Catholic Church declared that Native Americans were childlike beings without the ability to think properly. This ruling explained the Indians' non-Christian beliefs and prevented them from being punished for heresy*. It also helped the Spanish feel justified in their sense of their own superiority.

Race was just one of the elements in a person's *calidad,* or status*. Also involved in determining an individual's standing in society were gender, age, place of residence, occupation, and ownership of land. People in the Spanish Borderlands recognized three races: Spanish, Indian, and African. The numerous people of mixed races were generally considered Indian or African.

In the second stage, between 1770 and 1800, the Spanish became increasingly concerned with race. The mixed-race population was growing rapidly, and noble families feared that by mixing with inferiors they would lose their honor and social standing. To preserve their sense of superiority, they placed greater emphasis on race than ever before.

The Spanish colonists became obsessed with racial categories. Civil and religious laws made dozens of fine distinctions that specified degrees of "whiteness," "blackness," or "Indianness." For example, people called the child of a Spanish father and an Indian mother a mestizo, the child of a mestizo and a Spanish woman a *castizo,* and the child of a Spanish man and a black woman a mulatto. Each category had its own rules.

Race became the main way that the ruling upper classes defined social position. The whiter a person's skin, the closer that person was to the honored status of being a Spaniard. People with darker skin, by contrast, were considered closer to the Indians or Africans. Although marriage between people of different races was not illegal, society disapproved of it. Most interracial relationships occurred outside of marriage.

The third phase of the mixing process lasted from about 1800 until Mexican independence in 1821. During this period, details about race and color

disappeared from legal documents. People were classified by their economic or social class or by whether or not they owned land—not by race. Though racism was still part of life, people in the Spanish Borderlands no longer used it as the legal basis for determining a person's status or rights.

French Colonies.   Attitudes toward race in the French colonies of NEW FRANCE and LOUISIANA changed over time, as did the French government's attitude toward racial mixing. From the beginning of colonization in New France, French men formed relationships with Indian women. Children born of these unions were called métis. At first the métis were fully accepted into Native American and white colonial society. Though fully aware of people's racial origins, the colonists classified them more by culture than by race. Later, as colonial society became more structured and the number of mixed-race individuals increased, racial prejudice and discrimination emerged.

In the early days, when the French colonies had few white women, the authorities encouraged intermarriage. The Catholic Church knew that relationships between French males and Indian women would occur and preferred these relationships to take place within marriage. The sponsors of the colony believed that intermarriage would help win the Indians' loyalty, increasing trading opportunities for the French and reducing conflict. By 1700, however, the royal government had started to discourage interracial marriage, fearing that the colony's population was becoming too mixed.

Because of this policy, intermarriage became rare by the mid-1700s, though the practice remained legal. By this time, however, the large métis population had grown into a new element in French colonial society. Peter Kalm, a Swedish traveler in the region, noted that "the Indian blood in Canada is very much mixed with European blood, and a large number of the Indians now living owe their origin to Europe."

Race relations in LOUISIANA involved whites, Indians, and blacks, both free and enslaved. In Louisiana both the church and state disapproved of interracial relationships and the children they produced. People of mixed Indian-French and French-black ancestry formed a small population that lived on the fringe of society. This racially mixed group was the foundation of Louisiana's CREOLES of color, who emerged in the 1760s as a significant ethnic group.

New Netherland.   Records from the short-lived Dutch colony that later became New York show that Native Americans, whites, and blacks did intermarry, although not in large numbers. One account notes that in 1660, during a war between the Dutch and the Indians, the Dutch tried to pay ransom for a young man whom the Indians had captured. The Native Americans refused, saying that "the boy has a wife there and the wife is with child, who will not let him go and he will not leave her." Indians also sometimes accepted escaped black slaves into their communities.

By the end of the colonial period, the regions that the Dutch had settled contained a few small, isolated groups descended from racially mixed populations. One such group, in the Ramapo Mountains between New York and New Jersey, was descended from Dutch settlers, free blacks, and—most likely—Native Americans. In 1979 the New Jersey legislature recognized them as an Indian tribe—the Ramapough.

British Colonies. From the beginning of settlement in the British colonies, authorities made efforts to keep the various races apart. In the early years—when survival was in doubt—cooperation and even friendship sometimes existed between whites and Indians. By 1700, however, the white colonists' ideas of racial categories had become fixed, along with the barriers between races.

Soon most colonies had laws that used race as a basis for slavery. The laws also regulated other forms of race relations, such as intermarriage—which was usually illegal. Native Americans, Europeans, and Africans lived and worked together and sometimes intermarried, especially on the FRONTIER. But equality was not built into the legal or social structure of the colonies. British North America was always racially diverse—but never officially integrated.

Outside the British settlements, racial mixing did occur. A number of European colonists and African Americans built new lives among the Indians. Some were captives who decided to remain with the tribes. Others joined the Native Americans of their own free will.

These whites and blacks who abandoned colonial society often brought new skills to their Indian communities, sometimes serving as interpreters and traders. They usually adopted Native American culture. However, in some cases, Indians, whites, and blacks blended to form new, truly interracial societies. Composed of runaway slaves and indentured servants*, outlaws, fugitives, survivors of Indian tribes killed by war or disease, or simply people who wanted to live outside society's limits, these MAROON COMMUNITIES consisted of racially mixed populations in out-of-the-way places. One was located in the Great Dismal Swamp on the border between North Carolina and Virginia. Authorities regarded these communities as a threat to social values—including the separation of the races—and did their best to stamp them out. (*See also* **Free Blacks; Native Americans; Roman Catholic Church; Slave Resistance; Slave Trade.**)

* *indentured servant* person who agreed to work a certain length of time in return for passage on a ship to the colonies

Raleigh, Sir Walter

ca. 1552–1618
English explorer and colonial promoter

* *courtier* person skilled in the manners and customs of a royal court
* *patent* official document conferring a right or privilege

* *privateering* raiding ships of enemy nations for treasure

Sir Walter Raleigh was an English soldier, courtier*, and explorer. Though he never set foot in North America, he did much to promote the colonization of the continent. In 1585 he founded ROANOKE ISLAND, more than 20 years before the establishment of JAMESTOWN.

Raleigh was the half brother of the explorer Sir Humphrey GILBERT, a favorite of Queen ELIZABETH I. The queen granted Gilbert a patent* to establish an English colony in North America, and when Gilbert was lost at sea, she agreed to transfer the patent to his brother.

Raleigh quickly set about making plans for a new colony. In early 1584, he sent an expedition to explore the coast of North America and select a suitable site. When the advance party returned to England later that year, they recommended that the settlement be located on an island off the coast of what is now NORTH CAROLINA, which they called Roanoke Island. Raleigh named all the new territory Virginia in honor of the unmarried Elizabeth, who was known as the Virgin Queen. Pleased with Raleigh's part in claiming North America for England, Elizabeth rewarded him with a knighthood.

Raleigh began recruiting settlers for Roanoke Island. To finance the colony, he raised money by privateering*. He also received funds from the queen on the condition that he remain at court because she feared he would

die at sea as his brother did. As a result, Raleigh appointed two other men to lead the expedition. He also sent along a scientist, Thomas Harriot, and an artist, John WHITE, who provided the first detailed information about the people, plants, and animals in this strange new land. Arriving in July 1585, the settlers remained at Roanoke Island less than a year. Disputes within the community, dwindling supplies, and fear of the Indians made returning to England seem advisable.

Though Raleigh had lost a fortune in the failed colony, he proceeded to organize another group of settlers. The new colonists arrived in North America in the spring of 1587 and established their settlement on the same spot as the first group. Shortly after, the leader of the expedition, John White, went back to England to report to Raleigh and to obtain additional supplies. Naval warfare with Spain delayed White's return to Roanoke Island for three years. When he finally arrived, he found the colony deserted. The fate of the Roanoke colonists remains a mystery to this day.

Raleigh made no further attempts to establish a colony in North America. He lost Queen Elizabeth's support for such ventures after he married secretly without her permission. Banned from court, Raleigh was free to travel and explore. In 1595 he sailed for South America in search of gold in the swamps and jungles along the Orinoco River. Although the expedition failed to find gold, Raleigh's writings about his adventures added to the growing knowledge about the Western Hemisphere.

The explorer's standing at court declined even further when King James I, who wanted to make peace with Spain, took the throne. Because of his open hostility toward the Spanish, Raleigh was convicted of treason and imprisoned in the Tower of London under sentence of death. After 13 years, he was released to lead a second expedition to South America in search of gold. On returning to England empty-handed, Raleigh was executed.

Ranching

anching involves the raising of livestock—primarily cattle, horses, and sheep—usually on flat or rolling grasslands. During the colonial period in North America, ranching developed in the Spanish Borderlands, the area now occupied by Florida, Texas, New Mexico, Arizona, and California.

The *estancia,* or ranch, played a crucial role in the economy of Spanish North America. Vast areas of the Borderlands had an arid or semiarid climate that was not well suited to growing crops. However, the region's dry grasslands could be used for grazing livestock.

When the early Spanish explorers and colonists came to North America, they brought cattle, sheep, and horses with them. The original herds of the livestock thrived, and ranching became a way of life throughout the Spanish Borderlands. It dominated the region's economy and culture during the entire colonial period. Although basically similar throughout the Spanish Borderlands, ranching developed in slightly different ways in each province.

Spanish colonizer Pedro MENÉNDEZ DE AVILÉS brought cattle to FLORIDA in the mid-1500s in the hope of starting a profitable breeding business. One of the first important cattle ranches, located near present-day Gainesville,

Ranching

See map in Spanish Borderlands (vol. 4).

belonged to the colony's royal treasurer. Other large ranches were established near ST. AUGUSTINE and present-day Tallahassee. Cattle ranching gradually grew into a successful business, despite periodic setbacks caused by Indian revolts, disease, and pirate raids. By the 1690s, the number of cattle had increased dramatically, causing the price of beef to drop because of oversupply. Ranchers faced greater problems in the early 1700s, when British forces from South Carolina overran Florida and destroyed many ranches. Many of the cattle that survived ran wild and roamed throughout Florida during the 1700s.

The founder of NEW MEXICO, Juan de OÑATE, brought the first livestock to the province in the late 1500s. Descended from ancient breeds, the cattle and sheep he introduced were tough enough to thrive in New Mexico's harsh climate. Their numbers increased rapidly, and raising livestock on ranches and missions soon became one of the principal occupations in the colony. The PUEBLO REVOLT of 1680, which drove the Spanish from New Mexico for 12 years, dealt a serious blow to ranching. But after the Spanish reconquered the territory in 1696, ranching recovered, and sheep became more important than cattle. Controlled by a few wealthy families, sheep ranching dominated the region's economy into the 1800s.

The Spanish missionary Eusebio Francisco KINO introduced livestock into ARIZONA in the early 1700s. Ranches grew up around the region's missions, and a profitable business soon began to take shape. By the mid-1700s, however, attacks by APACHE INDIANS had drastically reduced the numbers of livestock. As relations with the Apache improved in the late 1780s, the livestock population began to increase. Although the herds remained smaller than those in other Spanish provinces, cattle and sheep ranching were undoubtedly the most important industries in Arizona.

Like the other Spanish provinces, CALIFORNIA developed a thriving ranching business. Introduced in the mid-1700s, livestock increased slowly at first. By the 1780s, however, almost all colonial settlements were heavily involved in ranching. Missions and presidios* raised thousands of animals for their own use. The Spanish crown also granted land to individuals to start ranches. By 1800 California had about 190,000 head of cattle, horses, and sheep. Horses became so numerous that many had to be killed to prevent them from damaging crops. Thousands of horses and cattle escaped from ranches and ran wild.

Cattle and horses were the dominant livestock in TEXAS, where ranching began in the early 1700s. By 1750 cattle herds had grown greatly in size, encouraging Texas ranchers to sell their extra animals outside the colony. Because Spanish policy prohibited exporting livestock, Texans began smuggling cattle into the neighboring colony of LOUISIANA and exchanging the cattle for trade goods. Such exports were made legal in 1780. Texas ranchers faced serious difficulties, including attacks by Apache and COMANCHE INDIANS. But the cattle business continued to grow, quickly becoming the center of a distinctive Texas culture. The Texas cowboy—descended from the Spanish vaquero, or cattle herder—developed into a legendary figure of the American West, an image that survives to this day. (*See also* **Agriculture; Animals; Economic Systems; Frontier; Missions and Missionaries; Presidios; Spanish Borderlands.**)

* *presidio* Spanish fort built to protect mission settlements

Recreation and Sports

*L*ife in the North American colonies involved plenty of hard work, particularly for the early settlers. Nonetheless, colonists still found time for recreation. They based many of their pastimes on European traditions and borrowed a few from Native Americans. Colonists also developed new leisure activities and sports to suit the conditions of life in the colonies.

Recreation and sports served many purposes for those living in North America. Besides providing an opportunity for relaxation and pleasure, they taught skills, strengthened community ties, and gave individuals the chance to test their abilities against others. Community events such as barn raisings allowed people to share their scarce labor resources and socialize at the same time. Among Native Americans, many sports also had religious or political aspects.

Native Americans

Physical activity and competitions played a large role in the existence of Native Americans at every stage of life. The distinction between work and play was often blurred. Some pastimes helped children learn skills they would need in adulthood. Boys played hunting games, for example, while girls imitated their mothers' farming and housekeeping duties. Hunting and fishing provided both enjoyment and food. Teenage boys and adult men held races and archery and wrestling contests that sharpened their survival skills.

Almost every Native American community enjoyed ball games. Tribes in the east and on the Great Plains played the game *baggataway*. Known to white colonists in variations called lacrosse or stickball, it involved a small hard ball and a stick with a net or cup on one end. Indians also participated in games consisting of kicking and throwing balls, which were sometimes played over great distances—for example, between two villages. Southeastern tribes invented a game in which players tossed a ball into a basket or container on top of a pole.

Indian women played many of the same games as men. Sometimes they joined in with men, and at other times they played by themselves. Frequently, they acted as spectators.

Indians often engaged in recreation purely for pleasure, but sports also had a spiritual side. Physical activities such as footraces were sometimes part of religious ceremonies meant to cure illness, prepare for war, bring fertility to people and animals, or produce rain. Dances brought men and women and all age groups together in an activity that often combined recreation and religion.

Group games and competitions—which sometimes turned violent—had important political meaning. Within a community, team sports gave people practice in leadership and decision making. They were also a way of settling disputes between communities without going to war. Native Americans took these competitions very seriously and prepared for them with great care, sometimes following a special diet beforehand.

Because of the link between their games and physical activities and their religion and politics, Indians rarely adopted European forms of recreation. But they did share an enthusiasm for gambling with many British and French

By Hook or by Crook

The Indian game *baggataway* had few rules and only two pieces of equipment: a hide-covered ball and a curved stick with a pouch attached to the end. Players used the stick to throw and catch the ball. Matches between tribes could last for two or three days, with more than 20 players on each team. French colonists called the game lacrosse because the curved stick resembled a shepherd's crook, known in French as a *crosse*. Although lacrosse became popular in the French colonies, the first recorded match between white players did not take place until 1844.

Most Indian tribes engaged in ball sports. This engraving of a painting by George Catlin shows the Choctaw "ball-play dance," a type of stickball.

frontiersmen. Both Europeans and Indians frequently bet on physical contests or games of chance. White colonists borrowed some Indian hunting and fishing methods and occasionally competed with Native Americans in physical contests.

British and Dutch Settlers

The British colonists enjoyed a wider variety of pastimes than any other settlers in North America. Sports and games had become popular in England. After establishing settlements, colonists made the most of their leisure time and turned to sports and other forms of recreation as an escape from the pressures of their daily lives.

Sporting activities in the colonies differed from those in England. The aristocracy* controlled the land and game animals in England, but in North America, common people could hunt almost anywhere they liked without interference from authorities.

* **aristocracy** people of the highest social class, often nobility

Colonial recreation was subject to some rules, however. Every colony had laws against playing sports on Sunday, the day that Christians were supposed to devote to religion. Yet these laws were hard to enforce—even in New England, which had the strictest Sunday laws of any region. By the early 1700s, many communities had given up trying to enforce Sunday restrictions.

Types of Recreation. Children played many familiar games from England and Europe, including tennis, badminton, marbles, hopscotch, leapfrog, bowling, and hide-and-seek. They also liked games that involved throwing, kicking, or batting balls.

Many adult recreational activities were versions of work or other everyday activities. Hunting and fishing, for example, combined duty and pleasure. Sports such as archery and target shooting helped develop important skills. Forms of transportation—horseback riding, running, boating, and swimming—became recreational activities.

Community residents often pooled their labor to help a neighbor with a big job such as raising a barn or husking a crop of corn. They usually turned the occasion into a social event with singing and dancing, large quantities of food, storytelling, and contests of strength and skill. Women had their own kind of work parties known as "bees." They gathered in groups to make an item such as a quilt for one of their members. They also held knitting and sewing bees.

Colonists—particularly those in newly settled areas—were constantly aware of the possibility of war or attack, and it was part of every man's duty to be prepared for military action. As a result, men throughout the colonies took part in combat sports such as wrestling, archery, fencing, and cudgeling, or fighting with sticks.

Blood sports involving animals were also popular in the British colonies. In cockfighting, two trained game birds with metal blades attached to their legs fought until one or both died. Bullbaiting and bearbaiting involved a pack of dogs that attacked a tied animal. In "gander pulling"—a sport begun by Dutch colonists—a man on a horse or in a boat tried to pull the head off a greased goose hanging from a rope.

Recreation in England revolved around religious holidays that included fairs, FESTIVALS, and games. Colonists did not celebrate many of the holidays observed by the Church of England. Instead, they substituted their own occasions for merriment, such as commercial trade fairs and school commencements. In Boston, for example, the entire town celebrated graduation day at Harvard College. Government occasions such as court days, elections, and militia rallies also provided opportunities for socialization and celebration.

Regional Variations. Each region in British North America had different policies about recreation. The PURITANS of New England took steps to ban sports and similar activities. They believed that most pastimes were immoral*. Puritan authorities also outlawed unnecessary travel and all holy day celebrations, including Christmas. The only occasion for group sports was the day when militiamen gathered for military training. Such gatherings were accompanied by drinking, gambling, wrestling, running, and shooting contests.

* *immoral* wicked

Recreation and Sports

Hunting became a popular sport among well-to-do British colonists. Unlike England, North America had a plentiful supply of game animals and no restrictions on hunting. This 1800 painting by an unknown artist shows an organized hunting party with horses and hounds.

The Puritans, however, did allow children to play games, especially ball games. They believed adults should exercise, but only in healthy, productive ways, such as hunting and fishing. Teenagers and adults were supposed to avoid activities that might lead to immoral behavior or distract them from their responsibilities to work, family, and God. Drinking, dancing, gambling, horse racing, and cockfighting were forbidden by the Puritans. Nevertheless, people throughout New England privately pursued these and other activities, although seldom on Sunday. As time passed and the influence of the Puritans weakened, New Englanders took a more relaxed, open attitude toward sports and other types of recreation.

In the middle colonies of New York, Pennsylvania, New Jersey, and Delaware, the mix of people from different backgrounds led to a great variety of sports and recreational activities. Swedish and Scottish settlers were especially fond of games of chance, horse racing, and community gatherings associated with harvests and barn raisings. The Scots also brought traditional games of the Scottish Highlands to the colonies, including footraces, throwing the caber—a heavy pole—and pole vaulting.

The short-lived Dutch colony of New Netherland, which later became New York, contributed bowling, hockey, and ice skating to the recreational life of the region. The English who took over New Netherland in 1664 introduced fox hunting and organized horse racing on oval courses.

Aside from field sports such as hunting and fishing, recreational activities caught on slowly in New Jersey and Pennsylvania because of opposition from the QUAKERS. But by the 1700s, racing, gambling, putting on plays, and socializing in TAVERNS had become quite popular in the region. Rural communities also celebrated at agricultural fairs and harvest festivals.

People in the South embraced sports and recreation more eagerly than any group in colonial America. For prosperous planters, elaborate and expensive leisure activities were a way of demonstrating wealth, style, and freedom. Eager to be seen as a privileged group within society, planters and their families imitated the way of life of English nobility, devoting themselves to

hunting, shooting, racing, dancing, and gambling at cards. Gambling fever reached a high point in the South, where people bet on everything from political elections to games of chance. Bets might involve a year's income, slaves, or an entire estate.

Cockfights—held in semisecrecy in the northern colonies—took place openly in the South with specially trained birds from England. Planters also imported horses to improve their stables of racing animals. Horse racing was immensely popular in the South, and people throughout the region prized Virginia's quarter horses, a breed that performed well on quarter-mile tracks.

Recreation on the frontier revolved around field sports and physical contests such as tug-of-war and wrestling matches. Settlers in the backcountry stubbornly resisted efforts to control their often violent sporting activities. These included "gouging," a no-holds-barred combat sport in which men kicked, bit, stomped, poked out eyeballs, and ripped off ears. Frontier communities sang and danced at loud hoedowns—square dances—and enjoyed themselves at bees. They also fished and hunted, often using techniques borrowed from Indians.

African Americans

The majority of blacks in colonial North America lived in the British colonies. In the northern colonies, free blacks took part in the same types of recreation and sports as lower-class whites—though separately. They did sometimes attend white sporting activities as spectators. The group activities of northern blacks included a handful of festivals celebrated with music, dancing, and parades.

African Americans in the South took part in a greater variety of sports. Sometimes they were involved in the white colonists' recreational world, as when slave children played with white children or black men rowed racing or pleasure boats for whites. Southern blacks also trained and rode race horses and joined whites as spectators at some sporting events.

African Americans had their own activities in the slave quarters of the southern plantations. Recreation was especially important as one of the few ways a slave could win status* or build self-esteem. Occurring away from white supervision, these pastimes also gave enslaved blacks a sense of freedom.

Despite the brutal realities of slavery, most slaves did have some opportunities for play. Weekends and holidays were the main time for recreation. Among African Americans' favorite pastimes were hunting and fishing, which provided food and sometimes a little income. Children played games such as hopscotch and jump rope. Gambling was a big part of leisure activities because it gave slaves a chance to increase their material goods. They eagerly bet prized possessions on the outcome of card or marble games, races, or cockfights.

The African heritage of slaves strongly influenced their singing and dancing. Group activities such as "ring shout" and "patting juba" involved rhythmic handslapping and singing that came from West Africa. For African Americans, dances served as tests of physical strength and skill. They also provided opportunities for slaves to express themselves and gain the praise of others.

* *status* social position

See color plate 4, vol. 2.

French Settlers

Spread out over a vast region, French settlers in North America could not continue the traditional community-based recreational activities that they had enjoyed in their homeland. Instead they developed new sports and pastimes shaped by the new land's climate and geography and influenced by Indian practices.

Rugged mountains, dense forests, and an abundance of lakes and rivers offered many recreational opportunities, as did the severe winter conditions that gripped Canada for as much as six months of the year. Roaming through forests richly supplied with game, French colonists soon learned new methods of hunting and fishing from the Indians. They also turned Native American forms of transportation into competitive sports—canoeing and footraces in the summer and skiing, ice-skating, and snowshoe racing in the winter.

To impress Native Americans with their courage and strength and earn Indians' respect, missionaries and frontiersmen engaged in physical contests against each other or against Indians. Footraces were the most popular kind of competition between Indians and Frenchmen. Following Native American tradition, these races usually covered distances of at least three miles. There was little horse racing in the French colonies because the few horses in the region were needed for work and travel. French settlers also played lacrosse, which they based on the Indian game *baggataway*. The sport gained popularity in part because of its similarity to a game played in France.

Gambling was a way of life in the backcountry, and the French found the Native Americans eager to take part in games of chance and betting. Military and combat contests such as target shooting and wrestling were also popular in the backcountry. Rail-splitting events and similar activities helped settlers turn work into pleasure and competition.

In frontier areas, people of different social classes sometimes participated in sports and other types of recreation together. But in Montreal and Quebec, the various levels of society generally enjoyed their leisure activities separately. The upper classes liked to ride or race carriages in the summer and sleighs in the winter and to attend dancing parties. The lower classes found entertainment in taverns, where they could play card games and gamble as well as drink.

After Great Britain took over France's northern colonies in 1763, British traditions spread into the former French territory. British soldiers introduced curling, a sport played on ice in which players push a polished stone across ice toward a target. The British also organized ice hockey and lacrosse into team sports and opened a horse track.

Spanish Settlers

* ***Spanish Borderlands*** northern part of New Spain, area now occupied by Florida, Texas, New Mexico, Arizona, and California

In the Spanish Borderlands*, Native Americans and Spanish settlers had their own separate pastimes. More than the French or British colonists, the Spanish in North America preserved many games and other forms of entertainment from their homeland.

The entire Spanish community—rich and poor—enjoyed theatrical events. In each village, a troupe of entertainers staged plays and musicals.

These spectacles strengthened the settlers' cultural traditions, as many plays dealt with Spanish history or with Christianity.

The fiesta—a large party or festival—was the most popular pastime in New Mexico, the first place in the Borderlands to have a sizable Spanish population. Of all social activities, the fiesta had the most "American" flavor. Instead of the music or dances of Spain, Spanish settlers at these events performed folk dances that had developed locally. Many of these dances included Native American elements.

Some fiestas celebrated religious holidays. Others marked important events in community or family life, such as a yearly market or a wedding. The wealthy people of the community competed to offer the most costly and extravagant party. Fiestas included a variety of games and contests, usually involving gambling. Gentlemen in the Borderlands often gambled to show off their wealth. They bet large sums—sometimes even entire ranches—on the roll of the dice, the turn of a card, or the speed of a horse.

Spanish men also favored activities they believed demonstrated their bravery and other "manly" qualities. One such activity was the horse race, which was a straight sprint. Another was the bloody "rooster race," in which players buried a chicken up to its neck and then galloped past on horseback and tried to pull the bird out of the ground by its head. Rival teams snatched at the bird until little was left of it. The rooster race was the only Spanish sport adopted by the PUEBLO INDIANS.

After 1821 Americans began flooding the Spanish Borderlands. Eventually, American sports became more popular than traditional Spanish ones, especially in large cities such as Santa Fe and El Paso. (*See also* **Drama; Music and Dance.**)

Regulators

*T*he Regulators were colonists in the frontier areas of the Carolinas who banded together in the 1760s to establish law and order, fight political corruption, and change local government. Their movement reflected the hostility between pioneers living in the backcountry, who felt they were not adequately represented in the colonial assemblies, and wealthy landowners and government officials of the coastal regions.

The most important Regulator movement began in NORTH CAROLINA in 1764. Settlers in the backwoods had grown angry with the corrupt legal system that imposed excessive taxes, charged high court fees, and forced immediate repayment of debts. After failing to convince colonial officials to change these practices, they organized groups to "regulate" local government. The Regulators harassed judges and other public officials, interfered with local courts, and refused to pay taxes. They sometimes resorted to violence, including whipping lawyers and destroying their homes. The colonial government finally decided to put an end to the troublesome movement by force. In May 1771, Governor William Tryon and a colonial militia* defeated the Regulators in the Battle of Alamance. Many Regulators fled west to Tennessee.

Another Regulator movement arose in South Carolina in 1767. At that time, bands of roaming outlaws were terrorizing settlements in the western

* *militia* army of citizens who may be called into action in a time of emergency

13

part of the colony. Leading colonists organized armed groups of Regulators to impose law and order. The Regulator movement in South Carolina ended in 1769, when the colonial assembly created local courts to administer justice in the backcountry. (*See also* **Frontier; Laws and Legal Systems.**)

Religions, Native American

*T*he religions of the early Native Americans were varied and complex, reflecting the diverse histories and cultures of the peoples. The religions also differed greatly from those of European colonists. Europeans tended to separate religion from everyday activities and to restrict religious rituals* and practices to specific occasions. Native Americans regarded religion and spirituality as part of the fabric of daily life, and their religious beliefs and ceremonies played a role in everything they did.

The Spiritual World. An important feature of all Native American religions was a deep belief in a spiritual world. The Indians described this world, which consisted of a variety of figures, forces, and powers, in their myths and legends. They attempted to communicate with it in their ceremonies. Some spirits were close at hand and could be easily contacted through ritual and prayer. Others were far removed from humans.

Many Indian tribes believed in an all-powerful spirit who inhabited all parts of existence. For the Algonquin peoples, this spirit was *manitou;* for the IROQUOIS, it was *orenda.* There were also countless forces or spirits associated with waters, winds, rocks, animals, plants, and other elements of the physical world. These forces had moral and religious power that shaped the daily lives of Indians. The villages of the OSAGE INDIANS, for example, were divided into two halves representing the spirits Earth and Sky that made the world fruitful. To maintain the balance and unity of these forces, Osage marriages were always between individuals from different halves of the village.

Expressing Religious Beliefs. The Indians did not have sacred writings or formal statements of religious doctrine*. Instead, they expressed their beliefs through rituals, ceremonial dances, costumes, masks, songs, prayers, and stories. Even architecture played a role in religion. Among the HOPI INDIANS, for example, the shape and location of kivas—underground chambers used for religious ceremonies—had great significance.

Complex religious ceremonies were held at important points in life. These often included dances and songs performed by individuals wearing costumes and masks representing spirits. The rituals were not performed to celebrate the occasion but to help bring about change. Thus, new year ceremonies brought about the change of the year, rites of passage* transformed a child into an adult, and funeral rites helped the dead make the transition from life to death.

In European religions, activities such as prayer and fasting generally focused on the needs and salvation of the individual. For Native Americans, by contrast, all religious rituals involved the community. Even ceremonies performed to assist individuals benefited the group because any advantage gained by a person strengthened the community. In the same way, violations

* *ritual* ceremony that follows a set pattern

* *doctrine* set of principles or beliefs accepted by a religious or political group

See color plate 3, vol. 2.

* *rite of passage* ceremony marking a change in a person's position in society, such as coming of age or marriage

of sacred traditions threatened not just the individual who committed the error but the community as well.

Native Americans expressed religious beliefs through a variety of symbolic objects and animals. In many of their cultures, religious symbolism centered on a single object, such as corn or tobacco, that had a variety of uses and meanings. Some animals—such as the eagle, bear, and wolf—also served as religious symbols. Among the NAVAJO INDIANS, the broken or open circle was a dominant religious symbol used in design and rituals.

Native American art was a form of religious expression as well. Masks, sand paintings, pottery designs, weavings, and other forms of Indian art played a part in many rituals. For Native Americans, the use of such objects in religious ceremonies—rather than their possession and display as art objects—was the primary reason for creating the art.

Religion and the Physical World.   European traditions tended to link religion with the idea of time and progress. Europeans believed that individuals could improve their souls over time, and they associated the passage of time with a movement toward perfection. They also worshipped on certain days and at regular times, with certain seasons and holy days marking high points of religious activity. Religious services, however, were not tied to a particular place and could be held anywhere.

Native Americans tended to think in terms of space rather than time. They regarded the physical world as a place of perfect balance and harmony, and instead of trying to change it, they sought to understand it. Religious beliefs and observances based on the physical world helped give meaning to their lives.

Indians believed that the physical world and everything in it was alive and filled with spiritual energy. Because of this, all things—from humans to

Artist Jacques Le Moyne produced a series of illustrations of the Indians of Florida in the late 1500s. Here, Native Americans perform a religious ritual in which they offer a deer's skin, stuffed and decorated with fruit, to the sun for a good growing season.

animals, rocks, and trees—were interrelated. Every object in the environment thus had religious significance and a place in the natural order. The religious character of the physical world was often reflected in practical activities. Hunting, for example, involved a religious relationship between people and animals. Before starting to hunt, Indians performed various ceremonies that helped create a spiritual bond between them and the animal they intended to kill.

For Native Americans, the natural landscape was the setting for the journey along the road of life, and the mountains, lakes, and other natural features of a particular region had special power and significance for the Indians who lived there. Each tribe had its own sacred places. The Sioux Indians of the Great Plains, for example, believed that the Black Hills of present-day South Dakota had great spiritual power. Blue Lake in New Mexico was sacred to the PUEBLO INDIANS.

The land thus played a major role in the cultural and religious identity of Native Americans. When Europeans forced Indian tribes out of their homelands, the effect on their culture was devastating because exile broke the bond between the Indians' environment and their religious beliefs. (*See also* **Missions and Missionaries; Native Americans; Protestant Churches; Roman Catholic Church.**)

Religious Groups

See *Jews; Protestant Churches; Religions, Native American; Roman Catholic Church.*

Religious Life in European Colonies

* Anglican of the Church of England

Religion played a very important role in the lives of most colonists in North America. Colonial governments supported religion and attempted to influence the way it functioned in society. Most people attended church when possible and believed firmly in their particular faith and its teachings. Although colonial religious life reflected practices in Europe, in time the colonies established their own traditions.

Many colonists had immigrated to North America in search of religious freedom. The PILGRIMS, PURITANS, and QUAKERS, for example, came to escape persecution for their beliefs and to form new societies where they could worship as they pleased. Settlers who moved for nonreligious reasons often hoped to recreate the patterns of religious life they had known in Europe. The early colonists of Virginia practiced the Anglican* faith. The French and Spanish brought Catholicism with them to North America, and the Dutch continued to worship in the Protestant Reformed Church.

Rulers in European countries often established one church as the state religion, prohibiting other faiths and sometimes persecuting those who practiced them. In the colonies of France and Spain, government authorities followed this pattern, making the ROMAN CATHOLIC CHURCH the official church. In England's North American settlements, however, a variety of churches appeared because the colonies were founded and settled by a number of different groups with their own religious views.

Protestantism dominated in all the English colonies except Maryland, which was created as a haven for Roman Catholics. In Massachusetts the Puritans established their faith as the official religion, and Anglicans did the same in Virginia and South Carolina. By the early 1700s, Maryland, too, had become an Anglican colony. But in the colonies of Pennsylvania, New York, New Jersey, and Rhode Island the connection between CHURCH AND STATE was weak. The main reason was that large numbers of people of other faiths settled in these colonies, which promoted religious diversity* and toleration*.

In the French and Spanish colonies, the Catholic Church possessed enormous power in the early colonial period. It ran schools, cared for the sick and aged, and helped keep public records. Catholic missionaries founded and ran MISSIONS and often led efforts to colonize new territory. Church officials had various privileges and played a role in political as well as religious affairs. In time, however, conflicts between the church and colonial authorities led to a weakening of the church.

In the British colonies, churches served as a focus of community life. They established schools, supported political causes, and helped support the poor. But the diversity of faiths and the tradition of religious liberty that developed generally prevented churches from assuming a central role in colonial politics.

A revival of religious feeling swept through the British colonies in the mid-1700s. Known as the GREAT AWAKENING, it had a major impact on colonial religious life. It increased church membership, promoted a more emotional religious experience, and changed the character of religious faith. But it also divided communities as some colonists abandoned their old forms of worship and embraced new ones. Because of the increasing diversity in religion, many colonists called for a greater separation of church and state. In time this weakened the hold of established church authority. (*See also* **Acts of Toleration; African American Culture; Bible; Calvinists; Deism; Enlightenment; Freedom of Religion; Jews; Protestant Churches; Religions, Native American.**)

* *diversity* variety

* *toleration* acceptance of the right of individuals to follow their own religious beliefs

See color plate 7, vol. 1.

See map in Missions and Missionaries (vol. 3).

Representative Government

See *Assemblies; Government, Provincial: British.*

Revere, Paul

1735–1818
American patriot and silversmith

*P*aul Revere is best known for his midnight ride of April 1775, when he warned American colonists that British troops were on the march. Revere made many other important contributions to the revolutionary cause, including taking part in the BOSTON TEA PARTY and manufacturing gunpowder for the colonial forces. He was also a master silversmith whose work can be seen in museums today.

Born and raised in Boston, Revere learned the trade of silversmith from his father, a descendant of French HUGUENOTS. In time the younger Revere opened his own shop, where he made teapots, bowls, plates, and many other items for colonial homes. Revere eventually expanded his business to include

Revere, Paul

Paul Revere, a Boston silversmith, won great fame as a patriot in the American Revolution. This portrait of Revere by French artist Charles Févret de Saint-Mémin dates from 1800.

---

* **patriot** American colonist who supported independence from Britain

* **artisan** skilled crafts worker

* **militia** army of citizens who may be called into action in a time of emergency

copper engraving, which he used to make political cartoons that often supported the patriot* cause. One of his most famous engravings was of the BOSTON MASSACRE of 1770.

Patriot. In the late 1760s and the 1770s, Paul Revere joined many Boston residents in opposing British policies. An enthusiastic supporter of the growing protest movement, Revere was a leader in the local SONS OF LIBERTY and persuaded other artisans* to join the organization. As a member of the local committee to decide on an appropriate response to the TEA ACT OF 1773, he helped plan and carry out the Boston Tea Party.

Long before his legendary midnight ride, Revere had become a familiar figure, galloping through the Massachusetts countryside delivering messages for the patriots. Many of his trips crossed colonial boundaries. He carried news of the Boston Tea Party to New York City in 1773 and of the Suffolk Resolves—recommendations for resistance to Britain's INTOLERABLE ACTS—to Philadelphia the next year. Revere became the official courier, or messenger, of the Massachusetts Provincial Assembly.

Paul Revere's Ride. On April 16, 1775, Revere rode to Concord, Massachusetts, to warn members of the militia* that the British planned to seize their weapons and ammunition. Two days later, he set out on his famous ride from Charlestown—on the Charles River across from Boston—to the town of Lexington, about 20 miles to the west. He wanted to alert patriot leaders John HANCOCK and Samuel ADAMS, who were staying in Lexington, that British troops knew of their location and planned to capture them.

On the night of April 18, Revere waited in a rowboat on the Charles River for a signal that would indicate the route of British troops. He had arranged with a lookout to hang one lantern in the steeple of Boston's Old North Church if the British were traveling by land, or two lanterns if they were crossing the river. On seeing two lights, Revere began rowing quietly across the river, using a woman's petticoat to muffle the sound of the oars.

After reaching Charlestown, Revere borrowed the first horse he could find—a sturdy workhorse—and headed off toward Lexington. As Henry Wadsworth Longfellow wrote in his poem *Paul Revere's Ride:*

A hurry of hoofs in a village street,
A shape in the moonlight, a bulk in the dark,
And beneath, from the pebbles, in passing, a spark
Struck out by a steed [horse] flying fearless and fleet;
That was all! And yet, through the gloom and the light
The fate of a nation was riding that night;
And the spark struck out by that steed in his flight,
Kindled the land into flame with its heat.

Alerting farmers along the way to take up arms against the British and avoiding several British patrols, Revere finally reached Lexington. There he woke Hancock and Adams and told them to flee.

At Lexington two other messengers—William Dawes and Samuel Prescott—joined Revere, and the three set out to warn patriots in nearby

Concord. British scouts, however, confronted them on the road. Prescott and Dawes managed to escape, but Revere was captured. After convincing the scouts that they were in danger from rioting colonists, Revere was set free—without his horse. He made his way back to Lexington to retrieve a trunk of important documents left behind by Hancock. In the morning, Revere saw the first shots of the AMERICAN REVOLUTION fired at Lexington.

See color plate 7, vol. 4.

The Revolution and Beyond.   Revere was in his 40s during the War for Independence—too old to be a foot soldier in the CONTINENTAL ARMY. As an officer of the Massachusetts militia, he did command a garrison at Castle William Island in Boston harbor for a short time, and he participated in military expeditions to Rhode Island and Maine. Revere's contributions to the war effort, however, came mainly as a skilled crafts worker. He manufactured gunpowder, copper balls, and cannons. He also designed and printed the first issue of Continental money and made the first official seal of the colonies.

* **ratification** formal approval

After the war, Revere continued to be active in public affairs. He campaigned tirelessly for the ratification* of the federal Constitution for the new nation. Revere also continued his work as a silversmith, producing some of his finest pieces. As an old man, he could be seen walking the streets of Boston wearing outfits from the Revolutionary War days. (*See also* **Lexington and Concord, Battles of.**)

Revivalism

See *Great Awakening.*

Revolutionary Thought

*T*he 13 British colonies on the Atlantic coast and the Spanish province of MEXICO both won their independence in wars of rebellion against their parent countries. In the years before each of these revolutions, colonial thinkers examined, discussed, and wrote about such topics as the proper relationship between a colony and its parent country, self-government, revolution, and independence. Their ideas gave shape and direction to the British and Spanish colonists' desire for political change, helping them move from discontent to action.

British Colonies.   For the most part, revolutionary thought in the British colonies took shape after Great Britain defeated the French in the FRENCH AND INDIAN WAR in 1763, gaining control of the eastern half of North America. The British then reorganized their empire to tighten their hold on the colonies. American colonists, who had grown used to managing their own affairs on a day-to-day basis, deeply resented this move. As the British Parliament began imposing new taxes and other laws that affected their lives, they began to express the view that they should not be subject to laws passed by a governing body in which they had no representatives.

People of all social classes expressed their anger at British policies through street riots and other acts. But the task of explaining the reasons for these actions fell primarily to the educated colonists who wrote pamphlets

and newspaper articles. These individuals hoped to persuade Britain to change the way it treated the colonies. However, their efforts produced something else—a philosophy, or set of ideas, that proclaimed their basic rights and called for self-government for the colonies and revolution against British rule. This philosophy appealed to different groups in the British colonies for different reasons. But in time the majority of the colonists came to agree that their own interests would be served by breaking their ties with Great Britain.

Revolutionary thinkers in the British colonies drew from several sources in developing their ideas. When discussing principles such as justice, equality, and the rights of citizens, they used examples from English common law* and interpreted them in ways that related to current events. They often tried to show that the British traditions of liberty and justice were being destroyed in the colonies by greedy and corrupt government officials.

The European intellectual movement known as the Enlightenment* also shaped revolutionary thought. By the 1760s, the ideas of English writer John Locke, a leading figure of the Enlightenment, were known and discussed throughout the colonies. Locke believed that people formed governments to protect their natural rights to life, liberty, and property and that a social contract, or agreement, existed between a government and the people it ruled. If the government broke that contract by threatening people's rights or acting in an unjust or unlawful way, the people no longer had to honor their agreement to obey the government. Colonial thinkers echoed the ideas of Locke and other Enlightenment figures in their own writings. The DECLARATION OF INDEPENDENCE is a clear and brief explanation of these ideas.

Republicanism—the idea that sovereignty* rests with the people—played an important role in revolutionary thought as well. To many colonists a republic consisted of more than a political system in which citizens elect their leaders. It also involved a set of virtues that included patriotism, courage, sacrifice for the good of the community, and civic responsibility. When the American Revolution broke out, republican ideals not only united American patriots* against the British but also gave them a sense of higher purpose—the belief that they were fighting to protect values important to all humanity.

A sense of moral superiority provided another basis for rebellion. Earlier in the 1700s, some English writers known as Commonwealthmen had charged that British society and government had gone steadily downhill since the late 1600s and that traditional values and liberties were disappearing. They claimed that Britain was becoming immoral and unjust and that the source of this decay was the greed and lust for power of British government officials. These ideas had a powerful effect in the American colonies. Many colonists came to see independence as the only way to preserve their liberty and to avoid the decline and decay that Britain was experiencing.

Spanish Colonies. Spain's North American empire consisted of a collection of far-flung provinces and regions, each with its own interests and political structures. Revolutionary thinkers in this territory known as New Spain* were not inspired by a sense of national unity. Instead, each area hoped to achieve self-government. The tendency of these regions to have a

* *common law* unwritten law based on customs and court decisions

* *Enlightenment* European intellectual movement of the 1600s and 1700s, based on faith in the power of reason and the idea that individuals have certain fundamental rights

* *sovereignty* supreme power or authority

* *patriot* American colonist who supported independence from Britain

* *New Spain* Spanish colonial empire in North America; included Mexico, the area now occupied by Florida, Texas, New Mexico, Arizona, and California, and various Caribbean islands

strong sense of their own identity was strengthened after 1808, when Napoleon Bonaparte of France conquered much of Spain and cut New Spain off from the parent country.

In the main province of Mexico, the struggle for independence from Spain was shaped primarily by tension between two groups of people. One group, the centralists, wanted the authority of a new Mexican state to rest with a strong central government. The regionalists, on the other hand, wanted the provinces or regions to have considerable authority. That tension has been a main theme throughout Mexico's history.

The Mexican struggle for independence was actually a series of civil wars sparked by several movements among different social classes. One movement originated among the wealthy, well-educated, white colonists who made up the highest levels of society. Another movement took shape among poor peasants at the bottom of society—the blacks, Indians, and people of mixed ancestry who accounted for about 80 percent of the population. The revolutionary ideas and activities of these groups were quite different.

Revolutionary thought among the Mexican upper classes was shaped by many of the same Enlightenment ideas that had influenced British colonists. However, it also had specific political, economic, and cultural causes. In the political area, the Creoles* of Mexico resented the fact that officials from Spain held all high colonial offices. In the economic area, wealthy Creoles protested Spanish reforms, which included high taxes and a plan to make colonists repay all the money they had borrowed from the Catholic Church, the only institution in Mexico that lent money. This plan would have caused financial ruin for most well-to-do colonists.

* **Creole** person of European ancestry, born in the Americas

An even more powerful push toward revolution came from a cultural movement called *Mexicanidad* ("Mexicanism"), which was widespread among all Creoles, not just the rich. The movement grew out of an awareness that Creoles were not simply Spanish people living in Mexico. They were Mexicans, members of a culture that combined European and Indian elements in a new way. In the late 1700s, writers expressed the idea of *Mexicanidad* in books and essays that created a growing sense of national identity. Along with that identity came a desire for an independent Mexican homeland ruled by people born and raised in Mexico, not by officials from far-off Spain.

Although the Creoles did most of the thinking, writing, and talking about revolution, action began with the peasants. In the century before the wars of independence, New Spain suffered a series of crop failures that brought financial ruin, misery, unemployment, and starvation to the poor people of the countryside. These problems provoked major outbreaks of unrest. For the most part, the Mexican peasants were not concerned with questions of national identity or sovereignty. They were struggling for their own survival.

* **mestizo** person of mixed Spanish and Indian ancestry

A farm crisis in the early 1800s was the spark that set off the rebellion among the Indian and mestizo* peasants led by Father Miguel HIDALGO Y CASTILLO. As that uprising spread, Creoles seized the opportunity to launch their own rebellions, and the Mexican fight for independence was under way. (*See also* **American Revolution; Enlightenment; Independence Movements; Mexican Independence; Paine, Thomas; Political Thought.**)

21

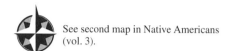

See second map in Native Americans (vol. 3).

*T*he smallest of the 13 original American colonies, Rhode Island was founded by English colonists from Massachusetts Bay who were seeking religious freedom. This commitment to liberty continued throughout the colony's history, and in the 1770s, Rhode Islanders strongly supported independence from Britain. The colony's many harbor towns helped make Rhode Island one of the major commercial centers of North America.

Earliest Inhabitants. A number of Native American tribes inhabited Rhode Island at the time the first English settlers arrived. The NARRAGANSETT INDIANS lived south of present-day PROVIDENCE, along Narragansett Bay. The coastal areas to the east were home to the WAMPANOAG, and the Nipmuck occupied the northern and western regions. The Niantic Indians lived in the southern part of Rhode Island.

Narragansett Bay, which cuts deep into Rhode Island, contains islands and miles of coastline. The Indians generally spent summers fishing in the bay and winters in the forests. The first European to sail into the bay was Giovanni da Verrazano, who explored the North American coastline for France in 1524.

Founding the Colony. In the 1600s, several groups of colonists left their homes in MASSACHUSETTS to found settlements in nearby Rhode Island. Most of the newcomers were dissatisfied with the strict policies of the Massachusetts PURITANS. One of the first to arrive was Roger WILLIAMS, who had been banished by Puritan leaders for his views on politics and religion. After purchasing land near the top of Narragansett Bay from the Narragansett Indians, he and his followers founded the town of Providence in 1636. The settlers agreed that the community's important decisions would be made by the will of the majority and that government would have no power over religious life.

In 1638 Anne HUTCHINSON, another religious dissenter*, fled Massachusetts for Rhode Island. Together with a number of other refugees, she settled Portsmouth at the northern end of Aquidneck Island (now known as Rhode Island). One of the leaders of Portsmouth, William Coddington, left the town after a year and moved to the southern end of the island. There he established the community of NEWPORT with the help of John Clarke. Samuel Gorton, another Portsmouth resident, set up the town of Warwick, on the bay south of Providence.

Settled by people with similar beliefs, these four towns decided to form a colony. Roger Williams went to England to make this proposal, and in 1644 he obtained a charter* from Parliament that combined the towns into a colony and confirmed the settlers' right to the land. Because the colony welcomed people of many religious faiths, it soon attracted a diverse population, including Baptists, QUAKERS, French HUGUENOTS, and JEWS from Europe and the other North American colonies.

Colonial Government. Local government in Rhode Island centered on TOWN MEETINGS, as it did in the other New England colonies. At the town meeting, the community elected officers who carried out duties such as keeping the peace, recording deeds, and maintaining roads. To handle issues beyond the scope of the towns, Rhode Islanders formed a colonial assembly. It met for the first time in Portsmouth in May 1647.

* *dissenter* person who disagrees with the beliefs and practices of the established church

* *charter* written grant from a ruler conferring certain rights and privileges

Naming a Colony

Two possible sources have been suggested for the name Rhode Island. When Italian explorer Giovanni da Verrazano sailed by the area in 1524, he remarked that one of the islands resembled the Greek island of Rhodes in the Aegean Sea. Almost 100 years later the Dutch explorer Adriaen Block referred to the same island as *Roodt Eylandt* (Red Island) because of the color of the soil. However, the colony consisted of more than islands—much of it was on the mainland. As a result, its official name became Rhode Island and Providence Plantations.

In 1663, after Charles II became king of England, Rhode Island managed to obtain a royal charter that gave the colonists an unusual degree of control over local matters. Although most colonies had governors appointed by the crown, Rhode Island would be allowed to choose its own governor. The charter also provided for a general assembly of elected deputies and granted complete religious freedom within the colony. This charter served as Rhode Island's basic law until 1843.

In 1675 the colony faced a devastating war. Local Native Americans, hoping to force the English colonists out of the region, began an uprising that became known as KING PHILIP'S WAR. Indian war parties burned many Rhode Island towns. One of the major battles of the war, the Great Swamp Fight, occurred in December near Kingston, Rhode Island. After a long and destructive war, the colonists finally defeated the Native Americans.

Culture and Economy. With the end of the war, Rhode Islanders were able to return to their farms and businesses. The population increased from 7,000 in the early 1700s to 60,000 in the 1770s. The colony's coastal towns, such as Newport, Bristol, and Providence, developed into trading centers and established a highly profitable pattern of commerce in rum, slaves, and molasses. Merchants shipped goods produced in the colony to the WEST INDIES, where the goods were traded for molasses, a by-product of sugar. Rhode Island distilleries made the molasses into RUM, a popular alcoholic drink, and then sent the rum to the west coast of Africa. In Africa the rum was exchanged for slaves, which Rhode Island traders sold in the West Indies and in other British colonies.

As the colony's business leaders became increasingly wealthy, they helped support cultural institutions. The Redwood Library of Newport, founded in 1747, housed a collection of books started with a gift from Abraham Redwood. In the 1760s, local Baptists established Rhode Island College in Providence, which later became Brown University. Successful merchants built elegant homes and hired leading artists to create works of art.

Rhode Island's dependence on commerce, however, and its tradition of self-government, caused the colonists to resent any interference in trade. When the British government began to impose taxes and restrictions on imports and exports, such as the SUGAR ACT OF 1764, the colonists strongly objected. In 1772 townspeople from Providence burned the British ship *Gaspée* in protest. A spirit of rebellion against British rule began to grow.

Revolution. On May 4, 1776, Rhode Island became the first colony to refuse continued allegiance to King GEORGE III. Several months later, British troops landed in Newport, which they occupied until October 1779. The presence of the British and the Revolutionary War disrupted Newport's economy. After the war, Providence became the state's more important commercial center and, eventually, its capital.

After the struggle for independence, Rhode Island was slow to join the new nation. Many residents feared they would lose control of their own government. Rhode Island finally ratified* the United States Constitution on May 29, 1790—the last of the 13 original colonies to do so. (*See also* **Freedom of Religion; Navigation Acts; Slave Trade.**)

* ratify to approve formally

23

Rice

* *cash crop* crop grown primarily for profit

Rice was one of the most important cash crops* in the southern colonies of British North America. As the rice trade boomed, SLAVERY in the region expanded. Rice cultivation helped make the South the richest area in the British colonies.

The colonial rice industry began in the 1690s along the coast of South Carolina, particularly in the area around CHARLESTON. Though Native Americans had harvested wild rice before the arrival of Europeans, colonists used seeds originally from Asia or Africa. By the early 1700s, South Carolina was already producing a surplus, and rice became the colony's major export crop.

The low-lying coast of South Carolina and parts of North Carolina and Georgia provided ideal growing conditions for rice—an average temperature of 70 degrees, 50 to 60 inches of rain a year, and rich, heavy soil. At first planters used the upland, or dry, method of rice cultivation, depending entirely on rainfall to provide needed moisture. Later they switched to flooding rice fields with water from nearby inland swamps. By the end of the colonial period, many planters used the tidewater method, in which they timed production according to the rise and fall of ocean tides. This practice, however, was limited to areas along the coast and along rivers affected by the tide.

* *thresh* to crush grains so that the seeds or grains are separated from the stalks and the husks
* *winnow* to remove seed coverings from grain by a current of air

Successful rice production in colonial times required a great deal of land—from 300 to more than 1,000 acres—and a huge amount of manual labor. Workers' tasks included clearing trees from fields, building dams and ditches to control water flow, planting the seeds, constantly weeding, and then cutting the rice crop and drying, threshing*, and winnowing* it. To meet the demand for labor, planters imported slaves from Africa. As rice production increased, so did the practice of slavery. By 1740 blacks outnumbered whites in South Carolina by two to one.

Planters shipped the harvested crop from plantation wharves to ports. Europe and later the WEST INDIES were the most profitable markets for South Carolina's rice. From time to time, European wars prevented rice ships from reaching their destination, disrupting South Carolina's economy. As part of the British empire, South Carolina rice growers also had to follow Britain's strict shipping regulations.

By the early 1770s, rice ranked fourth in value among colonial products—after tobacco, flour and bread, and dried fish—and the lower South was the wealthiest area in the colonies. When the British captured Charleston in 1780 during the Revolutionary War, they seized the entire rice crop, leaving no seeds. The rice industry revived a few years later, after Thomas JEFFERSON smuggled new rice seeds out of Europe. (*See also* **Agriculture; South Carolina; Trade and Commerce.**)

Rittenhouse, David

1732–1796
American engineer, astronomer, and mathematician

David Rittenhouse, a brilliant scientist, designed and constructed superb mathematical instruments that were more accurate than any others made in colonial times. During the Revolutionary War, he served the patriot* cause as an engineer.

Rittenhouse grew up on a farm in Pennsylvania. Although he had little opportunity for formal schooling, he studied mathematics and mechanics on his own, using tools and books inherited from an uncle. Rittenhouse trained

* *patriot* American colonist who supported independence from Britain

himself to make clocks, designing a special pendulum that kept more accurate time than standard ones. At the age of 19, he opened an instrument shop on his father's farm.

Expanding on his knowledge of clockmaking, Rittenhouse began to produce measuring devices such as thermometers, barometers, compasses, and levels. Using many of his own instruments, he became the leading surveyor in the British colonies. Rittenhouse gained such a high reputation for accuracy in surveying that he was often called on to settle boundary disputes. In the 1760s, he laid the groundwork for the survey, carried out by Charles Mason and Jeremiah Dixon, that established the boundary between Pennsylvania and Maryland.

Rittenhouse next applied his considerable skills to the field of astronomy, becoming famous for his calculations on the movements of planets and solar and lunar eclipses. In 1767 he designed his famous orrery, an amazing instrument that showed the movements of the solar system—an early version of the modern planetarium. He also constructed the first telescope made in America. In 1770 Rittenhouse moved to Philadelphia, where he became a professor of astronomy at the University of Pennsylvania.

* *mint* the place where coins are made

Well known in scientific circles, Rittenhouse was also involved in civic activities. When the American Revolution began in 1775, he served as an engineer on Pennsylvania's Committee of Safety, which supplied the army and carried out other functions of government during the war. At the same time, Rittenhouse participated in Pennsylvania's assembly and the constitutional convention before going on to become state treasurer. After the war, George WASHINGTON appointed him to be the first director of the federal mint*. In 1791 Rittenhouse succeeded his longtime friend Benjamin FRANKLIN as president of the AMERICAN PHILOSOPHICAL SOCIETY, a post he held until his death in 1796.

Roads

* *Spanish Borderlands* northern part of New Spain, area now occupied by Florida, Texas, New Mexico, Arizona, and California

*I*n the early years, colonists in North America depended largely on waterways for transportation and communication. But as more settlers arrived and communities sprang up farther inland, roads became more important. In the Spanish Borderlands*, roads were needed to transport supplies to missions and forts in frontier regions. In the British colonies, they were essential for carrying farm products to market. Roads also helped colonists communicate with each other.

Construction proceeded at an uneven pace throughout the continent. The well-populated British colonies of Maryland, Connecticut, Massachusetts, and Delaware established an extensive network of roads. However, the vast, thinly populated Louisiana territory had almost no roads. The difficulty of the terrain also affected road construction. The many rivers running through the land route from Quebec to Montreal kept French settlers from building a highway between the two settlements until the late 1700s.

During the colonial period, planning, building, and maintaining roads involved several different levels of government. In the British colonies, governors and provincial assemblies approved the construction of new highways, planned routes, and provided funding for materials and labor. These

Roads

Most colonial roads were made of dirt, and they were often in poor condition. This illustration from Charles Fraser's *A Charleston Sketchbook* shows the deep ruts in the road that ran past the Stony Creek Meeting House in South Carolina.

* *viceroy* person appointed as a monarch's representative to govern a province or colony

functions were carried out in NEW SPAIN by the viceroy* and in NEW FRANCE by a surveyor known as the Grand Voyer. Local governments were responsible for building and maintaining the roads. Communities found a number of ways of meeting this obligation. In Georgia all males aged 16 to 60 had to spend six days each year on road work. Other colonies relied on taxes to pay for road maintenance.

Colonists often followed Native American trails when laying out roads. Before the arrival of Europeans, Indians in every region of North America had developed extensive and complicated networks of footpaths. These trails usually provided the best route over mountains and through river valleys. In some places—especially on the frontier—roads were simply Indian footpaths widened by moving oxcarts and wagons over them.

In many parts of the continent, colonists developed a network of main roads with smaller roads branching off them. The most traveled highway in the British colonies was the Great Wagon Road, which was started in the 1730s. Based largely on old Indian trails, it eventually stretched 800 miles from Pennsylvania to Georgia. El Camino Real, the "Royal Highway," was even longer and older. Established by explorer Juan de OÑATE in 1598, this 1,800-mile road connected Mexico City and Santa Fe, New Mexico, and the journey from one end to the other by wagon train took about six months. Toward the end of the colonial period, several roads extending westward were started. The most famous of these was the Wilderness Road. Marked by Daniel Boone in 1775, this route led settlers through the Cumberland Gap in the Appalachian Mountains to Kentucky.

Travel on colonial roads presented numerous difficulties. Roads were often crooked, bumpy, rocky, full of ruts and holes, and blocked by overhanging

branches or fallen trees. Most were constructed of dirt or sand, which turned to mud whenever it rained or snowed, making them impassable. In swampy areas, builders sometimes laid 10- to 12-foot logs side by side to create a solid base, but these so-called corduroy roads frequently came apart. Because of cost and lack of engineering knowledge, colonists rarely attempted to build straight roads. Instead, the routes twisted and turned to avoid ravines, gullies, and streams.

During the mid-1700s, road travel began to improve. Longer and more extensive road networks gave rise to such features as stone markers—which told travelers the number of miles to their destinations—road maps, and guidebooks on the best taverns and hotels along the way. (*See also* **Knight, Sarah Kemble; Transportation and Travel.**)

Roanoke Island

*E*ngland's first two attempts to establish a colony in North America took place on Roanoke Island, a 12-mile-long, 3-mile-wide island off the coast of North Carolina. Both attempts failed, and the second ended in the mysterious disappearance of what has been called the "Lost Colony." However, the short-lived Roanoke settlement was of lasting importance because it established England's claim to the land that would later become the colony of Virginia.

Gilbert, Raleigh, and Virginia. England's colonial ventures in the Americas began with Sir Humphrey GILBERT, who thought England should enlarge its overseas territories to keep Spain from becoming too powerful. In 1578 Queen Elizabeth I granted Gilbert a patent* to start and govern a colony in "remote, heathen, and barbarous lands not actually possessed of any Christian prince, nor inhabited by Christian people." The queen promised to treat the colonists as English citizens. Gilbert died before establishing his colony, so the queen transferred the patent to Sir Walter RALEIGH, Gilbert's half brother. In 1584 Raleigh sent a scouting expedition to explore the North American coast and find a good site for a settlement.

Raleigh's scouts spent several weeks with the friendly Indians of Roanoke Island, returning to England with high praise for the "plentiful, sweete, fruitfull and wholsome" soil of the region. Queen Elizabeth, who was known as the Virgin Queen because she was not married, agreed to let the area be called Virginia in her honor. In 1585 Raleigh sent 108 men to build a supply post on Roanoke Island for the English privateers* who were attacking Spain's ships in the Caribbean.

Things did not go well for this first group of colonists. They spent their time searching for GOLD instead of growing food and building houses. Some members of the group were gentlemen adventurers who had no practical skills and were unwilling to work. The local Indians, tired of supplying the colonists with food, turned hostile. When Sir Francis DRAKE visited with his fleet in 1586, he found the settlement in danger and agreed to take the colonists back to England. Sir Richard Grenville, leader of the ill-fated colony, left 15 men on Roanoke Island to secure England's claim to the region until a new group of colonists could arrive.

* *patent* permission to found a colony

* *privateer* privately owned ship authorized by the government to attack and capture enemy vessels; also the ship's master

The Lost Colony. Raleigh sent a second expedition to North America in 1587. This group included more than 100 men, women, and children. The settlers' goal was to recreate a typical rural English community in the American wilderness. Two leading members of the group had taken part in the earlier attempt to colonize Roanoke. They were John WHITE, a skilled mapmaker and artist whom Raleigh made governor of the second expedition, and Thomas Harriot, a scholar and mapmaker.

White had explored part of the CHESAPEAKE BAY during his first visit to the region and wanted to set up the colony there. But the expedition's pilot refused to take the ships beyond Roanoke Island. Upon reaching the island, the colonists looked for the 15 men who had stayed behind but found only bones and signs that the settlement had been attacked. Despite these gloomy discoveries, the new arrivals had no choice but to settle on Roanoke. Soon after they landed, White's daughter gave birth to the first English child born in the Americas, Virginia Dare.

About a month after the colonists' arrival, White sailed back to England to gather supplies and reinforcements. But when he got there, he found the country on the brink of war. Spain had built a massive fleet of warships and was threatening to invade England. Queen Elizabeth would spare no ships for a voyage to the new colony.

White could not return to Roanoke Island until 1590. Instead of finding a flourishing colony, he discovered on his arrival that the settlement had been abandoned. The only clue to the settlers' fate was the word *Croatoan* carved into a doorpost. White believed that this referred to a Native American tribe that lived about 50 miles south of the island. Its chieftain, Manteo, had been friendly, and White thought that the colonists had fled to him for shelter when other Indians attacked. He could not persuade the captains of his ships to go in search of the missing settlers, however, and so he returned to England without knowing what had happened at Roanoke. Modern historians believe that the people of the Lost Colony probably moved north to live among the Chesapeake Indians, who were killed in 1606 by the Indian chieftain Powhatan. A period of great drought may have played a role in Roanoke's failure.

White and Harriot saved some of their drawings and notes from the first expedition. Harriot wrote a book about Virginia, and in 1590 an illustrated edition appeared with reproductions of White's drawings. Published in four languages, this volume gave many Europeans their first images and descriptions of the landscapes, plants and animals, and native inhabitants of North America.

Rolfe, John

1585–1622
English colonist

John Rolfe played a significant role in ensuring the survival of the JAMESTOWN COLONY of Virginia during the uncertain years of the early 1600s. His marriage to a Native American woman led to a temporary peace between the colonists and the local Indians. In addition, Rolfe developed an improved variety of TOBACCO that became the chief product of the Virginia colony.

Born in Norfolk, England, Rolfe emigrated to North America in 1609. His voyage was interrupted by a shipwreck in Bermuda, delaying his arrival

in Jamestown by several months. After a few years, Rolfe began to experiment with tobacco plants, trying to produce stronger, more pleasant-tasting tobacco. The variety he developed grew well in Virginia and became popular in Europe. Tobacco was soon Virginia's most valuable export.

In 1613 Rolfe met POCAHONTAS, the daughter of the Indian chief Powhatan. The colonists had captured Pocohontas and brought her to Jamestown as a prisoner. The following year she and Rolfe married, and the resulting truce between the POWHATAN INDIANS and the Jamestown colony lasted for eight years. Rolfe and Pocahontas went to England in 1616, but Pocahontas died there, and Rolfe returned to Virginia the following year. He served as secretary and recorder of the colony until 1619 and, two years later, accepted a position on the Council of State. He died shortly thereafter during an Indian raid on his home. (*See also* **Virginia.**)

See color plate 1, vol. 3.

Roman Catholic Church

Although the Roman Catholic Church existed in the Spanish, French, English, and Dutch colonies of North America, its place in colonial society varied according to the religious affiliation of the parent country. As the official religion of both Spain and France, Catholicism played a major role in the colonies established by these powers. However, in the colonies founded by the Protestant nations of England and the Netherlands, Catholicism struggled to survive. The Dutch banned the Catholic Church in NEW NETHERLAND but allowed Catholics to live there.

Catholicism in the Spanish Borderlands

From the very beginning, Spain's effort to colonize North America was both political and religious in nature. In 1486 the pope gave Spanish monarchs Ferdinand and Isabella special privileges and responsibilities to spread and protect the Catholic faith. Known as the Real Patronato, or "royal patronage," this papal* order was originally intended to apply to the reconquest of European lands held by Muslims. However, when Christopher COLUMBUS discovered a "New World" in 1492, the order was extended to the territory on the other side of the Atlantic. The Real Patronato lay at the heart of the Spanish conquest and administration in North America.

Conquest, Conversion, and Rule. After Spain's soldiers conquered a region in North America, Spanish missionaries and clergy* began the task of establishing the Catholic Church there. In the Spanish Borderlands*, missionaries were responsible for converting Native Americans to Christianity. They accomplished this by setting up a system of MISSIONS, which introduced the Indians to Catholic teachings and Spanish culture. Largely independent from the main church and government authorities of NEW SPAIN, each mission was supported by funds from the religious order that ran it—mostly the Franciscans in California and New Mexico and the JESUITS in Arizona—and by its farming and ranching activities. During the early colonial period, the missionaries served as agents of the Spanish crown, with responsibility for the protection, care, and growth of the communities that sprang up around the missions.

* *papal* of the pope

* *clergy* ministers, priests, and other church officials

* *Spanish Borderlands* northern part of New Spain, area now occupied by Florida, Texas, New Mexico, Arizona, and California

See map in Missions and Missionaries (vol. 3).

Militant Missionaries

Not all the missionaries in the Spanish Borderlands were tolerant of the Native Americans' traditional beliefs. In New Mexico, Franciscan missionaries tried to impose the Spanish language and culture on the Pueblo Indians along with Catholicism. They destroyed Pueblo religious artifacts and physically punished those who continued to practice their old religion. This harsh treatment finally caused the Pueblo to revolt in 1680 and drive the Spanish out of New Mexico for 16 years.

* *rite* ceremony or formal procedure
* *confirmation* ceremony marking admittance to church membership

See color plate 7, vol. 2.

* *lay* not linked to the church by religious vows or clerical office

Spanish clergy, rather than missionaries, attended to the spiritual needs of the European colonists in the Borderlands. The priests followed the rules and orders of church authorities in Mexico and Spain. They had little to do with Native Americans until the late 1700s, when control of the missions passed to the colonial government. The priests then took over responsibility for the Indians, but they were less successful than the missionaries had been in gaining Christian converts. Through the clergy and missionaries, Spanish authorities pursued their religious goals and also accepted responsibility for schools, hospitals, and other social services.

Success of the Church. Catholicism enjoyed great success in the Spanish Borderlands, mainly because it could be adapted to fit the beliefs and practices of Native Americans. Many missionaries realized that it would be impossible for the Indians to abandon their own religious traditions completely, and they worked instead to build a gradual understanding and acceptance of Catholic ideas. They tried, for example, to appeal to the Native Americans' reverence for nature by holding church services outdoors. They also staged processions and ceremonies that involved acting out religious themes because the Indians were accustomed to expressing religious feelings in active ways, such as by dancing and singing rather than by silent prayer.

Despite a willingness to adapt Catholicism to cultural differences, missionaries did not allow Indians to participate in certain rites* of the church. They often withheld the rite of baptism until they were sure that converts truly accepted and understood their new faith. The church also never allowed Indians to become priests. However, church rites such as confirmation* and marriage were freely given because they helped bind Native Americans to the Catholic Church and to Spanish culture.

The decline of the mission system was accompanied by a weakening in the influence of Catholicism in much of the Spanish Borderlands. Although the church had enjoyed remarkable success, it gradually lost the strong hold it had over many Indians. Local priests put most of their efforts into serving Spanish colonists, and they became more concerned with controlling Native Americans than in converting them. Harsh treatment at the hands of the clergy and colonial officials led many Native Americans to practice their own versions of Christianity outside the church. With no strong Indian support, Catholicism suffered a decline as Protestant settlers from the United States arrived in the early 1800s.

Catholicism in New France

NEW FRANCE was a Catholic colony that banned all other religions. CHURCH AND STATE were closely linked, and French religious and government authorities together controlled the political, social, and spiritual worlds of the colonists.

New France had very few French settlers before 1650. The representatives of the Catholic Church who were there had come to convert Native Americans to Christianity. These Franciscan and Jesuit missionaries were joined by various female religious orders, such as the Ursulines, and also by a number of devout lay* individuals. Catholic officials in France did not

parish church district

appoint a bishop for New France and did not establish parishes* there until the 1650s.

Efforts to convert Native Americans to Catholicism were less successful in New France than in the Spanish colonies. Franciscan missionaries chose to live near French settlements rather than among the Indians. This separation limited the missionaries' influence on the people they were trying to convert. The Jesuits, who generally made an effort to stay with the Indians and learn their languages, had more success. Yet, like Spanish priests, they were reluctant to administer church rites to the converts. Most Indians were baptized only when near death or after long periods of devout living. The missionaries' refusal to allow Native Americans to participate fully in the church hindered their attempt to attract large groups of young Indians to Christianity.

By the late 1650s, French immigrants were beginning to outnumber Native Americans, creating a demand for regular parish churches and priests. From this time forward, the Catholic clergy directed most of their energy to the spiritual needs of French colonists rather than to converting Indians. In 1663 a seminary* was founded in Quebec to train priests, and the first Catholic bishop for New France was appointed in 1674.

seminary school that trains individuals for the priesthood

The Roman Catholic Church played a major role in the political, social, and cultural life of New France. The high moral standards of the clergy set a strong example for colonists, resulting in a remarkably low level of crime and disorderliness. The church also established schools and gave assistance to the sick and the poor. The clergy had a great deal of influence in civic life as well, filling important functions such as keeping government records. The French crown granted the church large amounts of land and substantial sums of money. By the end of French rule in 1763, the church held about 25 percent of the land. Even the British recognized the important role of the Catholic Church in the colony. After defeating the French and taking control of Canada, they passed a law known as the QUEBEC ACT (1774), which allowed the French settlers to remain Catholics.

Catholicism in the English Colonies

England was officially a Protestant country, and Catholics there were not treated as equals under the law. Catholicism was banned in most of England's colonies in North America, but Catholics who settled in the colonies faced little serious persecution.

In 1634 Cecil Calvert, an English lord who was Catholic, founded MARYLAND as a haven for people of his religion. In the early years, Catholics provided the colony's political and economic leadership, even though Protestants outnumbered them. Maryland adopted a policy of religious toleration*, and Catholics and Protestants lived together peaceably for a number of years. When Protestants gained control in the colony, however, they placed some restrictions on Catholics. In 1649 the Maryland assembly passed an ACT OF TOLERATION that allowed freedom of religion to all Christians. But the act was repealed* five years later, and Catholicism was banned.

toleration acceptance of the right of individuals to follow their own religious beliefs

repeal to undo a law

Conditions improved in 1660, when the English king Charles II returned control of Maryland to the original proprietors*. The Act of Toleration was restored, and Catholics held important positions in colonial

proprietor person granted land and the right to establish a colony

society and government. In 1691 Maryland became a royal colony with the Church of England as its official religion. Catholics were barred from public office and denied the right to vote. However, the influence of wealthy and prominent Catholics in Maryland helped protect others of that religion from persecution.

There were few Catholics elsewhere in the British colonies. Virginia had a fairly sizable Irish Catholic population but not an organized church. The Carolinas and Georgia had no Catholics in colonial times, except for occasional Spanish missionaries. In Pennsylvania and Delaware, Catholics enjoyed toleration but were barred from holding public office or practicing certain professions, such as teaching and law. The situation was similar in New Jersey, where Catholic services were forbidden but Catholics were permitted to settle. Although New York passed laws against Catholicism in the late 1600s, Catholics enjoyed some toleration there. The colonies of New England, with their strong Puritan heritage, discouraged Catholic settlers. Even Rhode Island, which was a haven for religious dissenters*, did not welcome Roman Catholics.

Anti-Catholic feeling erupted briefly throughout the British colonies with the passage of the Quebec Act by Parliament in 1774. Colonists condemned the act—which granted French Canadians freedom to practice Catholicism—as a danger to the religious rights of all Americans. The American Revolution overshadowed concerns about religion, and the revolutionary period and the years following brought new ideas about religious toleration and the relationship between church and state. (*See also* **Freedom of Religion; Protestant Churches; Religious Life in European Colonies.**)

* **dissenter** person who disagrees with the beliefs and practices of the established church

Rowlandson, Mary

ca. 1635–ca. 1678
Indian captive and author

* **genre** type of literary or artistic work

*M*ary Rowlandson, a Massachusetts colonist, was captured and held hostage by Indians in 1676. The account she wrote of her sufferings became one of the most popular books in the English colonies and the first example of the literary genre* known as the Indian captivity narrative.

Mary White Rowlandson lived in the frontier village of Lancaster, Massachusetts, with her husband, Joseph, who was the local minister, and their three children. Their life was uneventful until 1675, when tensions with New England Indians led to a conflict known as KING PHILIP'S WAR. In February 1676, Indians staged a bloody attack on Lancaster. Before setting fire to the village, they seized Rowlandson, her children, and 19 other residents. Rowlandson's youngest child died almost immediately from exposure to the cold.

For three months, Rowlandson and her two remaining children were forced to accompany the Nipmuck, WAMPANOAG, and NARRAGANSETT Indians. Driven westward by colonial forces, the Indians and their captives suffered from hunger. In general, Rowlandson was treated well, partly because she made shirts and knitted stockings for her captors and partly because the Indians expected to receive a ransom for her. Finally, in early May, Rowlandson's husband and local officials negotiated her release in exchange for a ransom of 20 pounds. Her children were freed soon afterward.

Throughout her captivity, Rowlandson held fast to her confidence in God. She wrote the account of her experiences to praise the goodness and mercy God had shown to her and to her children. Published in Cambridge in 1682, the narrative captured the attention of readers in both England and the colonies and became a best-seller. The book provides a vivid picture of how the Indians lived during the war and of the scorn with which they were viewed by English colonists. (*See also* **Literature.**)

indigo plant used to make a blue dye

See map in Trade and Commerce (vol. 4).

*I*n the 1600s, colonists in New England developed an international trading network based on the sale of rum, a popular alcoholic drink. They produced rum from molasses, one of the by-products of sugar refining. Selling rum—or trading it for other goods—became a highly profitable business and helped transform several northern cities into major commercial centers.

The New England colonies began to deal in rum because, unlike other regions, they had few products to export. The South produced crops, such as tobacco, rice, and indigo*, that could be sold overseas easily. The WEST INDIES exported sugar. But the land in New England was not suitable for large-scale cultivation, and the English were not interested in the region's products. As a result, New England merchants sold timber, fish, and other items to the sugar-producing islands of the West Indies. Most of the molasses they received in exchange went to the rum industry.

Colonists throughout the north, especially in Boston, Newport, Philadelphia, and New York, opened distilleries where molasses was turned into rum. Much of it was sold and consumed in the colonies, but the surplus was exported. Merchants shipped rum to the west coast of Africa, where European slave traders exchanged it for slaves. The New England shippers then headed for the West Indies, where the sugar planters readily accepted the slaves in return for more molasses. This three-sided commercial arrangement, often called the triangular trade, greatly enriched New England.

The rum trade became a source of conflict between Britain and its colonies. New England colonists obtained much of their molasses from French, Dutch, and Spanish islands, where they could buy it cheaply and sell their own trade goods. Britain tried to force the colonists to trade only with British sugar planters by passing the MOLASSES ACT in 1733 and the SUGAR ACT in 1764. These laws placed high taxes on foreign sugar products, but colonial merchants avoided the taxes by SMUGGLING. (*See also* **Merchants; Slave Trade; Trade and Commerce.**)

*T*hroughout the colonial period in North America, the vast majority of people lived in the countryside rather than in towns or cities. Most settlers in the British, Dutch, and French colonies inhabited a rural world, where they often could not see another house and where each family household formed a self-sufficient community of its own. In the Spanish Borderlands*, by contrast, rural homes were typically clustered together in small

This view of New Jersey appeared in the *Columbian Magazine* in October 1789. It shows a typical rural landscape in the late 1700s—wide stretches of land cleared for farming with the forest that once covered the region in the background.

* **Spanish Borderlands** northern part of New Spain, area now occupied by Florida, Texas, New Mexico, Arizona, and California

* **tenant farmer** person who farms land owned by another and pays rent with a share of the produce or in cash

* **artisan** skilled crafts worker

settlements. It was these settlements, rather than individual households, that characterized the rural communities of Spanish America.

Farm-Based Society. Country life was based on farming. Nearly every rural family worked the land in some way. At one extreme were wealthy plantation owners who rarely visited the fields of their large estates. At the other extreme were tenant farmers* who labored and lived on land that belonged to someone else. Between these extremes were most colonial Americans— small landholders who owned and farmed their own land with the help of family members, occasional hired laborers, or perhaps one or two servants or slaves.

Rural households produced most of what they needed, from food and clothing to furniture, tools, and buildings. Few households, however, were completely self-sufficient. Neighbors often worked together on big jobs, such as barn building. Families also exchanged surplus goods—for example, trading butter for eggs or woven cloth for candles. If rural settlers lived near a town market, they sold or traded farm produce there. Those who possessed a little cash might buy manufactured items such as ribbons and needles at town markets or from traveling salesmen called peddlers. Some rural residents were artisans* who crafted goods such as wooden barrels and iron tools in addition to practicing farming. By selling surplus produce and handicrafts, rural families added to their income and improved their standard of living.

Patterns of Settlement. The way in which settlements formed had an impact on the nature of rural life in colonial North America. Early English settlers wanted to reproduce the English countryside, dotted with villages and

small towns whose inhabitants traveled to their fields during the day to work. But in North America few English colonists lived in villages. For the most part, they spread out in individual farmsteads scattered throughout the countryside. Isolated farms or plantations became the standard type of settlement in most British colonies outside New England.

The Dutch colony of NEW NETHERLAND was almost entirely rural. Aside from the large towns of New Orange (now Albany) and New Amsterdam, the greater part of the settlers lived on self-contained farms located around the countryside. With close-knit families, these rural colonists faced the common task of providing for their needs. Many supplemented their incomes by trading with Native Americans for furs.

Country life in NEW FRANCE developed around a handful of trading outposts. The SEIGNEURIAL SYSTEM of land ownership created large rural estates. These consisted of small farms strung along the rivers that served as the main routes of travel and transport. This arrangement, in which neighboring farms were set closer together than in the British colonies, discouraged the formation of villages. Living far from towns and markets, the rural residents of New France practiced subsistence farming* and developed a spirit of independence and self-sufficiency. Still, many farmers found it necessary to supplement their income by engaging in the FUR TRADE or working in logging camps during the winter months.

Rural life in the Spanish Borderlands was shaped by government regulations and differed significantly from that in other colonial regions. Spanish colonists did not have the freedom to stake out land claims wherever they wished. Instead, settlement was a government-licensed process in which the church, the army, and individuals worked together to build forts, MISSIONS, and communities. As a result, most colonists lived in farming or ranching villages called pueblos rather than on isolated homesteads. A typical pueblo had a central plaza, or square, surrounded by houses, private farm plots, and shared grazing land. Settlers lived in the town and worked on the outlying lands, blending elements of rural and urban life.

During the 1600s, the eastern region of North America was covered with thick forests that isolated neighbors. Cutting trees to clear land for planting was a major task in the endless toil of rural life. Another aspect of rural life common to all colonial regions was the presence of Native Americans—as neighbors, allies, and enemies. By the 1700s, the rural landscape in the eastern part of the continent had changed. Most forests had been cleared for planting. The Indians had been driven off most of their land. A growing network of roads, bridges, and ferries connected individual farms to towns and cities. The result was a new rural landscape of shrinking forests, open fields, and interconnected rural communities.

Social Ties. The family was the basic unit of rural colonial society. But other social bonds were also important to rural people whose contact with the world was limited. Rural men, women, and children spent most of their time working. They snatched at any chance to enjoy such festivities as weddings or holidays that broke up the daily and seasonal round of chores.

Most rural settlers, except those who were extremely isolated, visited their neighbors regularly and attended church together. The church was

See
color plate 3,
vol. 1.

* *subsistence farming* raising only enough food to live on

35

central to rural social life. Men in some areas frequently went to the nearest village or town to do business at the market and to attend court sessions or TOWN MEETINGS. Women came to town less often, so their social lives generally were confined to the family and to their neighbors.

Like people in all times and places, colonial Americans looked for opportunities to visit, gossip, and flirt. Mills, taverns, churches, and stores were meeting places for the rural colonists of New Netherland. Country folk in New France often gathered at homes in the evening for dancing, drinking, and STORYTELLING. The people of the Spanish Borderlands got together at FESTIVALS and visited the homes of relatives and friends to sing, tell stories, and play games. Rural Americans found relief from the loneliness and toil of rural life in such activities and in the warmth and support of a shared community. (*See also* **Agriculture; Family; Frontier; Population Growth in North America; Ranching.**)

Russian Settlements

Russia led the way in the exploration of present-day Alaska and the PACIFIC NORTHWEST. Russian scientists studied the plants, animals, and peoples of the region. Russian hunters and trappers probed the coast and the interior in search of fur-bearing animals. A chain of Russian TRADING POSTS stretched from the Bering Strait of northwestern Alaska to northern California. Russian Orthodox missionaries came as well to bring Christianity to the native peoples of the region. Today remnants of Russian architecture, religion, and culture survive in scattered communities in the coastal areas of Alaska.

Yet history books often overlook the role that Russia played in the colonizing of North America. One reason, perhaps, is that the Russians got a late start—arriving only in the mid-1700s. Furthermore, during the century or so they were active in the region, the number of Russians never exceeded 1,000. The outposts* they built in North America were intended for trade rather than as starting points for settlement. Finally, most Russian activity took place in the northwestern corner of the continent, far, far away from the other American colonies.

* outpost frontier settlement or military base

Early Fur Voyages. Unlike the other nations that established colonies in North America, Russia approached the continent from the west, sailing across the North Pacific Ocean. The Russian venture was part of a process of territorial expansion that began in the country's heartland in the late 1580s, when people started moving eastward into the area of Asia known as Siberia. They were looking for "soft gold"—the fur of a forest-dwelling animal called the sable, which at that time was the most valuable fur on the world market. This search carried Russian trappers and hunters—*promyshlenniks*—across Siberia on a wave of conquest and exploitation*. They reached the Pacific in 1639.

* exploitation relationship in which one side benefits at the other's expense

By the early 1700s, the *promyshlenniks* had all but wiped out the fur-bearing animals of Siberia. Russia then launched a series of expeditions to explore the North Pacific Ocean, searching for a good route to North America. Peter the Great, Russia's ruler, declared that the goal of these expeditions

was to "find glory for the state through art and science." But the explorers also were looking for new sources of furs.

In 1741 an expedition led by Vitus Bering, a Danish navigator working for Russia, made the first landing on the Alaskan peninsula. Although Bering died on the return voyage to Russia, his crew brought back a load of sea otter pelts. These glossy, waterproof furs quickly became more valuable than sable. Between 1743 and 1800, Russian trading companies made more than 100 voyages to the coastal regions of Alaska—known at first as Alakshak—and to the Aleutian Islands that extend southwest from Alaska. Their ships carried hundreds of thousands of sea otter and seal pelts back to Russia.

These voyages lasted from one to ten years. They were organized and paid for by small trading companies formed by merchant families from European Russia and Siberia. The crews were Russian peasants and Siberians. They relied heavily on the hunting and seafaring skills of Native Americans in Alaska, whom they forced to work for them. At first the Russians lived in temporary camps in Alaska. But by the late 1700s they had established their first permanent settlements in the Aleutian Islands.

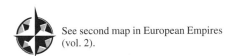

See second map in European Empires (vol. 2).

The Russian-American Company. The early phase of Russia's Alaskan adventure ended in 1799, when the Russian crown organized a single trading firm, the Russian-American Company, to manage all activities in North America. The company's first colonial governor was a tough, experienced merchant named Alexander Baranov. In 1799 he founded a colonial capital at New Archangel, later called Sitka, on a coastal island in southeastern Alaska. By the early 1840s, the town had three churches, two schools, and more than a hundred wooden houses for its 983 residents.

Baranov founded several settlements on the coast of northern California, including Fort Ross, just north of the San Francisco Bay. Besides hunting for seals and sea otters, the Russians who lived in this region grew grain and vegetables and raised livestock for the Alaskan settlements. They also traded with the Spanish colonists farther south along the California coast.

As the Russian-American Company expanded, it faced increasing hostility from some Native Americans, especially the TLINGIT INDIANS. In the early 1800s, the Russians fought several battles with the Tlingit. British and American traders also became a problem, presenting the Russians with serious competition in the Alaskan fur trade. When sea otters became scarce in the early 1800s, the Russians turned inland, exploring and fur trapping in the Alaskan interior.

The fur supply began to run out in California as well, and in 1841 the Russian-American Company abandoned its claims there. Meanwhile, Great Britain and the United States forced Russia to accept boundaries that confined its activities to Alaska. By the early 1860s, the population of Russian settlements in North America included about 7,700 Native Americans, 600 Russians, and 1,900 Creoles—people born to Russian fathers and Indian mothers. Russia found it increasingly difficult to supply and protect these distant settlements. To gain the United States as an ally and to create a buffer* between Russian Siberia and British Canada, Russia sold Alaska to the United States for $7.2 million in 1867. (*See also* **Aleut Peoples; Eskimo Peoples; Fur Trade.**)

* *buffer* protective barrier between two rivals

St. Augustine, Florida

St. Augustine, Florida

* **outpost** frontier settlement or military base

See map in Spanish Borderlands (vol. 4).

In 1565 Pedro Menéndez de Avilés founded St. Augustine, now the oldest city in the United States. This picture, originally published in Montanus's *New World,* shows the settlement as it looked in 1671.

Founded by the Spanish in 1565, St. Augustine survived numerous attacks and other difficulties to become the oldest permanent European settlement in the United States today. Until the mid-1700s, the town served primarily as a defensive outpost*, protecting Spanish interests in FLORIDA and guarding the sea routes between Spanish America and Europe.

In the mid-1500s, French Protestants, known as HUGUENOTS, established Fort Caroline in northeastern Florida (near present-day Jacksonville). The Spanish saw the French settlement as a threat to their territorial claims in Florida as well as to the Spanish treasure fleets that sailed along the coast on their way to Spain from the WEST INDIES.

In 1565 Pedro MENÉNDEZ DE AVILÉS, the captain of Spain's Caribbean fleet, led an expedition to drive the French from Florida. After destroying Fort Caroline, the Spaniards marched about 50 miles to the south, where Menéndez founded St. Augustine on September 8 at the site of an Indian village. Over the next several years, Menéndez established several other settlements in Florida, but only St. Augustine survived.

Menéndez obtained supplies and colonists to help St. Augustine survive the difficult early years. Provisions were often scarce, and the community lived under the threat of Indian attack. In later years, Spanish missionaries converted many Native Americans to Christianity and made them loyal to

Spain, thus ending the Indian threat. Supplies remained a problem, however, and the settlement depended greatly on shipments of goods from other parts of Spanish America. St. Augustine faced other dangers as well.

privateer privately owned ship authorized by the government to attack and capture enemy vessels; also the ship's master

In 1586 the English privateer* Sir Francis DRAKE attacked and burned St. Augustine. The Spanish rebuilt the settlement, but a hurricane and fire destroyed it again in 1599. Once more the colonists rebuilt the town. After English pirates attacked and plundered St. Augustine in 1668, Spain expanded its defenses. This included construction of a massive stone fortress, the Castillo de San Marcos. In the early 1700s, the British attacked Florida again from a base in South Carolina. Though they gained control of parts of the colony and burned the town of St. Augustine, they were unable to capture the fort. Two sieges led by James OGLETHORPE of Georgia in the 1740s also proved unsuccessful.

In its early years, St. Augustine sprawled haphazardly on its site. Eventually, however, the settlement developed in a more orderly fashion. The fort protected the entrance to the harbor. The town itself, which occupied higher ground, had wooden houses laid out in blocks. Like most Spanish communities, St. Augustine had a public square and market at its center. Over time the colonists constructed better-designed and sturdier buildings.

Throughout Spanish rule, St. Augustine remained an economically undeveloped military outpost and mission, often unable to raise enough food to feed itself or to produce a valuable export. Outwardly, the town reflected Spanish culture. But by the 1600s, it had a diverse population that included Spaniards, Native Americans, mestizos*, blacks, Italians, Greeks, and other ethnic groups that had come to Florida to work on plantations.

mestizo person of mixed Spanish and Indian ancestry

In 1763, under the terms of the TREATY OF PARIS, Britain won control of Florida. Nearly 3,000 Spanish residents left the colony. During the American Revolution, Loyalists* from the northern colonies arrived seeking haven in this area still under British rule. When Spain regained possession of Florida in 1783, the British settlers went elsewhere. St. Augustine became part of the United States after Spain ceded* Florida to the young nation in an 1819 treaty. (*See also* **Cities and Towns; Colonial Administration; European Empires; Spanish Borderlands.**)

Loyalist American colonist who remained faithful to Britain during the American Revolution

cede to yield or surrender

St. Lawrence River

See map in New France (vol. 3).

See third map in Exploration, Age of (vol. 2).

The St. Lawrence River flows from the eastern end of Lake Ontario to the Gulf of St. Lawrence. One of the most important waterways in the North American colonies, it provided easy access to the interior of the continent for explorers, fur traders, and settlers. The French settlements along this valuable waterway formed the core of NEW FRANCE.

Jacques CARTIER was the first European to navigate the St. Lawrence River. In 1534 he explored the Gulf of St. Lawrence, which lies between the mouth of the river and the Atlantic Ocean. The following year Cartier returned and sailed up the river. He stopped at the present site of QUEBEC, where he established a temporary settlement, and continued as far as modern-day MONTREAL. Rapids prevented the explorer from traveling farther.

In the 1500s, French fishing boats regularly sailed to the St. Lawrence to take advantage of the plentiful fish in the river and nearby coastal waters. On shore the fishing crews encountered the HURON, OTTAWA, and other Native Americans, sometimes obtaining furs from them. The Europeans used Tadoussac—located where the St. Lawrence meets the Saguenay River—as a fishing and trading station.

The first permanent settlement on the St. Lawrence was Quebec, founded in 1608 by Samuel de CHAMPLAIN. From there the French spread westward along the river, founding Trois-Rivières in 1634 and Montreal in 1642. In the years that followed, the COMPANY OF ONE HUNDRED ASSOCIATES, a French group in charge of colonizing North America, granted large tracts* of land on both banks of the river to nobles and high-ranking officials. Known as seigneurs, these colonial landholders divided their estates into long, narrow farms with one short end on the water, so that each household had access to the river for transport and communication. A continuous ribbon of farms formed along the river banks between the large towns.

* **tract** area of land

Navigating the St. Lawrence River presented some difficulties. Thick fogs, treacherous reefs, and strong currents made travel hazardous at times. During the long winters, ice blocked the route for months. Nevertheless, the colonists managed to use the river as a highway almost year-round. In warm weather, they traveled in birchbark CANOES, and in the winter, they glided over the ice in horse-drawn sleds. By the 1730s, a road was completed along the bank between Quebec and Montreal, making movement by horseback possible.

See color plate 6, vol. 1.

Travelers used the St. Lawrence to reach distant points on the continent as well. They could follow the river to the GREAT LAKES and continue down the MISSISSIPPI RIVER to the Gulf of Mexico or take one of the various rivers heading into the Rocky Mountains. They could also head north from the St. Lawrence along the Saguenay River to James Bay and Hudson Bay. For this reason, the St. Lawrence was of enormous strategic* importance to the French and became a military target during conflicts with Britain. Although the French built forts in the area, riverfront settlements were exposed to attack. By 1763 both Quebec and Montreal had fallen, and the British, as the new rulers of Canada, gained the right to use the St. Lawrence River. (*See also* **Fur Trade.**)

* **strategic** key part of a plan; of military importance

Salem, Massachusetts

Salem, a village on the northeastern shore of MASSACHUSETTS, was one of the earliest English settlements in New England. Founded after PLYMOUTH but before BOSTON, Salem played a major part in the political and religious history of the Massachusetts Bay colony. In 1692 the town gained lasting fame as the site of the SALEM WITCHCRAFT TRIALS.

Salem had its start in 1626, when an English colony established at Cape Ann failed financially. Some of the bankrupt colony's settlers moved to a place the Indians called Naumkeag, where the land was better for farming than at Cape Ann. In 1628 a group of PURITANS took over Naumkeag. Calling their group the Massachusetts Bay Company, the Puritans acquired a royal charter* to the land the following year. Settlers began to arrive in Naumkeag, including two ministers who founded the Congregationalist Church, the first Puritan church built in North America. The colonists renamed their settlement

* **charter** written grant from a ruler conferring certain rights and privileges

Salem, possibly a shortened version of Jerusalem, and it became the first town in the Massachusetts Bay colony.

In 1630 a fleet of Massachusetts Bay Company ships, under the leadership of Governor John WINTHROP, landed at Salem. But the new settlers decided that Salem was not a suitable place for the colony's capital. Instead, they moved southwest and founded the town of Boston on a site that offered a good harbor.

Before long the citizens of Salem came into conflict with the authorities in Boston. The town's former minister, Roger WILLIAMS, got into trouble with the colony's leaders for opposing their religious and political views. Most of the people of Salem supported Williams, and they protested when colonial officials decided in 1635 to banish him from the colony. A few of Williams's followers left Salem and joined him in founding the new colony of RHODE ISLAND.

Salem developed into a thriving fishing and shipping center. In the early 1690s, the town became caught up in a frenzied witch-hunt. Over the course of a year, some 250 people were accused of practicing witchcraft. Although many of Salem's leading citizens thought the accusations were false, 19 "witches" were hanged. Shortly afterward, most judges and jury members admitted that the executions had been a mistake.

Twice during the 1700s, Salem served as the temporary capital of Massachusetts. In February 1775, as patriots* in the American colonies began to prepare for the fight for independence, a clash occurred at the North Bridge of Salem. It was the first armed resistance of the American colonists to British troops. When the American Revolution came at last, Salem Bay was the home port of about 200 privateers* who attacked British ships.

See color plate 3, vol. 4.

* *patriot* American colonist who supported independence from Britain

* *privateer* privately owned ship authorized by the government to attack and capture enemy vessels; also the ship's master

Salem Witchcraft Trials

* *hysteria* extreme, uncontrollable fear

* *charter* written grant from a ruler conferring certain rights and privileges

* *supernatural* related to forces beyond the normal world; miraculous

*I*n the 1600s, many people in Europe and North American colonies believed in MAGIC AND WITCHCRAFT. In the town of SALEM, MASSACHUSETTS, this general belief combined with certain tensions in the community to produce an outbreak of witch-hunting hysteria*. A series of witchcraft trials were held in 1692 and 1693, leading to the sentencing and death of more than 20 colonists.

The PURITANS of New England had come to North America with the dream of creating God's kingdom on Earth. But the fulfillment of this glorious project had not gone smoothly. The colonists were battered by Indian wars such as KING PHILIP'S WAR and frustrated by political developments in England that resulted in Massachusetts losing its charter* and becoming part of the DOMINION OF NEW ENGLAND. Many Puritans saw these difficulties as signs that Satan was attacking their community. Ministers such as Cotton MATHER warned that the devil was trying to overthrow the kingdom of Christ, using witches as his servants. The witches made a bargain with Satan and received supernatural* powers to harm others, generally by causing the illness or death of people or their livestock.

These smoldering tensions burst into flame in Salem Village, a small rural offshoot of Salem (now the town of Danvers). Several children and teenage girls claimed to be under the spell of evil spirits summoned by witches. The

Salem Witchcraft Trials

This undated drawing, entitled "The Salem Martyrs," shows townspeople watching a public execution. Nineteen accused witches were hanged in Salem, and several more died in prison, before the witch-hunting craze died down.

See color plate 3, vol. 4.

* **magistrate** official with administrative and often judicial functions

first to be accused of being a witch was Tituba, a slave in the home of Samuel Parris, the town's minister. Tituba confessed to practicing witchcraft and named others who were supposed to have made bargains with the devil. Soon more townspeople—mostly young women—were "possessed," falling into fits before the church officials and civil magistrates* who were investigating the matter.

In the beginning, only people without any power in the community were charged with witchcraft—the slave Tituba and some poor, old women who had earned reputations as troublemakers, scolds, or users of traditional folk magic. Later, as the hysteria spread to Andover and other nearby towns, the accusations widened to include wealthy, respectable women and some men related to them. Even Lady Phips, wife of the governor of Massachusetts, and George Burroughs, a former minister of Salem, were accused.

A special court met in Salem in early summer 1692 to try the witchcraft cases. The first person to be sentenced to death was Bridget Bishop, who was hanged for witchcraft on June 10. By late September, the court had executed 14 women and 5 men. Another man died under torture, and several people perished in prison. Interestingly, those who admitted to practicing witchcraft escaped the death sentence. Only those who were convicted and refused to confess faced execution.

Even before the court began its grim work, some people in the community spoke out against accusing people on extremely flimsy evidence. Many of the charges were based on testimony that someone had been tortured by an apparition—a supernatural image—of the supposed witch. Several ministers, including Increase MATHER, claimed this kind of vision was insufficient evidence of witchcraft because Satan might take the shape of an innocent person. After a few months of convictions and executions, other colonists came to believe that the witch-hunt was a terrible mistake.

Governor Phips disbanded the special court in October. In early January, another court sentenced three more people to death, but they were not executed. In all more than 250 people, 80 percent of them women, had faced accusations of being witches. Afterward some judges and jury members publicly confessed that they had been tragically wrong.

Scholars have suggested many reasons for the outbreak of witch-hunting in Salem. The accusers were mostly young women who lacked power in colonial society. The attention they received for their role in the trials, combined with the psychological stress of adolescence, may have encouraged them. Old grudges, personal quarrels, economic hardship, and social tensions also provoked accusations of witchcraft. Generations of American writers and historians have found the Salem witchcraft trials a fascinating subject—and a frightening example of how fear and hysteria can tear a community apart. (*See also* **Gender Roles; Law and Legal Systems; Women, Roles of.**)

Santa Fe

* **Spanish Borderlands** northern part of New Spain, area now occupied by Florida, Texas, New Mexico, Arizona, and California

* **viceroy** person appointed as a monarch's representative to govern a province or colony

See map in Spanish Borderlands (vol. 4).

* **pueblo** Indian village

*F*ounded in about 1609, Santa Fe was the second capital of the Spanish colony of NEW MEXICO. It became the largest town in the colony and a frequent target for attacks by the PUEBLO INDIANS. Eventually, the residents made peace with the Indians, and Santa Fe emerged as a major trading center of the Spanish Borderlands*.

In 1598 Juan de OÑATE, New Mexico's founder, had established a capital called San Gabriel on the Rio Grande. When the viceroy* in MEXICO sent Don Pedro de Peralta to replace Oñate as governor, he gave instructions to move the capital to a new location. The reasons for the move are not clear—perhaps the viceroy felt that San Gabriel was too close to the farmlands of the Pueblo or too exposed in case of attack. At any rate, Peralta found a better site 25 miles to the southeast in a small, uninhabited, well-watered valley. He ordered construction of the province's new capital to begin.

Peralta gave the new capital the name Santa Fe, which means "Holy Faith." A city of that name had been built in Spain as a model for organizing cities in Spain's American colonies. Peralta and the men elected to the first town council laid out the city according to that model, with a central plaza, space for government buildings, and house and garden lots for the citizens. But as Santa Fe took shape, it began to resemble an Indian pueblo* because many of the builders were Indian workers who used traditional Southwestern materials and techniques. Houses were flat-roofed, with walls of adobe, or baked-clay bricks, covered with plaster.

By 1630 Santa Fe's population included 250 Spaniards and about 800 Indians or people of mixed blood. Along with the rest of New Mexico, Santa Fe

suffered a serious setback in 1680, when the Indians of the region rebelled against the Spanish in a violent uprising known as the PUEBLO REVOLT. The Indians killed some of the residents of Santa Fe, drove the rest out of New Mexico, and turned the governor's palace into a pueblo. Santa Fe remained in Indian hands until the Spanish reconquered the province in 1692.

During most of the 1700s, Apache, Ute, Comanche, and Navajo Indians from the border mountains frequently swept down in raids on Santa Fe. The Spanish finally made peace with these tribes in the 1770s. By that time, Santa Fe had already begun attracting traders from Mexico and LOUISIANA. The main goods offered for sale in its markets included sheep, wool, and skins.

After the British colonies won their independence, the United States began sending out expeditions to explore the Southwest. In 1807 Spanish troops arrested an American army officer named Zebulon Pike who had strayed into Spanish territory and imprisoned him in Santa Fe. Upon his return to the United States, Pike described the New Mexican capital as a backward place with "miserable houses" where cloth sold for an exorbitant price but sheep were extremely cheap.

American traders saw the city as a market for manufactured goods from the United States. In 1821 Americans from Missouri made the first journey to Santa Fe over what came to be called the Santa Fe Trail, beginning a busy wagon-train trade. Twenty-five years later, during the Mexican-American War, the United States gained control of New Mexico. Santa Fe became an American city and the capital of the state of New Mexico, but its Indian and Spanish heritage has remained alive.

Savannah, Georgia

* **buffer zone** neutral area between two enemy areas

* **charter** written grant from a ruler conferring certain rights and privileges

 See map in British Colonies (vol. 1).

* **evangelical** Christian movement emphasizing the importance of personal faith in leading to salvation

*F*ounded in 1733, Savannah was the first British settlement in the colony of GEORGIA. The town was built about 18 miles inland from the Atlantic Ocean on a plateau along the banks of the Savannah River. It served as the colony's capital until 1786.

In 1526 the Spanish made an unsuccessful attempt to establish a colony in present-day Georgia. They later founded several missions along the coast but abandoned them in the 1680s. During the early 1700s, the British became interested in using the area as a buffer zone* between their colonies in the Carolinas and Spanish FLORIDA.

In 1732 King George II granted a charter* to James OGLETHORPE and 20 other individuals to establish a colony in the region. In February of the following year, Oglethorpe and a group of colonists arrived at the Savannah River. They chose a site for a settlement and named it after the river. Oglethorpe quickly laid out the plans for the town—a rectangular layout of streets surrounding a series of open public squares. These squares, which eventually became individual parks, remain one of the distinctive features of the city today.

By the mid-1730s, Savannah had about 40 houses, each with a garden plot and about 50 acres of farmland. Around this time, the British preachers John and Charles Wesley came to town to spread their Methodist faith. Another evangelical* preacher, George WHITEFIELD, arrived soon afterward. In 1739 he founded the Bethesda Orphan Asylum, the first orphanage in North

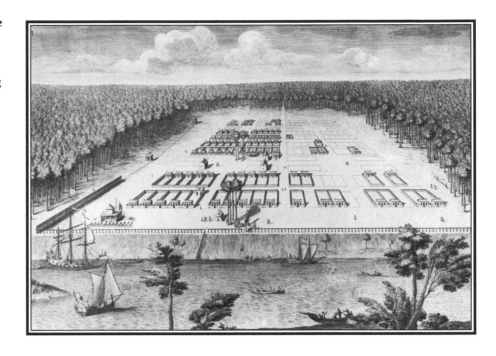

James Oglethorpe, founder of the British colony of Georgia, laid out the streets of Savannah in neat rectangles surrounding open public squares. Peter Gordon's 1734 engraving presents an early view of the city.

* **Anglican** of the Church of England

* **proprietor** person granted land and the right to establish a colony

America. It included a school that was free to the children of Savannah. Whitefield also established Christ Church, the first Anglican* church in the colony. Other religious groups followed, and by the mid-1700s, the town also contained a small but significant Jewish population.

Savannah developed slowly under the leadership of Oglethorpe and the other proprietors*. After the opening of its port in 1744, trade increased steadily, largely as a result of the expanding PLANTATION economy based on COTTON. Georgia came under the control of the British crown in 1752 and started to grow more rapidly. By the 1770s, Savannah had developed into one of the main cities of the South—but it was much smaller than CHARLESTON, SOUTH CAROLINA, or the cities of the northern colonies.

In the years leading up to the AMERICAN REVOLUTION, Savannah emerged as a center of opposition to British rule. By 1776 the city had become so anti-British that the royal governor was forced to flee the city. In December 1778, however, British troops attacked and captured Savannah. The following year a combined force of more than 6,000 French and American soldiers failed in an attempt to retake the city. The British remained in Savannah until July 1783, when American troops led by General Anthony Wayne forced them to evacuate. (*See also* **British Colonies; Cities and Towns; Government, Provincial.**)

Schools and Schooling

Schooling in colonial North America differed considerably from modern methods of education. Most instruction took place in the home, where parents or tutors taught children basic skills—reading, writing, and sometimes arithmetic—that would be useful in everyday life. Colonists did establish some public and private schools. Their curricula usually revolved around basics, but a few institutions offered more advanced subjects, such as history, geometry, astronomy, and languages.

British and Dutch Colonies

Settlers in the British and Dutch colonies generally placed great emphasis on education. Dutch children received instruction at home or in a small number of schools supported by colonial authorities and the Dutch Reformed Church. Parents who wanted their children to have more education than was available locally sent them to Europe or to schools in New England.

Education in the British colonies had its roots in England of the 1500s and 1600s, where religion and schooling were closely related. The Church of England controlled or influenced most schools, though PURITANS and Catholics took an active role in education as well. School founders and promoters in the colonies drew on this English tradition in establishing their own system of education.

New England. The Puritans associated education with religious devotion and social stability, and they took the lead in creating schools in New England. Although education was considered the realm of boys rather than girls, most white children received some instruction. Those who did not attend school often learned basic skills at home or as part of an apprenticeship*.

Massachusetts set the pace in establishing schools. As early as the 1630s, individuals in various towns began teaching basic skills to small groups of students in their homes. Most of the instruction was free, but few children attended. Some towns started higher-level grammar schools—such as the Boston Latin School, which was founded in 1635 and still exists today—that offered Latin, Greek, and other advanced courses. These early schools were supported primarily by public funds from taxes or rental of public lands. Qualified teachers, however, were generally in short supply.

* *apprenticeship* placing of young people in the care of a merchant or crafts worker to learn a profession

In 1774 at the Union Grammar School in New London, Connecticut, teacher Nathan Hale made special arrangements to teach "young ladies" in the early morning hours before the regular students—all male—arrived. Hale left teaching the following year to join the patriot cause. He later gained fame as a spy in the Revolutionary War.

Discouraged by the limited scope of education, colonial leaders in Massachusetts passed a law in 1647 to encourage the creation of schools. The law required towns with at least 50 families to establish a "petty" school to teach reading and writing. Towns with at least 100 families were directed to set up a grammar school, with a qualified teacher. These public schools would be funded through either public or private sources, depending on each town's circumstances. The other New England colonies soon began establishing public schools as well.

By the early 1700s, New England had a variety of public and private schools, with different levels of education. Local "petty" and grammar schools existed throughout the colonies, providing instruction in basic skills and more advanced studies. "Dame schools," run by women in their homes, offered basic instruction in reading and writing to boys and girls as young as age two or three. The women who ran the schools charged a fee to parents or were paid by the town. "Moving schools"—so called because they moved around a community—provided instruction for children in outlying areas of the towns. Only a few students had the opportunity to continue their education at COLLEGES in the region.

The Middle and Southern Colonies.   In New England, the Puritans led the way in creating a public school system. The middle colonies of New York, New Jersey, Pennsylvania, and Delaware, with their great religious diversity*, had no strong central force to organize an educational system. Schooling in those colonies was provided by communities, individuals, and various religious groups, such as the QUAKERS, Presbyterians, and Anglicans*. The groups established numerous schools, offering a mix of academic, practical, and religious subjects similar to those taught in the schools of New England.

Pennsylvania boasted a rich assortment of schools known for the high quality of their instruction. The Friends School in Philadelphia, founded by the Quakers in 1701, was one of the finest grammar schools in the colonies. Many students came from other areas to attend Philadelphia's boarding schools and day schools. New York and New Jersey had schools sponsored by various religious denominations*, including the Dutch Reformed Church, which continued to conduct classes in Dutch until the 1770s. New York City possessed a number of religious schools, even one established by Jews.

The middle colonies also had dame schools and a variety of nonreligious private schools. Some private schools offered both day and evening classes. Evening schools, which combined academic and practical instruction, were especially popular in towns with large numbers of young people.

The southern colonies had little organized education at any level. Schooling was a private matter, provided in a rather haphazard way. Setting up schools was difficult because the region had few large towns or cities and the population was scattered throughout the countryside. Wealthy planters and merchants often hired private tutors for their children. The few schools that did exist concentrated primarily on reading, writing, and arithmetic. The city of Charleston in South Carolina probably offered the greatest variety of schools in the South, including free schools and charity schools that served the needs of poor residents.

* *diversity* variety

* *Anglican* member of the Church of England

* *denomination* organized group of religious congregations

French and Spanish Colonies

The colonists of NEW FRANCE and NEW SPAIN placed less importance on education than the English and Dutch settlers did. Moreover, schooling in these colonies was closely connected to religion. Both the French and the Spanish developed their own educational systems.

French Colonies. In the British colonies, Protestant churches supported education so that people would be able to read the Bible. In the French colonies, schools had a larger responsibility. They were required to teach Roman Catholic doctrine* and to promote loyalty and obedience to the French crown.

The majority of French colonists lived on farms in rural areas and had little use for formal education. Nevertheless, the Catholic Church and the French crown hoped to place a school in each parish, or church district. To provide the priests and schoolmasters needed to achieve this goal, the authorities established a seminary* in Quebec in 1659. However, the crushing labor of colonial life and the rigorous nature of Catholic instruction discouraged many settlers from seeking much schooling. Despite such obstacles, colonial and church officials founded many parish schools by the mid-1700s.

Some religious schools in the French colonies provided an excellent course of study that matched that of schools in France. Among these were a school in QUEBEC founded by the Jesuits* and a school in MONTREAL established by the Sulpicians, another religious order. Most students in these schools were children of government officials and wealthy merchants. Boys from the lower classes obtained schooling through apprenticeships or at local parish schools. By 1707 a number of religious schools had been established in rural parishes to educate girls of the middle and lower classes. Daughters of wealthy French colonists attended schools at Quebec, Montreal, and Trois-Rivières.

Educational opportunities outside of New France were extremely limited. Most children in the colony of LOUISIANA received only basic instruction from their parents. The only successful school there was founded and operated by a group of Catholic nuns. The Catholic Church failed to establish a seminary in the colony. Louisiana colonists who wanted their children to receive any higher education had to send them to France.

Spanish Colonies. As in the French colonies, religion played a vital role in education in the Spanish colonies. Most schooling in the Spanish Borderlands* took place at Catholic MISSIONS, founded to teach Christian beliefs and practices to Native Americans.

Missionaries and priests typically brought the children of prominent Indians to live at the missions and made them follow a tough educational program. These youth, called *doctrineros,* then taught other Indians, translated sermons and religious writings, and accompanied missionaries to other regions. The education of villagers in the missions consisted of weekly sermons and daily lectures. The missionaries also taught agricultural techniques, crafts, and other practical matters.

There were few schools outside of the missions until the late 1700s, when the colonial government took responsibility for education. Until then

---

* *doctrine* set of principles or beliefs accepted by a religious or political group

* *seminary* school that trains individuals for the priesthood

* *Jesuit* Roman Catholic religious order
* *Spanish Borderlands* northern part of New Spain, area now occupied by Florida, Texas, New Mexico, Arizona, and California

A Hard School

Catholic education in the French colonies was a difficult experience. At the seminary in Quebec, boys typically rose at four in the morning and attended classes and religious services until eight at night. Their hair was cut short, and meals provided just enough nourishment to keep the boys healthy. All forms of amusement were forbidden. Students were required to avoid contact with their parents and family to keep from forming ties with the nonreligious world. Little wonder that nearly 80 percent of the boys dropped out before graduating.

the children of most Spanish colonists learned how to read and write at home from their parents or private tutors. Parents also had an obligation to teach their children the basic principles of the Catholic faith.

When formal schools began to emerge, they served the children of both a village and the surrounding areas. As in other colonial regions, some young people received instruction in basic skills through apprenticeship. The Spanish Borderlands had no colleges, so students seeking higher education had to travel to Mexico or Europe. (*See also* **Books; Education; Libraries and Learned Societies; Literacy; Roman Catholic Church.**)

Science

Science played a small but important role in colonial society. In the early colonial period, explorers, missionaries, and colonists contributed to scientific knowledge by making MAPS AND CHARTS; writing descriptions of the land and its inhabitants; and gathering samples of rocks, plants, and animals. Such activities had great practical value because they encouraged further exploration of the continent and aided the search for natural resources.

During this period when Europeans were exploring and colonizing North America, scientific thinking in Europe changed. A movement known as the ENLIGHTENMENT, which placed great emphasis on reason and on detailed observation and measurement, swept through Europe. Influenced by this movement, scientists in the colonies gathered information and attempted to fit facts into theories that would explain how the natural world operated. At this time, educated people took a great interest in "natural history"—a subject that covered many topics now considered to be separate sciences, such as botany, geology, and zoology.

Dutch Colony. The Dutch colonists made scientific contributions mainly in mapmaking and in describing the land, plants, and animals of New Netherland and the Native Americans who lived there. The earliest maps and charts of the colony came from the observations of Dutch fur traders and explorers. In the mid-1600s, a colonist named Adriaen van der Donck wrote *A Description of New Netherland* (1655). The book contained information on the geography, plants, animals, and weather of the region, as well as notes on Indian culture and folklore.

British Colonies. Beginning in the late 1500s, the English explorers in North America made notes and drawings of the people and landscape and collected samples of plants and animals to take back to Europe. Illustrations and accounts by early settlers such as John WHITE and John SMITH of Virginia gave people on the other side of the Atlantic Ocean their first ideas of what the "New World" was like.

Most of the colonists involved in scientific work in North America were not professional, full-time scientists, but amateurs. Working as farmers, ministers, merchants, and printers, they had a keen interest in natural history, ASTRONOMY, and other branches of science. Among the leading amateur

Science

Many colonial scientific experiments dealt with electricity. This undated engraving shows an early demonstration of static electricity.

* *alchemy* study aimed at turning common metals into gold

* *anthropology* study of past human cultures, usually by digging up ruins

* *naturalist* person who studies plants and animals in their natural surroundings

scientists were Connecticut governor John Winthrop, Jr., an avid student of alchemy* and astronomy; New England minister Cotton MATHER, who wrote extensively on natural history; Cadwallader COLDEN, a prominent official in New York, who published works on medicine, physics, anthropology*, and botany; his daughter Jane COLDEN, who became a well-known naturalist*; and political leader Thomas JEFFERSON, who provided detailed information on the geography of his native region in *Notes on the State of Virginia* (1784).

Science instruction in colonial schools and colleges was very limited, and scientific instruments such as telescopes were scarce. Europe remained the center of scientific study. Bookstores in all the large colonial cities offered English and European books on science, and many amateur scientists from the colonies corresponded with researchers and thinkers overseas.

Colonial scientists eventually established their own scientific societies. The first such organization was the AMERICAN PHILOSOPHICAL SOCIETY, founded in Philadelphia in 1743. Noted as a center of scientific activity, Philadelphia was the home of the tireless researcher and inventor Benjamin FRANKLIN, whose experiments with electricity made him one of the leading scientists of his day. Botanists John and William BARTRAM and the astronomer David RITTENHOUSE also lived there. Boston acquired its own scientific society, the American Academy of Arts and Sciences, in 1780.

* *New France* French colony centered in the St. Lawrence River valley, an area known as Canada; included the Great Lakes region and, until 1713, Acadia (present-day Nova Scotia)

French Colonies. Scientific study in New France* was broader and better organized than in the British colonies. The colony was closely controlled by the French crown, and science was an official activity encouraged and supported by the state. To gain as much information as possible about the territory they ruled, French administrators instructed commanders at remote fur-trading posts and military forts to collect minerals, plants, and animals and to observe how the Indians used plants for medicine.

Much of the scientific activity in New France centered on measuring the earth, which included mapmaking and surveying. Among the leading

mapmakers were Samuel de CHAMPLAIN, one of the finest geographers of the 1600s, and Jean Deshayes, who surveyed and charted the St. Lawrence River in the late 1600s and early 1700s. The study of natural history attracted the interest of people such as Michel Sarrazin, a naval surgeon who spent 25 years collecting and studying plants and animals in North America. Jean-François Galtier arrived in New France in 1742 and for the next 14 years made a detailed study of the local plants, all the while keeping a daily record of the region's temperatures.

French officials also authorized the religious order of the JESUITS to gather information about the geography of New France. Besides mapping much of northern North America, the Jesuits made valuable contributions to ethnography—the study of native peoples and cultures—through their observations and writings on Indian life.

In 1670 the Royal Academy of Sciences in Paris began sponsoring expeditions into the interior of North America. These expeditions resulted in mapmaking and in studies of river systems and astronomy that remained unsurpassed long after the colonial period. The Royal Academy also appointed officials to oversee science in New France. As a result, scientific activity there became highly organized and stayed under the control of French authorities. As in the British colonies, scientists in New France maintained a lively correspondence with researchers and scientists in Europe.

Spanish Colonies. For the Spanish, science was closely linked to exploration and the drive for empire. The Spanish crown encouraged early explorers to make maps and record what they saw. Maps and information gathered on plants, animals, resources, and Indians helped in the planning of settlements.

Much scientific activity in the Spanish Borderlands* was undertaken by the Royal Corps of Engineers, a special unit within the colonial army. Its members were trained in mathematics, mapmaking, engineering, and other subjects. In the course of surveying territory, preparing maps, and planning and building forts, bridges, and towns, the corps made detailed observations on geography, weather, wildlife, and other scientific topics.

In the late 1700s, Spain sent large expeditions to the western coast of North America, including California. These expeditions focused on natural history and the systematic observation of plants, animals, minerals, and Indian cultures. Throughout this period, scientists in Spanish America and Europe exchanged information and ideas. Such international cooperation resulted in the collection and analysis of enormous amounts of data. Yet because of political turmoil, changes in government, and simple neglect, some of the greatest scientific achievements of this region remained unpublished until long after the colonial period had ended. (*See also* **Education; Libraries and Learned Societies; Technology.**)

* *Spanish Borderlands* northern part of New Spain, area now occupied by Florida, Texas, New Mexico, Arizona, and California

Sculpture

See *Art.*

* *militia* army of citizens who may be called into action in a time of emergency

*I*n September 1774, colonial representatives gathered in Philadelphia at the FIRST CONTINENTAL CONGRESS to discuss their complaints about British rule. Before adjourning, the members agreed to meet again if the British government did not change certain policies they found objectionable. By the following spring, the colonists concluded that the British had made no attempts to deal with their complaints. More importantly, fighting had broken out between colonial militia* and British troops in the Battles of LEXINGTON AND CONCORD. On May 10, 1775, delegates from all the colonies except Georgia arrived in Philadelphia for the Second Continental Congress.

The Delegates to Congress.   The new congress struggled with the rapidly worsening state of affairs and the growing conflict with Great Britain. At their first meeting, the delegates expressed a wide range of opinions. The conservative members believed that the British government had simply misunderstood colonial concerns and demands. They insisted that the two sides could still resolve their differences and restore their former relationship.

Other representatives rejected such arguments. They believed that the British government was deliberately trying to take away the rights of the colonists. They argued that separating from Britain and declaring independence was the only way to maintain their freedom.

The majority of delegates fell somewhere in between. They hoped that Britain and the colonies could work out their differences but were not convinced that this would be possible. Although not ready to declare independence, they were willing to use armed force if it might bring their relationship with Britain back into balance.

All the members agreed on certain issues. They firmly supported the need to defend colonial rights, with military action if necessary. They rejected British efforts to tax the colonies and insisted that PARLIAMENT repeal* all such laws. They also condemned the INTOLERABLE ACTS, which imposed restrictions on Massachusetts colonists in punishment for the BOSTON TEA PARTY.

* *repeal* to undo a law

Congress Begins Its Work.   The delegates to the Second Continental Congress faced serious problems. The most important was how to respond to the outbreaks of fighting. Following the Battles of Lexington and Concord, British and colonial forces also clashed at BUNKER HILL and at Fort Ticonderoga, which Ethan ALLEN and his GREEN MOUNTAIN BOYS captured from the British.

Faced with these outbreaks of violence and the possibility of others like them, the delegates—even the conservative ones—decided that they must prepare a military defense against the British. In June 1775, the congress created the CONTINENTAL ARMY and appointed George WASHINGTON its commander in chief. To help pay for colonial defense, it issued paper currency.

In July the congress issued two documents to explain its position. The first, adopted on July 6, was the Declaration of the Causes and Necessity for Taking Up Arms. It explained that the colonies had adopted military measures simply to defend their liberties from the tyranny* of Parliament. It raised the possibility of independence but declared that the colonies would not break away from Britain if matters could be resolved otherwise. The other

* *tyranny* unjust use of power

document was the OLIVE BRANCH PETITION, which asked the king to use his influence in Parliament on behalf of the colonists and to restore peace.

Changing Sentiment in Congress. In the fall of 1775, the congress continued preparations for colonial defense while waiting for a response from the British government. In October its members received news that the king had refused to receive the Olive Branch Petition. Moreover, he had condemned the colonists as rebels and had ordered additional troops to the colonies.

By December 1775, independence had become the subject of constant debate both in and out of the congress. Several events pushed the delegates toward separation from Britain, including the fact that a number of colonies had established new, independent governments. As the debate continued, the congress took on greater responsibility for coordinating colonial activities and preparations for war.

By early 1776, a majority in the congress favored independence, but the delegates were hesitant to take that step without strong public backing. The writer Thomas PAINE helped build that support with his pamphlet *Common Sense,* which argued the cause of independence. Meanwhile, new British policies made separation seem more likely. In December 1775, Parliament had passed the Prohibitory Act, which banned all trade with the colonies and authorized the seizure of all American ships. Two months later, colonists discovered that Britain was hiring foreign troops to fight in North America. The idea that Britain would enlist foreigners to make war against its colonies convinced many that reconciliation* with Britain was impossible. The movement toward independence gained momentum.

In March 1776, the congress appointed Silas Deane envoy* to France and instructed him to request aid and arms. The congress also authorized American privateers* to attack British trade, and on April 6, it closed American ports to the British. By the end of April, independence and war seemed certain.

Independence and Afterward. On May 15, the congress authorized all colonies to establish governments independent of the king and Parliament. By this action, the colonies withdrew their loyalty to the crown and cut the final ties that bound them to Britain. Although some delegates still feared independence, they now supported it.

On June 7, Richard Henry LEE of Virginia introduced a proposal in the congress to declare independence from Britain. However, a final decision on the matter was put off until July. Meanwhile, a congressional committee began preparing a DECLARATION OF INDEPENDENCE. A draft of the document was presented to the congress at the end of June, and it was adopted a few days later. After making some changes in the text, the congress approved the final version of the Declaration on July 4.

Throughout the period of the AMERICAN REVOLUTION, the Second Continental Congress functioned as a national government. Besides supervising the war effort and managing political and economic matters, it began drawing up a plan for a permanent union of states. In November 1777, the congress adopted a loose framework of government—the Articles of Confederation.

* **reconciliation** reaching agreement after a dispute

* **envoy** person representing a government abroad

* **privateer** privately owned ship authorized by the government to attack and capture enemy vessels; also the ship's master

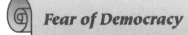

Fear of Democracy

By spring 1776, much of the opposition to independence focused on fears of the disorder and bad government democracy might bring. Even patriot John Adams worried about such a possibility:

I fear that in every Assembly members will obtain an influence by noise, not sense; by meanness, not greatness; by ignorance, not learning; by contracted hearts, not large souls. I fear, too, that it will be impossible to convince and persuade people to establish wise regulations.

* *ratification* formal approval

With the ratification* of this plan by the states in 1781, the congress became known as the Congress of the Confederation. This congress remained in existence until 1789, when the states adopted the U.S. Constitution, forming a new national government. (*See also* **Independence Movements.**)

Seigneurial System

* *New France* French colony centered in the St. Lawrence River valley, an area known as Canada; included the Great Lakes region and, until 1713, Acadia (present-day Nova Scotia)
* *tract* area of land
* *feudal* relating to an economic and political system in which individuals give service to a landowner in return for protection and the use of land

*I*n 1627 the COMPANY OF ONE HUNDRED ASSOCIATES, which managed the French colony of New France*, introduced the seigneurial system of landholding in the St. Lawrence Valley. The company distributed tracts* of land called seigneuries to nobles, high-ranking military officers, senior government and religious officials, and a few wealthy merchants. After the company was dissolved in 1663, the French crown took over the task of assigning seigneuries.

The seigneurial system was modeled after the feudal* system of France. Landholders, or seigneurs, kept only a small portion of their land for their own use. The rest they parceled out among farmers called *censitaires,* who legally owned the land and could sell it or leave it to their heirs. Anyone who asked could receive one of these plots of land. *Censitaires* had to give their seigneurs a yearly payment known as the *cens* and a share of the profits if they sold their property to anyone other than a legal heir. Seigneurs enjoyed certain ceremonial privileges, such as the right to carry a sword and be buried within a church. They also had the power to establish courts of justice. In exchange for their privileges, they had certain obligations. Seigneurs had to pay the state a share of any profits from the sale of land, and they were required to build flour mills for the *censitaires.*

The seigneurial system promoted settlement in the St. Lawrence Valley and established agriculture as the basis of the economy. Although seigneuries were also granted in the province of ACADIA, the system did not have much success there. In French LOUISIANA, the pattern of landholding was somewhat different. Instead of having seigneurs distribute land, the company that ran the colony gave land grants directly to the *censitaires.* (*See also* **Class Structure in European Colonies; Land Ownership.**)

Seminole Indians

*D*uring the 1700s, the Seminole Indians lived in FLORIDA and traded with both the Spanish and the British colonists. After the United States gained possession of Florida in 1819, the Seminole fought a long and unsuccessful battle to avoid losing their land in the region.

The earliest Seminole, a group of the CREEK INDIANS, had left their homeland on the Chattahoochee River in GEORGIA and migrated to northern Florida in the early 1700s. Survivors of various conquered tribes, as well as runaway slaves from Georgia plantations, joined the group. Sometime around 1775, the tribe came to be known as the Seminole Indians, from the Spanish word *cimarrón,* meaning "wild" or "runaway."

The Seminole lived in towns and produced most of their food by farming, along with some hunting and fishing. Through trade with the European colonists, they obtained items such as tools and cloth. The Seminole also herded cattle, which they sold to the Spanish missions in Florida and the British colonies to the north.

During the late 1700s, control of Florida passed back and forth between Spain and Great Britain. The Seminole had generally peaceful relationships with both sets of rulers. After the American Revolution, however, the tribe came into conflict with citizens of Georgia who objected to the Seminole's policy of taking in runaway slaves. During the War of 1812 (1812–1815) between Britain and the United States, the Seminole conducted several raids on the Georgia border. American troops struck back in 1817, beginning the conflict that would became known as the First Seminole War. Troops under the command of Major General Andrew Jackson, who later became President, defeated the Indians in 1818.

The following year, the Spanish agreed to transfer ownership of Florida to the United States, and the Seminole came under American control. In the 1830s, Congress passed a law requiring all Indians in the eastern part of the country to relocate to lands west of the Mississippi River. The tribe resisted this move. Led by a warrior named Osceola, the Indians fought for seven years in the Second Seminole War, the longest and most expensive Indian war in America's history. Eventually, the Seminole were defeated, and most were forced to move to Oklahoma. However, a small number managed to avoid capture by American forces and they remained in the swamps of southern Florida.

Seneca Indians

See *Iroquois Confederacy.*

Separatists

* **dissenter** person who disagrees with the beliefs and practices of the established church

* **ritual** ceremony that follows a set pattern

* **Anglican** of the Church of England

Separatists were PURITANS who broke away from the Church of England in the late 1500s and established their own churches. Persecuted because of their beliefs, many of these dissenters* left England. A small group of them, known as the PILGRIMS, migrated to North America and founded PLYMOUTH COLONY.

The Puritans objected to the rituals* and structure of the Anglican* Church and disagreed with some of its teachings. Their demands for change led to a movement of reform within the church. The Separatists, however, thought that the church had become so corrupt that they must break away from it completely.

The Separatists wanted to establish independent congregations that did not have to answer to a higher church authority. They believed that each congregation should be able to choose its own leaders and dismiss them at will. The Church of England and royal authorities condemned such ideas and persecuted the Separatists.

In the early 1660s, many Separatists fled to the Netherlands, which allowed them to practice their religion. But a number of them found life in a foreign country discouraging. They worked hard for little money and feared that their children were losing touch with their English heritage. Moreover, they saw little chance of advancing their faith in the Netherlands.

In 1619 a small group of Separatists received permission from the VIR-GINIA COMPANY OF LONDON to establish a colony in North America. They set sail the next year, accompanied by a number of other English settlers. Arriving in what is now Massachusetts, the Pilgrims established the Plymouth colony. (*See also* **Freedom of Religion; Protestant Churches.**)

Serra, Junípero

1713–1784
Spanish missionary

See map in Missions and Missionaries (vol. 3).

See color plate 3, vol. 3.

Known as the "Apostle to California," the Spanish missionary Father Junípero Serra founded a chain of missions along the coast of CAL-IFORNIA. These missions helped strengthen Spanish control of the region and spread Christianity to thousands of Native Americans living there.

Born in Spain, Serra joined the Franciscans—a Roman Catholic religious order—in 1731. Over the next two decades, he had a brilliant career as a teacher and preacher. In 1749 Serra left Europe to become a missionary in NEW SPAIN. After working among the Indians of central MEXICO for nine years, he became an administrator of a Catholic college in Mexico City.

In 1767 Serra was appointed head of missions for Baja (Lower) California. Around this time, colonial officials decided to establish missions in Alta (Upper) California as a way of strengthening Spanish claims to the region and discouraging Russian expansion along the Pacific coast. Father Serra was put in charge of the new mission system.

In 1769 Serra accompanied an expedition to Alta California led by Gaspar de PORTOLÁ. Arriving in present-day San Diego, the Franciscan father founded his first mission there on July 16. The next year he started the mission of San Carlos Borromeo on Monterey Bay, which became his headquarters.

Over the next 14 years, Serra established seven more missions in California. He worked tirelessly to maintain the missions and to minister to the spiritual and material needs of the Indians. Serra became a vigorous defender of Native Americans and of their rights—a position that often put him at odds with authorities. Yet at the same time, he was often harsh with his Indian charges. They were forced to work to support the missions and sometimes severely beaten for disobedience.

Under Serra's guidance, the California missions prospered. Thousands of Indians converted to Christianity and learned skills known to Europeans, such as ranching and blacksmithing. Serra continued to visit all the missions he had founded until his death at the mission of San Carlos Borromeo, near Monterey. (*See also* **California Indians; Missions and Missionaries; Roman Catholic Church; Russian Settlements.**)

Seven Cities of Cíbola

One of the most powerful forces driving European exploration of North America was the lure of GOLD. Spain's conquest of the Aztecs of MEXICO in 1521 and the Inca of Peru in 1533 brought the nation immense wealth in gold and silver. For years afterward, the Spanish searched for other golden empires to conquer, chasing rumors of gold across North and South America. No rumor led to a greater disappointment than the tale of the Seven Cities of Cíbola.

* conquistador Spanish explorer and conqueror

* viceroy person appointed as a monarch's representative to govern a province or colony

See first map in Exploration, Age of (vol. 2).

In 1536 a conquistador* named Alvar Núñez CABEZA DE VACA reached Mexico after years of wandering through the Southwest. Cabeza de Vaca repeated stories he had heard from Indians about seven fabulously rich cities in the lands north of Mexico. Three years later the viceroy* of NEW SPAIN sent a priest named Marcos de Niza to look for the cities. ESTEBAN, an African who had traveled with Cabeza de Vaca, served as the expedition's guide. Hostile Indians killed Esteban, but Marcos de Niza returned to Mexico with the exciting news that he had glimpsed the golden cities.

In 1540 the viceroy sent out a large expedition under the command of Francisco Vásquez de CORONADO to find and conquer Cíbola. Father Marcos guided the troops north to the cities in what is now New Mexico. But to Coronado's dismay, the rich cities turned out to be a group of Zuni Indian pueblos, or villages. Although Coronado's men extended their search far into the Great Plains, they never found the seven fabulous cities of gold. (*See also* **Exploration, Age of; Zuni Indians.**)

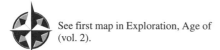
Seven Years' War

See *French and Indian War.*

Shawnee Indians

The Shawnee of Pennsylvania and Ohio formed alliances at various times with the French and the British. This engraving of a Shawnee man by Jean Baptiste Tardieu appeared in George Collot's *Voyage in Northern America,* published in Paris in 1826.

Driven from their Ohio River homeland by the Iroquois Indians, the Shawnee migrated repeatedly during the colonial period. At various times, they lived in present-day Tennessee, South Carolina, and Pennsylvania before returning to Ohio. They strongly resisted British colonists' efforts to expand their settlements on the western side of the Appalachian Mountains. The Shawnee fought against the British in the mid-1700s and with the British against the Americans during the Revolutionary War.

In the period before the Europeans arrived, the Shawnee Indians consisted of five groups, possibly five separate tribes. Each division lived independently with its own chief, though they did have some responsibilities to the larger tribe. The Shawnee hunted, farmed, and—after the Europeans arrived—engaged in the FUR TRADE.

Though the Shawnee had dealt with French fur traders in the Ohio Valley, they gave most of their business to the British. Yet the British consistently cheated the Shawnee and sold them large amounts of rum—a beverage that caused many problems in the Indian community. The Shawnee began to side with the French, but the British in Pennsylvania tried to regain their favor. British authorities convinced their powerful Indian allies, the Iroquois, to try to persuade the Shawnee to abandon their dealings with the French. But when the colonial government of Pennsylvania failed to establish an Indian department that would regulate trade, the Shawnee came to the conclusion that the British could not make their traders behave.

During the FRENCH AND INDIAN WAR (1754–1763), the Shawnee sided with the French against the British, attacking settlements in central and western Pennsylvania. However, the tribe later turned on the French, hastening the end of the war and British victory in North America.

See second map in Native Americans (vol. 3).

Disappointed by Britain's failure to keep its promise to abandon western forts and lands when the fighting ended, the Shawnee joined the rebellion of Chief PONTIAC against the British in 1763. The following year, they fought against Virginia colonists in Lord Dunmore's War. In this conflict, the Indians tried to stop Virginians from moving into what is now Kentucky.

With the outbreak of the American Revolution, the Shawnee turned to their former enemies, the British, for help in removing American settlers from Indian hunting grounds in Kentucky. For many years afterward, the Shawnee continued to struggle against American expansion westward. (*See also* **American Revolution; Iroquois Confederacy; Native Americans.**)

Ships and Shipbuilding

*F*rom the start, the North American colonies depended on ships to carry people and supplies from Europe and to carry their exports to market. By 1700 merchant vessels and navy ships were regularly crossing the Atlantic Ocean. Closer to shore, coastal trading ships and fishing boats moved around in the waters bordering the colonies. To meet the demand for vessels, a shipbuilding industry grew up in the colonies.

Colonial shipbuilding in the Americas began in 1496, when Christopher Columbus's crew assembled a vessel from the wreckage of three ships. During the period of exploration and early settlement, ships' carpenters often used trees growing close to shore to construct small boats for use in local waters. The French in Florida produced oceangoing vessels in 1562, and in 1607 the English built a ship in Maine.

During the colonial period, European settlers from Quebec to South America found they had plenty of timber for constructing ships. Spain was the only power to place any restrictions on shipbuilding. To keep control, Spanish authorities banned shipbuilding in their colonies except on Mexico's Pacific coast. They concluded that it made more sense to produce vessels there than to sail them through the treacherous waters around South America.

In the other European colonies, settlers built boats and ships—generally small ones—as they needed them. The shallop, the most common vessel, was an all-purpose ship about 30 feet long that could make ocean crossings. Barks and ketches were a bit larger and could carry more cargo than shallops. These boats were often used for coastal trade and fishing. For longer voyages, colonists built cargo ships modeled on the Dutch *fluyt,* a broad, shallow vessel that could hold boxes, barrels, and bales in every corner. Such ships commonly transported 100 to 200 tons of cargo.

New France* possessed more waterways than roads. In 1663 French authorities decided to launch a shipbuilding industry in the colony. But lacking skilled shipwrights*, the new industry began with prefabricated ships sent from France in kits and assembled in North America. Soon, however, the colony's crafts workers were capable of building ships from scratch. Quebec alone produced 230 vessels by 1763, and shipwrights in the interior constructed and launched more than a dozen vessels on the Great Lakes.

The shipbuilding industry in the English colonies got under way in the 1600s. Although all of the colonies built ships, New England became the most successful. Massachusetts and Connecticut assigned officials to inspect

* *New France* French colony centered in the St. Lawrence River valley, an area known as Canada; included the Great Lakes region and, until 1713, Acadia (present-day Nova Scotia)

* *shipwright* carpenter skilled in ship construction and repair

With a plentiful supply of timber, North American colonists quickly developed a thriving shipbuilding industry. Oceangoing ships ranged from the 30-foot shallop to the large, two-masted schooner.

vessels produced in their shipyards to oversee quality. They also welcomed master shipwrights from Europe who wanted to go into business for themselves.

The English Parliament gave colonial shipbuilding a boost when it passed the NAVIGATION ACTS of 1651 and 1660. The acts required, among other things, that all trade and commerce with the colonies take place on ships built and owned by English subjects. Having banned the use of foreign-owned vessels, the act created a great demand for English ships, including ships made in the colonies. With their ample timber supply and low labor costs, the colonies could build ships more cheaply than England could. They began selling their ships to English buyers. By the 1770s, about one-third of the British merchant fleet was American-built.

Though Boston was the first colonial shipbuilding center, the shipyards of New York and Philadelphia expanded as traffic in those ports increased during the 1700s. Shipbuilders experimented with new kinds of vessels, chiefly by changing the arrangement of the sails. Because English merchants had to be prepared to face enemies at sea, they preferred ships that could sail fast and fight, as well as carry large loads. Such ships could be brought into the navy if additional warships were needed. One of the most popular new vessels was the schooner, a two-masted ship that combined cargo capacity with speed. Although it carried a large amount of sail, the ship was designed so that a small crew could manage it. By the end of the 1700s, the schooner had become the most common cargo vessel. Shipbuilders on both sides of the Atlantic continued to tinker with its design to make it even faster and roomier.

artisan skilled crafts worker

The shipbuilding industry employed a number of skilled artisans*—not just shipwrights but also ironworkers, rope makers, and sail makers. In addition, forest industries were closely linked to shipbuilding. To seal and waterproof a vessel's planking, the shipping industry used great quantities of pitch and tar, sticky substances made from pine trees. The production of naval stores—pitch, tar, timbers, and cordage for cables and rigging—became an important colonial industry during the 1700s. (*See also* **Merchants; Trade and Commerce; Transportation and Travel.**)

Shoshone Indians

See *Great Basin Indians.*

Silver

* *conquistador* Spanish explorer and conqueror

*A*t the beginning of the colonial period, each of the European powers viewed its colonies as potential sources of three precious metals—gold, silver, and copper. Of these, silver played perhaps the most important role. Silver became the basis of Spain's colonial economy; silver coins served as currency throughout North America; and making fine products out of silver developed into a skilled craft in the colonies.

The discovery of gold and silver by the early Spanish conquistadors* quickly turned European exploration into a competition for these precious metals. The monarchs of England, Spain, and France encouraged expeditions into newly discovered territories in search of gold and silver deposits because they generally received the rights to any minerals found. For all their efforts, however, neither the English, the French, nor the Dutch located much silver or gold in the regions they explored and colonized.

Only the Spanish succeeded in their search for precious metals. By the mid-1500s, they had discovered rich silver deposits in central MEXICO. These deposits soon changed the focus of Spain's efforts in North America from conquest to mining. Mining towns sprang up throughout NEW SPAIN, and silver mining—often using the labor of Indian slaves—became the backbone of the Spanish colonial economy. It provided material for coins, created jobs, and encouraged long-distance trade.

By the 1680s, one-third of all the world's silver came from mines in Mexico. Most of it went to Spain and helped support Spanish power in Europe. Treasure fleets carrying silver and gold were a favored target of PIRATES and of privateers* backed by rival European nations.

* *privateer* privately owned ship authorized by the government to attack and capture enemy vessels; also the ship's master

Spanish silver served various functions in the European colonies. Coins produced in Mexico and other parts of Spanish America made up a large part of the money supply in the Dutch, English, and French colonies. The coins reached the colonies primarily through trade—both legal and illegal. Although the gold ones were the more valuable, silver coins were more common. The most popular Spanish coins in North America were the silver *reales,* known as "pieces of eight" because a *reale* was one-eighth of a silver dollar. They became the model for the coinage system of the United States.

From the 1600s onward, silver played an important role in colonial CRAFTS. In the English and French colonies, silversmiths fashioned jewelry, dinnerware, church objects, and other items. Silversmithing was a highly skilled craft that required many years of APPRENTICESHIP. The most famous colonial silversmith was Paul REVERE of Boston. Silversmiths in the Spanish

* *Spanish Borderlands* northern part of New Spain, area now occupied by Florida, Texas, New Mexico, Arizona, and California

Borderlands*, including Indians who learned much about the craft from colonists, became known for their skill in making fine silver jewelry. (*See also* **Economic Systems; Exploration, Age of; Gold; Mercantilism; Money and Finance; Trade and Commerce.**)

Sioux Indians

See *Plains Indians.*

Slavery existed in all the colonial regions of North America, and along with the slavery came resistance from the people who were forced to live and work in brutal, inhumane conditions. Native Americans resisted the Europeans who enslaved them. So did black slaves brought from Africa during the colonial period and their descendants born into bondage in the Americas. Recent historians have concluded that slaves opposed their masters in the colonies more frequently than was once thought. This resistance took many forms, ranging from attempts to escape enslavement to outright rebellion.

Escaping From Slavery. One of the most common forms of resistance to slavery was the attempt to escape. Enslaved Native Americans ran away whenever possible, fleeing colonial settlements and rejoining Indian communities. Because escape was so common, early colonists often arranged for Indian slaves to be sold in the WEST INDIES or other distant places where it would be harder for them to blend into the local population after escaping.

Many African slaves attempted to escape from traders in Africa or during the Middle Passage—the horrendous ocean voyage from Africa to the West Indies. Some Africans jumped ship and drowned during the crossing rather than remain in bondage. Others rebelled in shipboard uprisings. In 1764 African prisoners aboard the *Hope,* a slave ship bound for the West Indies, took advantage of the confusion caused by a shipboard mutiny to stage a revolt. Eight slaves died in the uprising, which failed. Once on American shores, many slaves tried to escape from captivity. As early as the 1520s, Africans brought to the continent to serve Spanish explorers fled and sought refuge with Native Americans.

Slaves tried to run away not only to escape bondage, harsh treatment, or the threat of being sold but also to maintain contact with family and friends. Some runaway slaves joined Indian tribes or fled to crowded seaports, where they hoped to blend in with FREE BLACKS. Some escaped to MAROON COMMUNITIES, interracial settlements located in remote places beyond the reach of colonial law. Slaves in South Carolina often tried to flee to Spanish Florida, which gave refuge to runaways. When the American Revolution broke out, the British offered freedom to slaves who left their masters to fight for the British. Large numbers of blacks did so. At all times, runaways risked harsh punishment if caught.

Driven to despair by the loss of freedom as well as by fear and brutal treatment, some slaves tried to escape their misery through suicide. During the 1500s, enslaved Indians sent to the West Indies often killed themselves by eating poisonous plants. To prevent African slaves from drowning themselves during the Middle Passage, ship captains had their crews string nets along the sides of the vessels to catch people who jumped overboard. Many slaves tried to starve themselves by refusing to eat during the voyage to the Americas. To keep them alive, slave traders pushed funnel-shaped devices down their throats and force-fed them.

Economic and Cultural Resistance. Slaves resisted captivity in various quiet and subtle ways, often resorting to some form of sabotage* against their masters. Many slaves pretended that they had difficulty learning to use farm equipment correctly. Others worked as slowly and clumsily as possible,

* *sabotage* act designed to interfere with work or damage property

61

breaking hoes and other tools. They sometimes deliberately ruined crops—for example, by flooding rice fields at the wrong time or picking unripe tobacco leaves. Slaves also withheld their labor by pretending to be sick.

Slaveholders had difficulty dealing with this type of resistance. If challenged, slaves could claim ignorance or argue, which only slowed the work further. Moreover, many masters hesitated to use harsh punishment unless certain that a slave was causing problems intentionally. Slaves represented a sizable investment. A slave who died or was unable to work as a result of punishment meant a substantial financial loss to the slaveholder.

One type of sabotage that was particularly damaging was arson—setting fires deliberately. Because it required no special strength and was difficult to prove, arson became a favorite form of resistance. Slaves set fire to fields, crops, barns, and houses. To halt arson attacks on crops, South Carolina passed a law in 1740 that set the death penalty for any slave, free black, or Indian found guilty of burning a crop. That same year, a fire in Charleston, South Carolina, destroyed 300 houses and burned down newly constructed fortifications. Authorities suspected slave arson but could prove nothing. Large fires in other cities were blamed on slaves as well, and white communities throughout the colonies lived in fear of slave arson.

Slaveholders were also terrified of being poisoned. They especially feared the female household slaves who prepared food and handled medicines. These women generally had a wide knowledge of plants, including how to obtain poison from them. Concern about poisoning led colonial assemblies to pass laws that punished those who taught others about poisons, restricted the occasions when slaves could administer medicine, and offered rewards for information. Like arson, acts of poisoning were difficult to prove. Those found guilty of using poison could be punished severely, even burned alive—a punishment reserved for witches and traitors.

Another form of resistance by blacks involved their efforts to keep their African customs and identity alive. Whenever they could—especially in their own quarters at night—slaves spoke African languages, wore African-style clothing, and ate African foods. They also practiced traditional ceremonies of worship and mourning and joined in African songs and dances. Such activities allowed slaves to maintain their sense of cultural identity and helped them keep alive the hope of further resistance—even freedom. Slaveholders realized that these practices presented a threat to their control. But they could do little to prevent blacks from following traditional African ways in the separate and relatively secret world of the slave quarters.

Slave Uprisings. White colonists probably feared organized slave rebellions more than any other type of resistance. Slave uprisings in North America were smaller and less frequent than those in the West Indies and South America, where slave populations were greater and the conditions of slavery were worse. Nevertheless, rebellions did occur in North America wherever large numbers of Indians or Africans were enslaved. Some historians have suggested that many of the Indian wars of the colonial period were really rebellions against the threat of enslavement.

The biggest slave uprising in the British colonies took place in 1739 at Stono, South Carolina. A group of about 20 slaves, recent arrivals from

See color plate 4, vol. 2.

Africa, broke into a store, seized guns, and marched toward Spanish Florida. Joined by others along the way, the rebels killed whites and burned plantations. Planters managed to put down the rebellion, but one slave leader avoided capture for nearly three years. More than 30 blacks and 20 whites died in the Stono Rebellion. To avoid future uprisings, South Carolina passed laws that placed restrictions on blacks moving about and gathering in groups.

Slave rebellions occurred in New York City in 1712 and 1741. In the first uprising, two dozen black slaves and several Indians set fire to a building, planning to kill any whites who tried to fight the fire. The rebels killed nine men and wounded seven others before they were overpowered by soldiers. Twenty-one of the rebels were eventually executed, and six more committed suicide rather than face capture. New York passed a series of laws aimed at preventing further uprisings, but slaves continued to resist. In 1741 a group of black slaves joined some poor whites in a crime ring that involved robbery and arson. White residents began to fear that the slaves were plotting to burn down the city. Authorities eventually arrested 150 slaves, executing 31 of them and banishing another 70.

During the 1770s, as social turmoil in the British colonies increased, black slaves up and down the Atlantic coast plotted to escape, to overthrow local governments, or to help the British. Others aided colonial patriots*, hoping that American independence might lead to black liberty. That hope died when slavery continued after the American Revolution. (*See also* **African American Culture; Antislavery Movement; Slave Trade.**)

* *patriot* American colonist who favored independence from Great Britain

Slave Trade

* *maritime* related to the sea or shipping

The slave trade—the business of buying and selling human beings—has flourished in many times and places. However, a new maritime* trade in black slaves that involved merchants from many nations began to develop during the colonial period. Part of an international trading network that moved manufactured goods, plantation crops, and human cargoes among three continents, this slave trade forced vast numbers of Africans onto ships bound for the Americas. It played a vital role in the colonial economies of Portugal, Spain, France, the Netherlands, and Britain.

The vast majority of African slaves went to the WEST INDIES, Central America, or South America. Only a small percentage ended up in the North American colonies. The British colonies relied on the slave trade as a source of labor. French, Dutch, and Spanish colonists in North America acquired slaves as well, but in smaller numbers than the British did.

By the time the slave trade officially ended in the early 1800s, it had brought untold misery to millions of Africans. It also changed racial patterns in the Americas by planting a large and growing black population there. Today the legacy of the slave trade continues to shape ethnic, cultural, and political life in North America's former colonies.

Development of the Atlantic Slave Trade

The Atlantic slave trade was an outgrowth of practices that had existed for centuries in northern Africa and the Mediterranean regions of Europe. As

Slave Trade

part of the trade in these regions, African slaves—often prisoners of war, criminals, people who owed money, or children sold into slavery by their parents—sometimes passed from African owners into European hands. Europeans began taking black slaves directly from Africa in the 1440s, when Portuguese seafarers exploring the west coast of Africa carried human captives back to Europe and sold them there.

Portugal Takes the Lead. Portugal was the first European nation to develop a large-scale overseas trade in African slaves. Portuguese adventurers and merchants established trading posts on the west coast of Africa, made alliances with coastal Africans, and bought slaves from them. When the supply of slaves ran short, the Portuguese equipped their African allies with weapons and organized slave raids into the interior.

At first the Portuguese sold their African captives in markets in Europe or in Atlantic islands such as the Azores. After about 1520, however, most of the slaves taken by Portuguese traders went to the fast-growing Spanish colonies in the Americas, which needed people to work in mines and on plantations. In the early years, the Spanish colonists had met their need for labor by enslaving Native Americans. But after disease and warfare killed large numbers of Indians, the Spaniards were forced to seek another source of workers. Portuguese traders, eager to exchange their human cargoes for silver from Spain's colonial mines, began delivering shiploads of slaves to Spanish America.

By the 1550s, the slave traders had found another large market for African slaves—the Portuguese territory of Brazil. Within 50 years northeastern Brazil had the world's largest sugar colonies and was importing as many as 5,000 slaves each year.

Dutch, French, and British Slave Trade. In time other nations took prominent roles in the Atlantic slave trade. In the 1640s, the Dutch seized Brazil and several Portuguese trading colonies along the west coast of Africa. Now in control of both a major source and a major market for slaves, the Dutch entered the trade. Portugal soon reconquered its colonies, but the Dutch remained active in the slave trade, providing African laborers to the island colonies of the West Indies.

The French and British joined the Dutch as important slave traders in the early 1700s. British sea captains entered the slave trade to sell Africans to sugar plantation owners on the Caribbean island of BARBADOS. They later extended their commerce in slaves to other West Indian islands and to Britain's mainland colonies. When Britain became the leading sea power in the 1700s, it also dominated the slave trade.

By the 1780s, British and French traders were bringing about 60,000 Africans to the Americas each year. As their business expanded, these Europeans found new sources of slaves in Africa. One region on the central west coast became known as the Slave Coast because it provided so many captives.

"Triangular Trade." The commerce in slaves was part of a transatlantic* trade pattern that became known as triangular trade because it included three "legs," or routes, that resembled a triangle. In the first leg of this trade pattern, merchants carried manufactured goods such as cloth and tools from Europe to

* *transatlantic* across the Atlantic Ocean

Africa and exchanged them for slaves. The second leg involved transporting the slaves from Africa to the Americas. The final leg of the triangle consisted of shipping sugar, tobacco, and other American crops to Europe. Few ships completed all three legs of the triangle. Many slave traders simply went back and forth between Africa and the Caribbean, sometimes sailing to North American ports with slaves they had not been able to sell in the West Indies.

New England developed its own version of the triangular trade. Massachusetts and Rhode Island merchants obtained molasses from the West Indies in exchange for beef and lumber. After making the molasses into rum, they shipped it to Africa, where they traded it for slaves. The slaves were transported to the West Indies to be exchanged for more molasses, which was brought back to New England to be made into rum.

The Slave Trade and the North American Colonies

North America was a minor part of the overall slave trade. Between the arrival of the first Africans in Virginia in 1619 and the outlawing of the slave trade by Congress in 1807, some 500,000 or 600,000 enslaved Africans were brought to the area that is now the United States. Although this number seems large, it represents only 5 to 10 percent of the total population of slaves transported to the Americas.

Once dominated by the Dutch and Portuguese, the North Atlantic slave trade eventually came under the control of the British. The island colonies of the West Indies were a major center for British and French slave dealers.

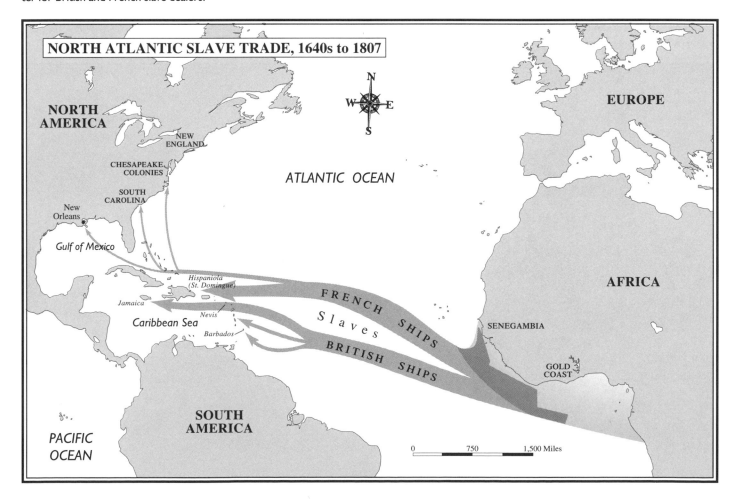

NORTH ATLANTIC SLAVE TRADE, 1640s to 1807

Slave Trade

* ***Spanish Borderlands*** northern part of New
Spain, area now occupied by Florida, Texas,
New Mexico, Arizona, and California

* ***New France*** French colony centered in the
St. Lawrence River valley, an area known as
Canada; included the Great Lakes region and,
until 1713, Acadia (present-day Nova Scotia)

* ***indentured servant*** person who agreed to
work a certain length of time in return for
passage on a ship to the colonies

This illustration from Thomas Astley's *A New
and General Collection of Voyages,* published in
London in 1746, shows a "slave factory" operated by traders in western Africa. The com-
pound is divided among the four European
nations most active in the slave trade—Portugal, France, Britain, and the Netherlands.

Spanish, Dutch, and French Colonies. Few African slaves reached
the Spanish Borderlands*. The early colonists of that region made slaves of
Native Americans, even after the Spanish crown banned the practice in 1542.
Spaniards who carried out raids against Indians and seized captives claimed
that they were not breaking the law but were engaged in a "war" against the
enemies of Christianity. Most of the Indians taken in raids in frontier lands
were sent to work in the mines and plantations of Mexico.

Some African slaves were brought to the Dutch colony of NEW NETHER-
LAND from the Caribbean, but only two shiploads of slaves are known to have
arrived there directly from Africa. The labor needs of the colony remained
too small to compete with other regions as a market for slaves.

The French trade in African slaves centered on the island colonies of the
Caribbean. New France* and the small French settlements of the lower Mississippi Valley met their need for labor largely by enslaving Indians. In the
1760s, French Canada had fewer than 1,000 black slaves, though about
28,000 black slaves had reached Louisiana. After the American Revolution,
imports of slaves into Louisiana increased as the lower Mississippi region became an important producer of sugar.

British Colonies. The slave trade got a slow start in British North Amer-
ica. Early planters in Virginia and the Chesapeake Bay region sometimes took
Indian slaves, but for the most part they relied on indentured servants* from
England for labor. In the late 1600s, when the flow of indentured servants

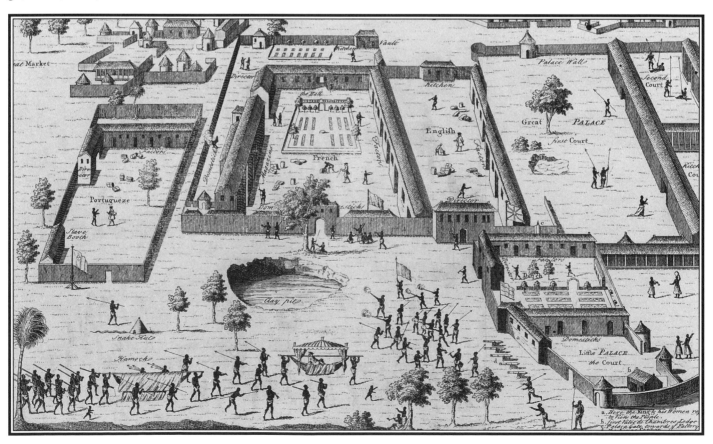

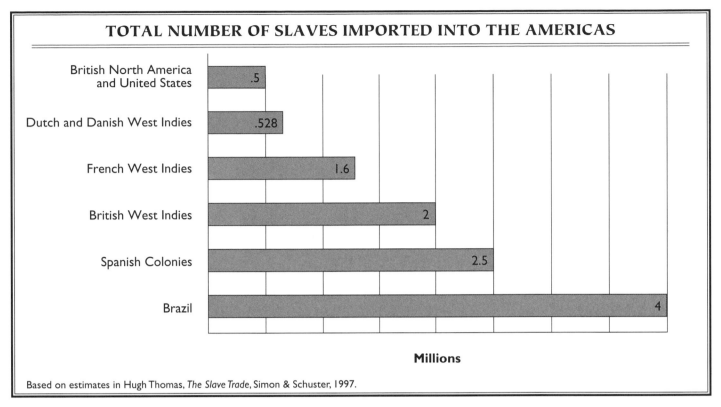

TOTAL NUMBER OF SLAVES IMPORTED INTO THE AMERICAS

British North America and United States — .5
Dutch and Danish West Indies — .528
French West Indies — 1.6
British West Indies — 2
Spanish Colonies — 2.5
Brazil — 4

Millions

Based on estimates in Hugh Thomas, *The Slave Trade*, Simon & Schuster, 1997.

Although slavery is associated with the American South, only about 5 percent of the slaves brought to the Americas ended up in the British colonies and later the United States. The majority went to South America and to the sugar plantations of the West Indies.

began to dry up, the planters began buying African slaves, mostly from the West Indies.

Around the same time, merchants in South Carolina developed a thriving business in Indian slaves, buying captives from Indian allies and sending them to other English colonies. This particular trade ended around 1720 as a result of a war between British colonists and the YAMASSEE INDIANS. The rice growers of the southern colonies then began buying large numbers of enslaved Africans from British traders. The Chesapeake region and South Carolina soon became the largest markets for slaves in the British colonies, with the city of CHARLESTON emerging as a major distribution center. North Carolina and Georgia also imported considerable numbers of enslaved Africans.

The middle colonies played a much smaller role in the slave trade. Merchants in New York, Pennsylvania, and New Jersey seldom became involved in the trade except to fill local needs for workers. In the mid-1700s, for example, New York merchants made five or six voyages to Africa each year, bringing back several hundred slaves. Pennsylvania, a colony founded by QUAKERS, who opposed slavery, took little part in the slave trade until 1760, when the need for labor prompted some Philadelphia merchants to send about a dozen ships to Africa for slaves. Many of the African slaves imported into the region were unloaded in New Jersey, where taxes were lower, and then smuggled into New York or Pennsylvania.

New England, where most people worked on family farms, had little demand for slave labor. Yet the commerce in slaves touched New England deeply because of its involvement in the "triangular trade." Rhode Islanders,

the leading slave traders in the North American colonies, shipped about 60,000 slaves from Africa to the Caribbean and North America between the 1750s and 1775.

See
color plate 5,
vol. 4.

The Middle Passage.   The ocean voyage from Africa to the Americas, which lasted from 40 to 70 days, was known as the Middle Passage. Enslaved Africans often had to endure atrocious conditions during the trip. On some ships, slaves were packed so tightly in the cargo areas below deck that they could not move. The crew brought them up onto the deck periodically for exercise in order to keep their blood circulating. At such times, the crew strung nets around the sides of the ship to keep the desperate and miserable slaves from jumping overboard and drowning. Packed in filthy, stifling quarters, with meager food, the slaves fell prey to disease as well as despair. Those who refused to eat were force-fed with a funnel-shaped device pushed down their throats. Between 10 and 20 percent of African slaves died during the Middle Passage, although on some vessels the death toll was much higher.

By the late 1700s, an ANTISLAVERY MOVEMENT began gaining strength in Europe and the United States. Both the British and the Americans passed legislation in 1807 that made slave trading illegal. Other nations later passed similar bans against the Atlantic slave trade, thus ending the horrors of the Middle Passage. (*See also* **Labor; Rum Trade; Slave Resistance; Slavery; Trade and Commerce.**)

Slavery

Slavery—the condition of being totally controlled by others through force, custom, or law—is probably as old as human history. It has taken many forms in different times and places. In North America during the colonial period, slavery developed as part of an economic system that included plantation farming, merchant shipping, and a transatlantic trade in slaves. Only about 5 percent of the slaves taken from AFRICA during this time ended up in the area that is now the United States. Most went to European colonies in the WEST INDIES, Central America, and South America.

By the time Christopher COLUMBUS reached the Americas in 1492, slavery had almost disappeared from most of Europe, except for the area around the Mediterranean Sea. Many of the slaves in that region were white—the word *slave* comes from Slav and refers to the Slavic people of eastern Europe. Black slaves also appeared for sale on Mediterranean shores, brought by Arab traders from Africa south of the Sahara. In the mid-1400s, the Portuguese began carrying shiploads of black captives—generally purchased from African traders—from the west coast of Africa to markets in southern Europe.

The European "discovery" and colonization of the Americas brought three new elements to the age-old institution of slavery. First, it introduced Europeans to a new race of people, Native Americans, many of whom were enslaved by Europeans. Second, colonization created a huge and endless appetite for labor. European settlers established mines, PLANTATIONS, and sugar mills that demanded a large and steady supply of workers. Each colony met its labor needs in its own way, but many relied heavily on slaves. Slavery eventually existed in all the North American colonies.

Third, slavery in the Americas became mixed with racial prejudice. Europeans of the 1600s associated slavery with the mysterious land of Africa, a place filled with heathens—evil people who did not accept Christianity or even the God of the Bible. For the English, whiteness meant purity and blackness suggested evil. The colonists came to regard African slaves as less than human and not deserving of the same treatment as white servants. This attitude allowed them to accept the permanent enslavement of blacks as natural, a form of prejudice that lasted for centuries.

British Colonies

Freedom and equality were foreign ideas during most of the age of colonization. In England the system of common law* protected most citizens from extreme cruelty or exploitation*. But tradition also tied individuals to a particular role in society. At the time, the great majority of people in England were peasants, servants, tenant farmers*, laborers, or others who took orders from their social superiors.

Because of their background, English settlers in North America were accustomed to a society in which some individuals controlled the lives of others. Slavery thus did not seem out of place. Even colonies with few slaves, such as Massachusetts, were involved in the SLAVE TRADE or made money by trading with colonies that depended on slavery.

The Development of Slavery in British North America.
The early English colonists made attempts to enslave Native Americans, either setting them to work within the colonies or sending them to plantation owners in the West Indies. However, there were not enough Indians to meet the colonists'

* **common law** unwritten law based on custom and court decisions

* **exploitation** relationship in which one side benefits at the other's expense

* **tenant farmer** person who farms land owned by another and pays rent with a share of the produce or in cash

Planters in the South relied on slaves for the production of labor-intensive crops, such as indigo. This 1771 engraving shows indigo being planted and harvested.

Slavery

indentured servant person who agreed to work for a certain length of time in return for passage on a ship to the colonies

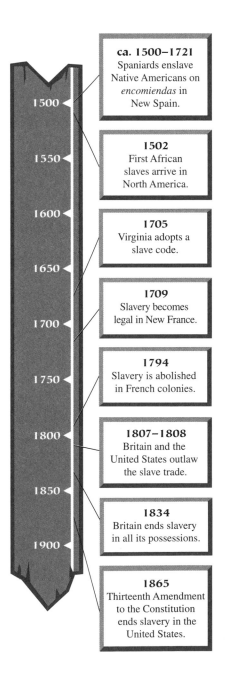

ca. 1500–1721
Spaniards enslave Native Americans on *encomiendas* in New Spain.

1502
First African slaves arrive in North America.

1705
Virginia adopts a slave code.

1709
Slavery becomes legal in New France.

1794
Slavery is abolished in French colonies.

1807–1808
Britain and the United States outlaw the slave trade.

1834
Britain ends slavery in all its possessions.

1865
Thirteenth Amendment to the Constitution ends slavery in the United States.

growing need for labor, and the Indians found many ways to escape into the wilderness. The colonists also relied on indentured servants*, but again the supply could not keep up with the demand for workers.

The first Africans to arrive in the English colonies came in 1619, when a Dutch ship left some 20 blacks in Virginia. It is not clear from historical records whether these people were slaves. The white colonists did not use the word *slave* and may have treated the blacks as indentured servants who would serve as laborers for a certain number of years. But early documents from Virginia also refer to "servants for life"—a term that suggests a situation not far removed from slavery.

In the 1640s, when England entered the transatlantic slave trade, North American colonists began acquiring slaves from Africa. Most of the Africans arrived in large English-owned ships. Sea captains involved in trade with the West Indies started to bring some slaves to New England. In 1641 Massachusetts passed a collection of laws known as the Body of Liberties. Among the many issues covered by these laws was the institution of slavery, which was defined and prohibited. Strangely, this made the colony the first to formally recognize slavery in its legal code. However, the first significant slave population developed in Virginia and the Chesapeake Bay region, where black slaves eventually replaced white indentured servants on tobacco plantations. By the 1650s, several hundred blacks—a few of them free—lived in Virginia.

Around this time, a change occurred in the way that colonists in some areas viewed black people. Virginians passed laws that placed African Americans at the lowest level of society and declared that children born of slaves would also be slaves. Blacks were barred from voting, holding public office, testifying against whites in court, serving in the military, owning firearms, and marrying whites. These laws transformed the early form of black servitude into the legal institution of slavery. In 1705 Virginia brought its scattered laws about slavery together in a single code. Other colonies produced slave codes in the 1700s. These codes governed every aspect of slaveholding, including the forms of discipline slaveholders could use, the punishments runaway slaves could receive, and the conditions under which slaves could be freed.

The form of slavery that emerged in Virginia is called chattel slavery. It regarded enslaved blacks as chattel—items of property no different from livestock or furniture—and thus treated them as less than human. As applied in the British colonies, chattel slavery included the idea of racial prejudice—whites were never considered chattel—and projected the image of blacks as inferior beings.

Regional Variations in Slavery. The number of black slaves imported into the Chesapeake Bay region increased slowly and steadily throughout the early 1700s, reaching a peak in the late 1740s. After that time, fewer new slaves were brought to the region. The black population began to grow fast enough to keep up with the demand for slave labor, and increased European immigration provided additional workers. The slave trade was also disrupted by wars and international disputes. Moreover, by the late 1700s, Chesapeake planters preferred slaves born in the colonies to those brought from Africa or the West Indies. American-born slaves were more useful because they spoke English and grew up familiar with plantation tasks.

Large plantations with many slaves were the exception in the Chesapeake region, not the rule. More than half of all black slaves in colonial Virginia lived in groups of 10 or fewer, including children. The majority of slaveholders owned only 1 or 2 slaves, while large tobacco plantations almost never had more than 35.

Chesapeake slaves performed tasks based on their age and abilities. Young boys often shared household and garden tasks with girls of the same age. Because planting, tending, and picking tobacco required more skill than strength, women often worked in the fields alongside men, especially during the busiest seasons. Female slaves also served as nursemaids, house servants, and cooks. Men worked as lumbermen and boatmen, and thousands became skilled artisans*. Those who survived to old age were given tasks that required experience rather than strength, such as tending livestock.

* **artisan** skilled crafts worker

Planters in the Chesapeake region did not often sell their slaves. They were more likely to give the slaves to their children—along with land and money—to help them start their own lives. In many cases a slave who had grown up with a planter's son or daughter would accompany that young person when he or she left home. More than half of Virginia-born slaves moved at least once in their lifetimes. Most such relocations were to places within visiting distance of the former home, so slaves often could maintain contact with family members left behind. Because slaves dreaded being separated from their families, slaveholders sometimes used the threat of sale to South Carolina or the West Indies as a way to bring disobedient slaves into line.

In some ways, the conditions of slavery were quite different in South Carolina and Georgia. The large plantations in this part of the South were the birthplace of the slaveholding culture that lasted for many years after the American Revolution and shaped our modern image of slavery.

In the early years, most slaves in South Carolina were captive Indians or blacks brought from the West Indies by planters who relocated to Carolina. Large-scale black slavery began about 1700, when the colonists developed rice as the leading cash crop*. Rice could be grown efficiently only on large plantations with many workers. Because white labor, including indentured servants, was scarce, slavery expanded along with the cultivation of rice. Colonists also relied on slave labor to produce cash crops such as indigo* and naval stores*. By 1740 more than half of South Carolina's 59,000 inhabitants were enslaved blacks.

* **cash crop** crop grown primarily for profit

* **indigo** plant used to make a blue dye
* **naval store** tar and other products from pine trees that were used on ships

Slavery was originally forbidden in Georgia, which had been founded as a place where criminals, the poor, and persecuted religious groups could build new lives. To help achieve that goal, the colony placed restrictions on both landowning and slavery. Georgia failed in its mission, however, and in 1752 its borders were opened to colonists from South Carolina, who had run out of room to grow rice. The South Carolinians brought slavery into the colony, and by 1773 the slave population of Georgia had risen from about 500 to almost 15,000.

By the end of the colonial period, blacks greatly outnumbered whites in the coastal lowland areas of both Georgia and South Carolina. Many black slaves lived in villages on large plantations. In comparison with the Chesapeake region, these colonies had fewer small plantations in which master and slave worked side by side and less interaction between blacks and whites. Black

Slavery

Massachusetts abolished the practice of slavery in its 1780 state constitution, which declared that "all men are born free and equal." By the time the first United States census was taken in 1790, several other states had also outlawed slavery.

BLACK POPULATION OF THE UNITED STATES, 1790

	Slaves	Free Blacks
Connecticut	2,648	2,771
Delaware	8,887	3,899
Georgia	29,264	398
Kentucky	12,430	114
Maine	0	536
Maryland	103,036	8,043
Massachusetts	0	5,369
New Hampshire	157	630
New Jersey	11,423	2,762
New York	21,193	4,682
North Carolina	100,783	5,041
Pennsylvania	3,707	6,531
Rhode Island	958	3,484
South Carolina	107,094	1,801
Vermont	0	269
Virginia	292,627	12,866
Other areas	3,417	361
TOTAL	697,624	59,557

Negro Population 1790–1860, U. S. Department of Commerce, Bureau of the Census, 1910.

slavery also took root in North Carolina, where migrating tobacco planters from Virginia established plantations in the 1650s. North Carolina later developed an important industry in naval stores produced by black slave labor.

The climate of New England and the middle colonies was not suited to plantation agriculture, so large-scale slavery did not develop in those regions. Yet there were slaves in all the northern colonies. Some worked for wealthy farmers who could afford a few slaves and had enough work to keep them busy year-round. Northern slavery was mostly urban, however. Wealthy urban residents purchased slaves to serve as house servants, dock and warehouse workers, sailors, and crafts workers. One Philadelphia merchant imported 150 African slaves in 1684 and sold them all within a few days. At least 4,000 slaves arrived in New York City during colonial times.

Slave labor played a vital role in the rapid economic growth of British North America. Yet by the end of the colonial period, the idea that slavery was wrong began gaining strength. This was not a new idea. As early as 1680, some colonists had spoken out against slavery, and people continued to raise

their voices against the injustices of slavery throughout the colonial period. In the early 1800s, the influence of a growing ANTISLAVERY MOVEMENT became strong enough to end the slave trade.

Dutch Colony

The Dutch were deeply involved in the Atlantic slave trade during the 1600s. But few slaves arrived in the Dutch colony of New Netherland. The DUTCH WEST INDIA COMPANY, the trading company that ran the colony, also shipped slaves from Africa to the Americas. Although the company tried to boost the demand for slaves in New Netherland, most of the Africans carried on Dutch ships went to Brazil or to the Spanish and English colonies.

Between 1654 and 1664, Dutch slave ships arrived at the colony more regularly. They often brought older slaves who had already labored in the West Indies because buyers in New Netherland could not compete for workers in their prime. When the English conquered New Netherland in 1664, the colony had about 500 slaves.

Though enslaved Africans lived throughout the colony, most resided in New Amsterdam, the colonial capital. Many of these slaves belonged to the Dutch West India Company, which provided them with housing and medical care. Their work consisted of clearing land, farming, and building and repairing the company's fort. The company occasionally allowed individual colonists to rent its slaves for specific periods of time. By the 1650s, some colonists were buying slaves of their own to serve as farm laborers, domestic servants, and skilled workers.

The colonists of New Netherland accepted slavery as a fact of life, but they did not make it a legalized institution. As a result, enslaved Africans in the Dutch colony had more opportunity than slaves elsewhere in North America to change their status*. The West India Company regularly freed slaves who had served well and gave them small plots of land. Although these former slaves generally had to provide labor for the company when the need arose, they received wages for their work. Such individuals, who could live independently with their families on their own farms, held a status called "half-freedom" or "half-slavery." Other slaves received complete freedom. At the time of the English conquest in 1664, about 75 FREE BLACKS lived in New Amsterdam. These people served as an inspiration to slaves with whom they came in contact.

* **status** social position

French Colonies

Slavery provided the labor needed for the sugar plantations and sugar mills of France's rich island colonies in the West Indies. Slavery also developed in the French mainland territories of North America—but on a much smaller scale.

Throughout the colonial period, most slaves in New France* were Native Americans from the western parts of the interior. France's Indian allies frequently sold captives from enemy tribes to colonial merchants, who resold them to settlers. African slaves also trickled into New France, sometimes from the French colonies in the Caribbean. Both African and Indian slaves worked as household servants and field laborers for the wealthier French settlers.

* **New France** French colony centered in the St. Lawrence River valley, an area known as Canada; included the Great Lakes region and, until 1713, Acadia (present-day Nova Scotia)

73

Some colonists objected to slavery, but a law passed in 1709 confirmed the legality of slaveholding. By the 1760s, the slave population of New France included about 1,000 blacks, most of whom lived in or near Montreal.

French settlers in LOUISIANA also took Native Americans as slaves. But after the 1720s, Indian slavery decreased, partly because the French wanted to improve relations with Indian tribes and partly because it was easy for Indian captives to escape and disappear. Thereafter, Louisianans shipped most Indian captives to the West Indies and relied on African slaves for labor. Most black slaves labored on indigo and tobacco plantations along the Mississippi River. But some worked as house servants, lumbermen, boatmen, and skilled artisans. By 1732 Louisiana's population included 4,000 black slaves, 2,000 white settlers, and fewer than 100 Indian slaves.

The upper reaches of the Mississippi River—the Illinois country—remained rather isolated from other parts of French America. The colonial population of the region was small, numbering only 800 white settlers, 450 black slaves, and 150 Indian slaves by the mid-1700s. Slaves in the region worked in mining, farming, and fur trading.

Both New France and Louisiana adopted the *Code Noir* (Black Code) in the early 1700s. Providing a legal basis for slavery, this series of laws imposed restrictions on slaves and responsibilities on slaveholders. In Louisiana the code was never fully enforced, partly because of vague, shifting boundaries between free blacks and slaves and the interracial mixing of whites, blacks, and Indians in the society.

Spanish Colonies

* ***Spanish Borderlands*** northern part of New Spain; area now occupied by Florida, Texas, New Mexico, Arizona, and California

Slavery in the Spanish Borderlands* was shaped by tradition, law, and religion. The conditions of slavery varied from brutality and total control to a situation in which workers were attached to the land and its owner but possessed certain rights. Spain's eastern Borderlands—Florida and, after 1762, Louisiana—had large numbers of African slaves. The western Borderlands had mostly Indian slaves. The Spanish generally treated black and Indian slaves differently.

Slavery and Spanish Law.
Slavery had a long history in Spain, dating back at least to the time of Roman rule. Although the Spanish Catholic Church did not forbid slavery, it set limits on what masters could do to their slaves. In the mid-1200s, Spain adopted *Siete partidas,* a legal code that gave slaves some rights and spelled out the ways in which a slave could obtain freedom.

The Spanish who came to the Americas brought European forms of slavery with them. Slaves were present on many of the expeditions of exploration, conquest, and colonization. From the beginning, the Spanish forced Indians into slavery, and they transferred Spanish customs and laws connected with slavery to their colonies. The *Siete partidas,* however, applied mainly to black slaves. The enslavement of Indians occurred under the Laws of the Indies, which regulated affairs in the Americas.

Spain harnessed the labor of captive Native Americans mainly through two institutions—*ENCOMIENDAS*, property grants that allowed landholders to

Early Spanish visitors to North America often made slaves of Native Americans. This engraving from Theodore de Bry's *America,* published 1590–1634, shows Indians being forced to carry gear for Spanish explorers.

use Indian labor, and MISSIONS, which compelled Indians to work at the missions while being converted to Christianity. The Spanish crown tried to protect Indians from outright slavery, passing at least ten laws against Indian slavery between 1530 and 1550 alone. But authorities found it difficult to enforce such laws, and colonists engaged in various activities that would enable them to continue enslaving Indians. For example, the law allowed the enslavement of Indians captured in war, so the Spanish colonists sometimes made war simply to take slaves.

Some people in Spanish America spoke out against the enslavement of the Indians. One leading defender of Indian rights, the missionary Bartolomé de LAS CASAS, urged the Spanish crown to protect Native Americans by importing white and black laborers to replace Indian slaves. To his dismay, many Spanish colonies in the tropical regions of America turned to large-scale black slavery, condemning tens of thousands of Africans to lives of misery.

A Black Slaveholder

Slavery was such a familiar part of life in colonial times that even some African Americans kept slaves. Anthony Johnson, a free black planter, lived in the Virginia colony before 1660. Johnson claimed that one of his black servants was "bound for life"—in effect, a slave. A neighboring white landowner disagreed, claiming that Johnson's servant was bound only for a limited time. The disagreement ended up in court. When the court learned that the white neighbor was keeping the servant for his own, it settled the case in Johnson's favor, returning his black "servant."

See color plate 3, vol. 3.

Regional Variations.   Many of the early slaves in Spanish Florida were Native Americans. In the 1700s, Florida became a refuge for both black and Indian slaves fleeing from the British colonies, and in 1738 the Spanish governor allowed free blacks to form their own community there. When Britain acquired Florida in 1763, the Spanish left for Cuba, accompanied by the colony's 87 free blacks and about 300 slaves.

From 1763 to 1800, Spain controlled Louisiana, where the original French colonists had imported a large population of African slaves. The Spanish left French slave laws in force but pressed landholders for better treatment of their slaves. In general, slaves working on small farms in Louisiana fared better than those on large plantations.

Slavery in Texas involved both Indians and Africans. In the colony's early years, conflicts arose over the question of Indian captives. Some settlers argued that it was necessary to enslave non-Christian Indians in order to protect those who had adopted Christianity. However, some Spanish authorities pointed out that the forceful methods used by priests and soldiers to round up Indians for conversion were not very different from enslavement. In any case, the number of slaves in the colony remained small—only about 20 in 1779, most of them black.

Spanish colonists in New Mexico enslaved Indians for local labor and for sale in Mexico. Indian tribes or communities that fought or resisted whites were considered fair game for forced servitude, sometimes combined with forced conversion to Christianity. The Spanish often bought Indians from other tribes that had captured them. Colonists seldom used the word *slave* in describing these Native Americans. Instead, they spoke of "rescuing" the Indians. In reality, though, Indian captives were removed from their families and societies by force and were treated as goods to be bought and sold. Yet Spanish law also limited the number of years these captives had to work for their masters, and while Indian slaves could be inherited, the children of slaves were not born into slavery. In addition, colonial officials sometimes stepped in and took away slaves who were badly treated, either returning them to their own people or sending them to missions.

Settlers in Arizona also used Indian captives as slaves, and the conditions of slavery were similar to those in New Mexico. Though less populated than New Mexico, Arizona may have had a higher proportion of slaves.

In California, Spanish priests and soldiers worked together to force Indians onto missions, where they provided labor and were converted to Christianity. The enslavement of captive Indians by other tribes was widespread, especially in northern California. The Spanish colonists did not consider Indian life at missions to be enslavement, but many people today disagree. Historians and Catholic scholars are still debating the question of whether the servitude of California's mission Indians was really slavery. (*See also* **Genízaros; Labor; Race Relations; Rice; Slave Resistance.**)

Smallpox

See *Diseases.*

Smith, John

ca. 1580–1631
English explorer and colonizer

---

* **apprentice** person placed in the care of a merchant or crafts worker to learn a profession

---

Captain John Smith governed the Jamestown colony from 1608 to 1609. He established peaceful relations with the local Indians and made sure that all colonists did their fair share of work.

*C*aptain John Smith helped establish the JAMESTOWN COLONY OF VIRGINIA, the first successful English settlement in North America. Although best known for his connection to Virginia, Smith also made important contributions to the colonization of New England.

John Smith was born to an English family with a small amount of property. When his father died, young John became an apprentice* to a merchant. At the age of 16, Smith decided against the life of a merchant and became a professional soldier in eastern Europe. After several dangerous adventures, he returned to England in 1604.

When the directors of the VIRGINIA COMPANY OF LONDON decided to establish a colony at Jamestown, they hired Smith to serve as the settlers' military adviser. After arriving in North America in the spring of 1607, the English colonists opened their sealed instructions from the company. They

discovered that Jamestown would be ruled by a seven-man council, which included Smith. However, John Smith spent little time governing the colony, preferring to explore the area around Jamestown.

On one of these expeditions, Smith and his companions encountered hostile Native Americans. The colonists were captured and condemned to die. According to Smith's account (which may have been his own invention) in his *Generall Historie of Virginia, New-England, and the Summer Isles* (1624), a young Indian woman named POCAHONTAS persuaded her father, Chief Powhatan, to spare his life. On returning to Jamestown, Smith discovered that his enemies had taken over the government. The council sentenced him to death for the loss of two men in his exploring party. However, the arrival of ships from England in January 1608 with fresh supplies and new settlers calmed the colony and saved Smith from hanging.

By the fall of that year, Smith's enemies in the colony had lost power. Rejoining the council, Smith was elected president and placed in charge of the settlement. Using his military skills and knowledge of the region, Smith saved the colonists from starving to death during their second winter at Jamestown. He negotiated peace with Chief Powhatan, obtained corn and other food from the Indians, and organized the colonists into work groups. He continued to explore the region and mapped the area around Chesapeake Bay. In October 1609, Smith returned to England for medical treatment of an injury suffered in a gunpowder explosion.

In 1614 a group of London merchants asked Smith to explore an area of the Americas north of Virginia. He returned from a voyage to the region—which he called New England—with a valuable cargo of fish and furs and the strong belief that the area could support settlement. In 1616 Smith wrote *A Description of New England.* The book's valuable information and accurate maps were later used by the people who settled PLYMOUTH COLONY. Smith spent the rest of his life at home in England, writing about his adventures in North America and promoting colonization. (*See also* **Literature; Military Forces; Powhatan Indians.**)

See color plate 1, vol. 3.

Smuggling

Smuggling is the moving of goods into and out of a country secretly and illegally, usually to avoid paying import or export duties. Smuggling was a common feature of colonial trade. Most colonists benefited economically from the activity, so few wanted to stop it. Efforts by colonial authorities to prevent or limit smuggling generally had little success and aroused resentment and opposition among the colonists.

Although smuggling took place in all colonial regions of North America, the British took the strongest steps against it. Beginning in the mid-1600s, England passed a series of restrictive trade laws known as the NAVIGATION ACTS. These laws, which required colonists to trade certain goods through England or on English ships, prevented colonists from finding the best markets for their products and buying raw materials and European manufactured goods at the cheapest prices. Instead of protecting English shipping, the Navigation Acts forced many colonists to turn increasingly to smuggling as a way of trading goods more profitably.

Smuggling flourished in the American colonies not only because it was an economic necessity but also because the Navigation Acts were difficult to enforce. English ships patrolled the seas looking for smugglers. But the coastline of North America was long, with many sheltered bays where smuggling ships could easily hide. Moreover, the English often were too busy with foreign wars to pay attention to colonial smugglers. The WEST INDIES, in particular, became a smuggler's paradise, and the French, Spanish, and Dutch colonies were important centers of smuggling activity as well.

Colonial Americans smuggled goods in various ways. They might disguise a product—for example, by packing tobacco in flour barrels or putting foreign wine in bottles made to hold New England rum. Smugglers also forged shipping documents, bribed customs officials, brought goods ashore in the dark of night, and transported goods overland from the Dutch, French, or Spanish colonies. Smuggling could be a dangerous business. Colonists caught trading with Britain's enemies could be convicted of treason.

Smuggling changed somewhat in the 1700s. Its focus shifted from European manufactured goods—most of which could now be imported more cheaply from Britain—to sugar, molasses, and rum from the French and Spanish colonies. The British Parliament tried to stop this trade by passing the MOLASSES ACT (1733) and the SUGAR ACT OF 1764. Laws such as the TOWNSHEND ACTS (1767) and the TEA ACT OF 1773 required colonists to pay high import duties on other products and imposed various trade restrictions. These laws angered the colonists and aroused opposition to British policies. Many considered the smuggling of items covered by the laws to be justified acts of resistance, and they viewed well-known smugglers—including John HANCOCK—as heroes. (*See also* **Mercantilism; Rum Trade.**)

Social Conflict in European Colonies

*T*he North American colonies were places of continuing change, sometimes of conflict. Not all conflict took the form of open warfare. Racial, ethnic, religious, and economic tensions resulted in social conflict in all the colonies.

Dutch Colony. The colonists who settled in NEW NETHERLAND (present-day New York) came from a number of countries besides the Netherlands and held a variety of religious beliefs. Their diverse backgrounds produced conflict. The DUTCH WEST INDIA COMPANY, which owned the colony, had allowed some English PURITANS to settle on Long Island. At times anti-Dutch feelings flared in these English communities, especially when England and the Netherlands went to war in the early 1650s. The relationship between the English colonists and their Dutch rulers remained uneasy until the colony came under English rule in 1664.

Religion led to social conflict as well. Although most of the settlers belonged to the Dutch Reformed Church, the colony also included English QUAKERS and Puritans on Long Island, Lutherans from Europe, and JEWS who had fled the Dutch colony of Brazil when it was recaptured by the Portuguese. The West India Company and Director General Peter STUYVESANT, who governed New Netherland from 1647 to 1664, refused these groups the

Social Conflict in European Colonies

* **clergy** ministers, priests, and other church officials

right to practice their religions. The Jewish settlers faced hostility not just from Stuyvesant but also from the Dutch Reformed clergy* and other colonists. They sought help from some wealthy, powerful Jews in the Netherlands, who were investors in the West India Company. Pressured by the company, Stuyvesant allowed the Jews to worship but not to build a synagogue.

British Colonies. The British North American colonies eventually numbered 13. Each had its own particular culture, economy, and problems, which changed over time. Conflicts existed within each colony as well as among the colonies.

Those conflicts grew out of three sets of problems. First, in the early 1600s, came the practical issues connected with establishing a settlement—how to transfer English power, people, and methods to a distant land. Second, in the late 1600s and early 1700s, came military and racial concerns related to expansion and growth—the Native Americans' struggle to deal with the white invasion, the English conquest of other settlements such as New Netherland, and the growth of the African American population. Third, beginning in the mid-1700s, came political and cultural problems as the gap widened between the maturing colonies and a parent country that remained determined to keep them under tight control.

The problems in each of these stages produced various social tensions. For example, during the early phase of settlement, Puritans in Massachusetts tried to build perfect, harmonious communities shaped by the religious beliefs they had brought from England. But the first generation of American-born children did not always follow the pattern their parents had set. They expected to be considered full members of the church without undergoing the adult religious conversions that their elders had experienced.

New Englanders also felt a deep tension between the Puritan belief that the community came first and the growing desire of individuals to improve their personal circumstances through trade. In the 1640s, one Boston merchant even stood trial because the community felt that he charged too much for the goods he sold. The trial showed the conflict between traditional ways and the new spirit of self-advancement. Such tensions continued as some individuals challenged authority, claiming the right to believe, marry, and do business as they pleased. At the same time, some New Englanders of later generations felt that their societies had failed to live up to the founders' visions.

Other social conflicts involved land. Most of the colonies' boundaries were uncertain, and maps made as late as the 1770s showed the same piece of territory claimed by two colonies. Border disputes occurred frequently between New Englanders and New Yorkers. Pennsylvania and Maryland argued over their borders for more than a century, finally hiring two English surveyors—Charles Mason and Jeremiah Dixon—to trace an official boundary line. Disputes over land were the main source of conflict between the colonists and Native Americans as well. Indians protested bitterly—and sometimes went to war—as the colonies expanded into tribal lands. Although the colonists usually defeated any tribe that took up arms against them, those who settled on the frontier had to live with the danger of Indian attack.

Land also lay at the root of the tenant-landlord conflicts that swept some colonies in the 1700s. Good farmland along the coast and the rivers had filled

 See map in British Colonies (vol. 1).

* **tenant farmer** person who farms land owned by another and pays rent with a share of the produce or in cash

* **militia** army of citizens who may be called into action in a time of emergency

* **oppression** unjust or cruel exercise of authority

up in the early years of settlement, wealthy families had claimed large estates, and many people had little choice but to become tenant farmers*. However, those who moved beyond the frontiers of crowded New England wanted to own their own farms, and they resisted the attempts of landlords to control the land. In the 1770s, tenant resistance turned to outright rebellion in the Green Mountains of VERMONT, where some settlers formed a militia* under the leadership of Ethan ALLEN to defend their rights against the demands of New York landlords. The rebels declared Vermont an independent republic in 1777.

In some cases, social conflict in the colonies erupted into riots or rebellions. Racial oppression* was one cause. Large slave uprisings occurred in Stono, South Carolina, in 1739 and in New York City in 1712 and 1741. The slaves who revolted in New York joined forces with free blacks, Indians, and poor whites who also felt oppressed by those in power. Finally, in the colonies as in the parent country, mobs sometimes took to the streets in protest when the local government failed to keep down the price of essential goods such as firewood, salt, and bread. But the fact that the colonies had some common problems does not mean that they were unified in any way. Only in the 1770s, when the British PARLIAMENT imposed new taxes and new restrictions on trade and local government, did people throughout the American colonies begin to see themselves as sharing common problems and interests.

French Colonies. NEW FRANCE, the French colony in what is now Canada, experienced no slave revolts, bread riots, urban crime waves, or political or religious rebellions. Yet it was not without social conflict. In a society where class and rank meant everything, those at the top regarded the common people as potentially dangerous.

In both New France and the colony of LOUISIANA, royal and church authorities believed it necessary to maintain constant control. They did so by limiting the officer ranks in the military to men of noble birth, by appointing mostly French-born clergy to high positions in the church, and by discouraging ordinary people from forming organizations—even craft guilds*—that might become sources of political power. French authorities dealt harshly with lower-class protests, yet people often resisted pressure to follow the "correct" social order. In Canada, for example, bishops felt it necessary to issue strict warnings to women to dress modestly, laborers to rest on Sundays, and men and boys to stop swearing, smoking, and horse racing during the hours of church services.

* **guild** association of crafts workers

Throughout the French colonial period, tension existed between people born in North America and those who had come to the colonies from France and therefore considered themselves superior. Although these tensions did not produce open conflict, they were felt at all levels of society.

Spanish Colonies. In Spain's North American colonies, race was the most important element of social class and social conflict. The colonial order rested firmly on racial identity, with Indian, black, and racially mixed people at the bottom and whites at the top. At the highest level were the *peninsulares,* or Spanish-born whites, who looked down on the white *criollos* born in the Americas. The *criollos,* nonetheless, held many of the most important local offices.

Government and church officials often took as much pride in their racial purity as in their positions of authority. Convinced of their cultural and racial superiority, white colonists believed they had the right and the duty to dominate other races. Tensions and conflicts arose when the goals of these groups differed, as they often did.

The Spanish Borderlands*, however, differed from some of Spain's large and well-established provinces in the Americas. Its population was small, spread over a vast area far from the main centers of Spanish authority, and generally fairly poor. As a result, class lines became a bit blurred in the Borderlands, where different groups had to cooperate with each other simply to survive.

* **Spanish Borderlands** northern part of New Spain, area now occupied by Florida, Texas, New Mexico, Arizona, and California

Still, social conflicts did exist. Some involved competition for resources, especially water, good land, and Indian labor. In California, for example, missionaries tried to prevent the Native Americans at their missions from working at nearby ranches.

Tension often surfaced in racial slurs. Most Hispanic settlers in the Borderlands were racially mixed, but they called themselves *espanoles,* or Spaniards. They resented attacks on their "Spanishness" and often fought over such insults. Although racial categories were less firmly fixed in the Borderlands than elsewhere in Spanish America, people at all levels of society felt the importance of racial distinctions. In 1743, for example, a Spanish missionary reported that Indians in Florida refused to wear burlap because blacks wore it.

Social tensions often took the form of individual acts that challenged the official idea of proper order, such as secret weddings and duels. There were also some larger conflicts, including the PUEBLO REVOLT in New Mexico in 1680 and the uprising of French settlers in Louisiana against the Spanish, who had gained control of the colony in 1762. However, these scattered cases of violent social conflict were the exception, not the rule, in the history of the Spanish colonies. (*See also* **Class Structure in European Colonies; Independence Movements; Land Ownership; Race Relations; Slave Resistance.**)

Social Customs

An English visitor to Boston during the 1600s remarked scornfully that in the colonies "neither days, months, seasons, churches, nor inns [were] known by their English names." Besides unfamiliar names, visitors also found customs and rules of behavior that were different from European traditions. The English, French, Dutch, and Spanish colonists—and people from other countries who settled in the colonies—attempted to reproduce the traditions and practices of their homelands, but the conditions they encountered in North America gave rise to new social customs.

British Colonies.   Like people in England, colonists of the 1600s and 1700s took the question of manners—how they ought to behave toward each other—seriously. They wrote and read books aimed at improving manners and behavior. The Massachusetts preacher Cotton MATHER produced manuals telling people how they should act in various circumstances. George WASHINGTON copied out for himself more than 100 "rules of civility and decent behavior in company and conversation."

Dueling

To defend their honor, or settle a dispute, American colonists sometimes resorted to duels. The man claiming to have suffered an insult formally challenged his opponent to a duel. The opponent then offered a response. Sometimes the dispute was settled without violence. If not, the two parties met to fight, usually with swords. The result might be serious injury or even death.

The custom of dueling was brought to North America by French and British officers who served in the colonies. Although dueling was illegal in many colonies, it became common, particularly among army officers in the French colonies.

* **militia** army of citizens who may be called into action in a time of emergency

* **magistrate** official with administrative and often judicial functions

* **gentry** people of high social position

Rules of behavior were especially important for children, who were expected to be polite and obedient to their parents at all times. In fact many colonies passed laws to punish disobedient children. Young people who struck their parents could be jailed, whipped, or even killed. Eleazar Moody's "163 Rules for Children's Behavior" (1715) was just one of a number of works on manners for children.

Manners and social customs served as signs of a person's position in the CLASS STRUCTURE. Colonists who belonged to the upper classes—or who wanted to look as if they did—adopted the new manners that had swept Europe in the 1600s. They made an effort to cover up body functions such as spitting and blowing their noses, and when eating they no longer wiped greasy fingers on their clothes. As table manners grew more elaborate, their use became a sign of high social standing. In a more general sense, "good behavior" came to mean not giving way to strong outbursts of emotion such as anger, sorrow, or even joy. Well-bred, well-behaved people prided themselves on self-control.

Yet the realities of colonial society created new kinds of behavior. In Europe the complex and interconnected worlds of church, government, and the nobility kept a close eye on people. These conditions did not exist in the colonies. In England traditional customs helped keep the social classes sharply separated from one another, but in the colonies the classes mixed more freely, and the old class distinctions were not so clear. For example, English harvest festivals provided by manor lords for the local peasants gave way in the colonies to cornhuskings where laborers rubbed elbows with landowners.

The use of weapons provided more evidence of changing social customs. In England only well-to-do landowners served in the military. The colonies, however, expected all healthy men to serve in the militia*. In England only the king's friends could hunt in the royal deer park. But any colonist was free to hunt in the nearest woods. In dozens of similar small ways, customs of dress, speech, and behavior changed in the colonies. Although class differences remained strong throughout the colonial period, the trend was toward greater equality.

People in the British colonies were well aware of the new freedoms open to them now that they were far from the controlling institutions of the homeland. Many of them rejected the customs by which English people showed respect to certain individuals. The diaries of leading landowners reveal their frustration when they could not force neighbors or even family members to obey them. Colonists frequently treated ministers, judges, magistrates*, and other authority figures with a degree of disrespect that would not have been allowed in England. Constables trying to maintain law and order in society received threats of violence from annoyed citizens. Soldiers challenged their officers to fistfights, refusing to serve under any man who could not beat them. Colonists displeased with court verdicts sometimes attacked their judges. A governor of North Carolina declared that the previous governors had all "lived in fear of the people." At its worst, such behavior was nasty rudeness. At its best, it was a crude form of democracy taking shape.

Some colonial gentry* and visitors from Europe were disturbed by what they saw as the breakdown of social order. Every colony passed so-called

Social Customs

Colonial women turned work into a social event at gatherings known as "bees." In this 1876 illustration of a late colonial quilting bee in Massachusetts, women of all ages came together to make a quilt—perhaps as a gift for a new bride or a mother-to-be.

* **New France** French colony centered in the St. Lawrence River valley, an area known as Canada; included the Great Lakes region and, until 1713, Acadia (present-day Nova Scotia)

* **clergy** ministers, priests, and other church officials

sumptuary laws trying to keep people from wearing clothes "above their station." However, these laws failed to keep ordinary citizens from imitating the dress of the gentry as soon as they had a little money to spend.

Fine dress and skillful dancing, like manners learned from a book, allowed people who had not had a "proper" upbringing to move in higher social circles. In their desire to seem fashionable, some colonial men and women went to extremes—wearing huge, awkward, powdered wigs that smelled and itched, for example. Such customs may have made people look ridiculous, but they also showed that many colonists viewed North America as a place where they were free to remake their identities.

French Colonies. Society in New France* and Louisiana was divided into classes that mirrored those of France: clergy*, nobility, and commoners. During the 1600s, there was considerable movement up the social ladder—and down it—in these colonies. By the 1700s, society was becoming more fixed, and members of the upper classes took steps to keep commoners from imitating their "betters." In 1721, for example, commoners were forbidden to carry swords.

Social customs and manners in the French colonies were set by the nobility, who established courtesy and consideration for others as prime values. After a 1749 visit to the French province of Canada, Swedish visitor Peter Kalm wrote:

> The common man in Canada is more civilized and clever than in any other place . . . that I have visited. . . . One can scarcely find in a city in other parts, people who treat one with such politeness both in word and deed as is true everywhere in the homes of the peasants of Canada.

He added that the manners of the Canadian nobles and clergy were as different from the behavior of English colonists as heaven from earth.

Other observers, however, noted that the nobility in the French colonies were often vain, hot-tempered, and wasteful. They spent money they could ill afford on banquets and entertainments. They were quick to respond to insults, whether real or imagined, and often settled disputes through duels, in which two people fought each other according to certain rules in the presence of witnesses.

Common folk also replied to insults with their fists, swords, or stones. By the early 1700s, mirroring the rejection of authority that was taking place in the British colonies, ordinary French settlers were beginning to show disrespect to the clergy. They came to church drunk, quarreled in the church lobby, and talked or sang during religious processions.

Spanish Borderlands. Customs and behavior in the Spanish Borderlands* were governed by the all-important concept of honor, which penetrated every level of the community. At first it was easy to identify those who possessed honor—they were white, Christian, and noble. As Spanish American society became racially and culturally more complex, however, it became harder for people to evaluate each other's level of honor. Land ownership, occupation, and family background all took on importance. A peasant who owned land could be regarded as having honor.

The entire community followed the code of honor. For women, honor was closely related to sexual virtue. Fathers, brothers, and husbands all felt a duty to protect the purity and honor of their womenfolk. This led to such social customs as the use of chaperons and keeping girls and women inside the house much of the time. An unfaithful wife brought dishonor to her husband. He could restore some of his honor by publicly shaming her, perhaps by cutting off her hair.

For men honor was linked to bravery and power. For example, a man accused of lying could restore his honor if he responded to the accusation with violence. A man who could not control his son's behavior lost honor, as did a son who disobeyed his father. The father could use physical punishment to restore his honor. He might even go so far as to curse his son, with such words as, "May the earth part and swallow you."

Customs designed to protect honor were based on *respeto* (respect). The young showed respect to the old, the child to the parent, the host to the guest. As in other colonies, the customs and manners accepted by most people in Spanish America served as a lubricant that kept the wheels of society turning smoothly. (*See also* **Clothing; Gender Roles.**)

* *Spanish Borderlands* northern part of New Spain, area now occupied by Florida, Texas, New Mexico, Arizona, and California

Society for the Propagation of the Gospel

See *Protestant Churches: Anglican.*

Society of Friends

See *Quakers.*

Sons of Liberty

After the British government passed the STAMP ACT in 1765—a law that imposed taxes on newspapers, legal and commercial documents, and playing cards—secret societies known as the Sons of Liberty sprang up in the colonies in protest. Outraged by what they considered to be "taxation without representation" and by Parliament's interference in colonial affairs, these organizations opposed the new law and tried to prevent the British from enforcing it.

The first Sons of Liberty society was formed in New York City in the fall of 1765. The name came from a speech made by a member of PARLIAMENT who criticized the Stamp Act and referred to the colonists as "sons of liberty." The New York group quickly established contact with similar societies elsewhere. By the early spring of 1766, a formal alliance of Sons of Liberty had been established in New England, and it soon expanded to include colonies in other regions.

Most organizations of Sons of Liberty were founded in the months following the first Stamp Act protests—usually in response to some local event. For example, one group formed in Albany, New York, after hearing rumors that a stamp official might be appointed to the area.

The members of these groups came mostly from the middle and upper classes of colonial society—merchants, businessmen, lawyers, journalists, public officials, and others. Samuel ADAMS and Paul REVERE were two of the society's most famous members. Once organized, however, the Sons of Liberty tried to broaden their appeal so that they would represent all colonists.

The Sons of Liberty rallied colonial opposition to the Stamp Act in various ways. They circulated petitions, published anti-British propaganda*, tarred and feathered* people they considered disloyal, threatened British officials, and hanged effigies* of unpopular officials. Britain found the Stamp Act too difficult to enforce, and the law was repealed*.

Although the Sons of Liberty called for an end to British tyranny*, they did not at first support revolution. In fact, they often expressed a deep loyalty to King GEORGE III and to Great Britain. Nevertheless, their activities encouraged colonial patriots* and helped bring the issue of greater rights for the colonies to the public's attention.

After the repeal of the Stamp Act, the Sons of Liberty continued to stir up opposition to British policies. They supported bans on British imports, and the Boston organization took a leading role in the BOSTON TEA PARTY. (*See also* **American Revolution; Daughters of Liberty; Independence Movements; Revolutionary Thought.**)

* *propaganda* information presented in a way to influence people
* *tar and feather* to punish a person by covering with hot tar and feathers
* *effigy* dummy of a person
* *repeal* to undo a law
* *tyranny* unjust use of power
* *patriot* American colonist who supported independence from Britain

South Carolina

The English began to colonize present-day South Carolina in the mid-1600s. But both the French and the Spanish had visited the area a century earlier and tried to establish settlements. Under English rule, South Carolina developed a flourishing agricultural economy that relied heavily on SLAVERY.

The Spanish and French. A Spanish expedition from the Caribbean island of HISPANIOLA, led by Lucas Vásquez de Allyón, explored parts of the

Blackbeard the Pirate

Edward Teach, known as Blackbeard, was one of the most fearsome pirates of the colonial period. In 1717 Teach anchored near Charleston and established a blockade of its harbor. Within days, he had captured several ships and taken their sailors hostage. Running low on bandages and medicine, Teach demanded that supplies be sent to his ship and threatened to kill the hostages if his demands were not met. Meanwhile, his crew took over the streets of the city, terrifying the residents. The colonial governor finally sent the supplies, the prisoners were released, and Blackbeard sailed on.

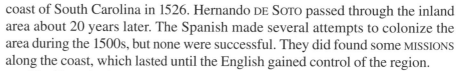

coast of South Carolina in 1526. Hernando DE SOTO passed through the inland area about 20 years later. The Spanish made several attempts to colonize the area during the 1500s, but none were successful. They did found some MISSIONS along the coast, which lasted until the English gained control of the region.

The French also were interested in the area that is now South Carolina. In 1562 Jean Ribault built a small fort at Port Royal and tried to establish a colony of French Protestants, or HUGUENOTS. The colony failed to take root, and later French attempts also proved fruitless. Lack of supplies, disputes between settlers, and attacks by Native Americans and European rivals doomed all these early attempts at colonization.

English Settlement. In the early 1660s, a group of influential Englishmen became interested in settling the area. Among them were Sir William BERKELEY, the governor of Virginia; his brother John Berkeley; and Sir George Carteret, who later founded the colony of New Jersey. In 1663 Charles II of England granted the men a royal charter* for a colony that was named Carolina in the king's honor. The charter gave its proprietors* title, or ownership, to all the land between Virginia and Spanish FLORIDA.

To encourage colonization, the proprietors issued a document that promised political and religious freedom, as well as land, to anyone who settled in Carolina. At the same time, they organized an expedition from the Caribbean island of BARBADOS to locate suitable sites for colonization. The Barbadians selected the Cape Fear region, and colonists from Virginia settled around Albemarle Sound. The proprietors divided Carolina into two regions—Albemarle in the north and Clarendon, including the Cape Fear settlement, in the south.

The Cape Fear community failed, mostly because the proprietors had invested very little in it. But Sir Anthony Ashley Cooper, one of the proprietors, was determined to see the colony succeed. He persuaded the other proprietors to supply funds for recruiting colonists and to provide an additional sum each year for several years to ensure that the colony would have sufficient resources.

Besides financial backing, Ashley Cooper believed the colony needed a stable social structure. With his secretary, political thinker John Locke, he drafted a document in 1669 called the Fundamental Constitutions of Carolina, which established a plan for the colony's development. The plan proposed a society dominated by the aristocracy*. Almost half of the colony's land would go to this group, with the rest being distributed among ordinary settlers. Representatives of the proprietors, the aristocracy, and the settlers would sit in a colonial assembly. However, a council of nobles, not the assembly, would make the laws. The colonists never adopted the plan.

In August 1669, a group of new settlers sailed from England. Arriving on the Carolina coast in March 1670, they proceeded to Port Royal Sound. Because of concern over their closeness to the Spanish in Florida, the colonists decided to move northward. They founded a settlement called Charles Town on the Ashley River. In 1680 their community—which soon became CHARLESTON—was relocated to the junction of the Ashley and Cooper rivers. A stretch of uninhabited country divided the settlers clustered around Charleston and those living to the north in Albemarle. In 1712 the two regions became the separate colonies of South Carolina and NORTH CAROLINA.

* **charter** written grant from a ruler conferring certain rights and privileges

* **proprietor** person granted land and the right to establish a colony

* **aristocracy** people of the highest social class, often nobility

See map in British Colonies (vol. 1).

Rice was a major cash crop in South Carolina throughout the colonial period. In this illustration from Charles Fraser's *A Charleston Sketchbook*, rice fields are irrigated by a network of ditches and floodgates. This system allowed planters to flood and drain the fields repeatedly.

* **cash crop** crop grown primarily for profit

* **indigo** plant used to make a blue dye

Proprietary Rule. In the beginning, the colony faced a shortage of food, and the settlers had to depend on supplies from England and food provided by local Indians. Despite this problem, Carolina began to attract settlers from other English colonies, including Barbados. By 1700 more than 5,000 people lived in what would become South Carolina.

In the early years, the colonists' main source of wealth was trading hides and furs with the Indians rather than agriculture. They raised enough corn and other crops to meet their own needs and grew some TOBACCO. In addition, they exported hogs, cattle, grain, and timber to the WEST INDIES.

In about 1685, Carolinians began to cultivate RICE, and within a few years, it had become an important cash crop*. Rice transformed the region. The crop soon dominated the colonial economy and brought great prosperity to many planters. It also changed the nature of Carolina society. To grow rice, fields must be flooded and drained several times—a process that could not be carried out economically on small farms. Large PLANTATIONS and many workers were required to produce rice profitably. To meet their labor needs, planters relied increasingly on African slaves, and slavery quickly became the dominant feature of South Carolina society. In the 1740s, the colonists began raising another important cash crop—indigo*. This crop also required large plantations and many workers, thus contributing to the growth of the slave population. The colony prospered, and the population increased.

South Carolina faced a serious crisis in 1715 when the YAMASSEE INDIANS started attacking colonists along the southern borders of the colony. During the Yamassee War, more than 400 colonists were killed, and large areas of land that had been cultivated were abandoned. At the same time, settlements along the coast suffered from increasing raids by PIRATES. The Indian war and piracy hurt the colonial economy and created discontent among the colonists.

When the Yamassee Indians were defeated, the proprietors seized Indian land and refused to distribute it among the colonists. This was too much for

the South Carolinians. They overthrew the proprietors in 1719, and the British government took control of the colony.

Royal Control.   In 1729 the proprietors of South Carolina sold their rights to the colony to the British crown. During the remainder of the colonial period, South Carolina was ruled by a series of royal governors. South Carolinians welcomed royal control at first, especially after the crises of the final years under the proprietors. Eventually, however, opposition arose to British policies, and the colonists joined the movement for independence.

During the 1700s, South Carolina continued to expand north and west from the original coastal settlements. In time this expansion led to tensions with Indians along the frontier. In 1760 war broke out between the CHEROKEE INDIANS and settlers in the South Carolina backcountry, the undeveloped inland area. Colonial troops from Charleston helped end the war after nearly two years of fighting.

The defeat of the Cherokee did not end the colony's troubles. Tensions soon arose between people living in frontier areas and colonial authorities. The backcountry settlers complained that colonial troops had taken their supplies and plundered their farms during the Indian war, causing great damage. Moreover, bands of outlaws continued to roam the countryside.

In 1767 groups of settlers called REGULATORS sprang up to combat lawlessness in the backcountry. The Regulators criticized the government for failing to protect them against bandits and for not establishing local courts or providing adequate schools. They also complained about the colonial tax system, which they considered unfair, and about the control of government by the coastal settlements. Tensions between the backcountry and coastal regions continued throughout the colonial period.

Most South Carolinians eventually grew weary of royal government, and opposition arose to British colonial policies. Wealthy merchants and planters led the revolutionary activity in the colony, and Charleston played an important role during the AMERICAN REVOLUTION. The British captured Charleston in 1780, but backcountry MILITIA held off the British until the CONTINENTAL ARMY drove them out of the colony near the end of the war. (*See also* **Agriculture; British Colonies; Colonial Administration; Government, Provincial; Slave Trade; Trade and Commerce.**)

Southern Colonies

See *British Colonies; Georgia; Maryland; North Carolina; South Carolina; Virginia.*

Spain

*L*ocated on the Iberian Peninsula of southwestern Europe, Spain and neighboring PORTUGAL both ventured out during the 1400s in search of sea routes to Asia. After Christopher COLUMBUS sailed across the Atlantic Ocean and landed in the Americas, Spain began to explore and colonize these "new" lands, hoping to gain great riches and glory from them. It built an enormous empire in North America that included New Spain* and the Spanish Borderlands*.

Spain

* *New Spain* Spanish colonial empire in North America; included Mexico, the area now occupied by Florida, Texas, New Mexico, Arizona, and California, and various Caribbean islands

* *Spanish Borderlands* northern part of New Spain, area now occupied by Florida, Texas, New Mexico, Arizona, and California

* *feudal* relating to an economic and political system in which individuals give service to a landowner in return for protection and the use of land

See map in Missions and Missionaries (vol. 3).

Muslim Rule. In the 700s, Muslims from North Africa, known as Moors, had conquered much of the Iberian Peninsula. Only the small mountainous region of Asturias in the northwest remained under Christian rule. Gradually, the rulers of Asturias gained control of neighboring lands, and by the end of the 900s, they had established the Christian kingdoms of León, Castile, Navarre, and Aragon. Although these Christians fought among themselves, they were united in their desire to recapture the peninsula from the Muslims.

The Reconquista. Around the year 1000, Moorish Spain began to break up into various small kingdoms. Clashes among the kingdoms weakened Muslim rule and allowed Christian forces to begin taking back large parts of the Iberian Peninsula. The *Reconquista,* or reconquest, of Muslim Spain by Christians began in earnest in the early 1200s, when the monarchs of Aragon and Castile won important victories.

During the 1300s, Spain's Christian kingdoms continued their campaigns against the Muslims. Conquest, new trade, and increasing contact with other European countries brought power and prosperity to the region and the winds of change to society. Growing conflict among social classes contributed to the gradual breakdown of the feudal* system.

The task of reconquest helped bring Spain's Christian kingdoms closer together economically and strengthened the power of their monarchies. But political unity did not occur until the late 1400s, when Isabella I of Castile wed Ferdinand II of Aragon. Although they kept their kingdoms separate, Ferdinand and Isabella extended their joint authority over much of Spain. In 1492 they completed the reconquest by driving the remaining Moors out of Iberia. That same year Isabella supported a voyage of exploration by Columbus that led to the European discovery of the Americas.

Spain and the "New World." After Columbus's voyage, Spain quickly built a large and immensely profitable colonial empire in the Americas. At first Spain had few rivals in this region with the exception of Portugal, which had begun to establish an empire of its own. Disputes between Spain and Portugal were resolved in 1494 by the TREATY OF TORDESILLAS. This agreement divided the world into two spheres of influence: one for the Spanish to claim and colonize, the other for the Portuguese.

The Spanish developed their colonial empire by conquering the Indians they encountered in the "New World" and establishing Spanish laws and culture. They converted and educated Native Americans through MISSIONS AND MISSIONARIES. They defended the frontiers of New Spain by building forts, or PRESIDIOS. GOLD and SILVER from South and Central America brought great wealth to the Spanish crown and helped make Spain the richest and most powerful nation in Europe.

Extending Spanish Power. The marriage of Ferdinand and Isabella had united the kingdoms of Aragon and Castile. But other Spanish kingdoms and small independent states still existed, each with its own separate laws and customs. In the early 1500s, King Ferdinand conquered the kingdom of Navarre. His successors continued efforts to unify Spain and expand its power.

Spain launched the exploration of North America when it sponsored Christopher Columbus's voyages across the Atlantic Ocean. In this engraving from the late 1500s by Theodore de Bry, Columbus prepares to set sail. The explorer hoped to discover a new sea route to Asia, but he found the Americas instead.

* **dynasty** succession of rulers from the same family or group
* **abdicate** to give up the throne voluntarily

Charles I, the grandson of Ferdinand and Isabella, gained the throne of Spain in 1516. From his other grandparents, Maximilian I of Austria and Mary of Burgundy, Charles inherited title to the Holy Roman Empire—which included Germany—and to the Netherlands. Charles founded the Hapsburg dynasty* of Spain. During his reign, Spain became involved in several international disputes, including wars with France for possession of territories in Europe.

Reign of Philip II. Charles abdicated* the throne in 1556. His son Philip II continued his efforts to expand Spain's empire but experienced several setbacks. One of Philip's most serious problems involved the Netherlands. Many Protestants lived in the Netherlands, and they resented rule by Spanish Catholics, leading to years of conflict. In 1581 the Dutch provinces of the Netherlands declared their independence from Spain. Thereafter, the Dutch built a strong fleet and presented a serious challenge to Spain's dominance.

Beginning in the 1560s, Spain's rivalry with England also heated up. In 1588 Philip sent a fleet, called the Spanish Armada, to destroy England's navy. Instead, the English—with the help of stormy weather—defeated the Armada, slowing Spain's drive to build an empire. Spain also became involved in a long

Spain

See first map in European Empires
(vol. 2).

See second map in European Empires
(vol. 2).

* ***Seven Years' War*** series of conflicts in
Europe, North America, Africa, and Asia that
involved two struggles—one between Austria
and Prussia and the other between Britain
and France; the American part of the conflict,
the French and Indian War, ended in 1763
with Britain defeating France and its ally Spain

* ***absolute monarch*** king or queen who
possesses unlimited power

series of religious wars in Europe that further weakened its power. In 1580 Philip united Portugal and Spain, but Portugal later rebelled and regained its independence in 1640.

Declining Power in Europe.
During the 1600s, art and literature flourished in Spain. At the same time, the country entered a period of political decline. Spain fought a series of wars with England, the Netherlands, and France that greatly diminished its influence in Europe. It remained a great colonial power, but other nations began challenging its supremacy.

In 1700 King Charles II of Spain died without a direct heir, and both French and Austrian relatives claimed the throne. The War of the Spanish Succession (1701–1714) brought a French dynasty, the Bourbons, to the Spanish throne.

Bourbon Rule.
The Bourbon rulers attempted to restore Spanish power and prestige by forming a close alliance with France. This helped Spain regain some of its former territory in Italy. However, it also brought Spain into the Seven Years' War*. In the TREATY OF PARIS (1763), which ended the war, Spain received the colony of LOUISIANA from France but lost FLORIDA to England. Spain regained Florida at the end of the American Revolution.

The Bourbons also began a series of reforms aimed at developing better administration in both Spain and its colonies. These reforms improved transportation and agriculture. They reorganized the central government and colonial governments to make them more efficient and increased the power of the state over the Catholic Church. The Bourbons also lifted many of the restrictions on colonial trade, which helped stimulate the economy of Spain and its colonies.

In 1793 revolutionaries who had come to power during the French Revolution executed the king of France. Spain responded by declaring war on France. The conflict was a disaster for Spain, as French armies invaded the country and captured Spanish territory. To limit the spread of French control and revolutionary ideas, Spain signed a treaty with France in 1796. The treaty drew Spain into a war with Britain. The British responded by cutting the nation off from its colonies in the WEST INDIES and opening their markets to British and American trade. This action dealt a serious blow to Spain's economy.

Independence in Spain and Its Colonies.
In 1808 the French dictator Napoleon Bonaparte sent troops into Spain, occupied the capital of Madrid, and forced King Ferdinand VII to abdicate. He then placed his brother Joseph Bonaparte on the throne and established a military government.

The Spanish resisted the occupation of their country by the French. In the Peninsular War—known in Spain as the War of Independence—the Spanish army suffered repeated defeats. But in 1814 Napoleon met his downfall after British troops, aided by Spanish forces, defeated his armies and drove them back to France.

The war left Spain economically ruined and politically divided. During the fight, Spanish rebels had adopted a new constitution that limited royal power. When Ferdinand VII regained the throne after the war, he refused to honor the constitution. Instead, he tried to rule as an absolute monarch*.

Efforts to restore absolute monarchy led to conflicts within Spain and contributed to INDEPENDENCE MOVEMENTS in Spanish America. By 1825 all Spanish colonies in the Americas—except several territories in the West Indies—had gained their independence. (*See also* **Colonial Administration; Conquistadors; European Empires; Exploration, Age of; Mexican Independence; New Spain; Spanish Borderlands.**)

Spanish Borderlands

* *buffer* protective barrier between two rivals
* *New Spain* Spanish colonial empire in North America; included Mexico, the area now occupied by Florida, Texas, New Mexico, Arizona, and California, and various Caribbean islands

A Salary With No Money

An important financial resource for most Borderland provinces was the *situado,* or military payroll. The *situado* formed the backbone of all provincial economies except that of New Mexico. Paid in Mexico City, most of the money never reached the soldiers. Instead, the frontier forts had agents in Mexico City who purchased needed supplies and luxury items and shipped them to the Borderlands. This merchandise was then "sold" to the soldiers, and the cost was subtracted from a salary credited in an account book. Soldiers on the frontier were able to buy items this way, but usually no money changed hands.

Beginning in the 1500s, Spain assembled a vast colonial empire that included much of South America, all of MEXICO and Central America, and parts of the present-day United States. This last territory was a frontier region that served as a buffer* between New Spain* and the French and British colonies of North America. Known as the Spanish Borderlands, it included present-day FLORIDA, TEXAS, NEW MEXICO, ARIZONA, and CALIFORNIA.

The Borderlands shared many of the features common to other parts of Spanish America. Yet these northern frontier provinces were also very different from the more settled colonies. They enjoyed greater independence because they were so far from authorities in Spain and Mexico City, and they developed institutions to meet the unique problems of a frontier region.

Exploration and Settlement. First explored in the early 1500s, the various regions of the Spanish Borderlands were colonized at different times. Spaniards founded the first permanent settlement in Florida, ST. AUGUSTINE, in 1565. The region never attracted large numbers of colonists, and it remained one of the least developed in the Spanish Borderlands. During the 1700s and early 1800s, Florida changed hands several times between Britain and Spain, eventually becoming part of the United States.

New Mexico, first colonized in the late 1500s, became one of the most successful and populated colonies in the Spanish Borderlands. A meeting place of Spanish and Native American cultures, New Mexico remained under Spanish rule until 1821. At that time, it became part of the newly independent nation of Mexico.

Spanish settlement of Arizona did not begin until the mid-1600s. Colonization proceeded very slowly, and large areas of the region remained isolated and unsettled throughout the colonial period. Like New Mexico, it became part of Mexico in 1821.

In the late 1700s, an increasing number of foreigners, including British merchants and Russian trappers, began moving into Spain's California territory. To strengthen claims to the area, Spanish authorities encouraged settlement in the region. Isolated from other Spanish lands and from colonial authorities in Mexico City, California enjoyed a great deal of political and economic freedom. When Mexico won its independence from Spain in 1821, California became a territory of the new nation.

The Borderland regions attracted far fewer settlers during the colonial period than did other areas of North America. The great distances between settlements, the poor state of transportation and of trading links, and Spanish policies restricting immigration all played a role in limiting population

Spanish Borderlands

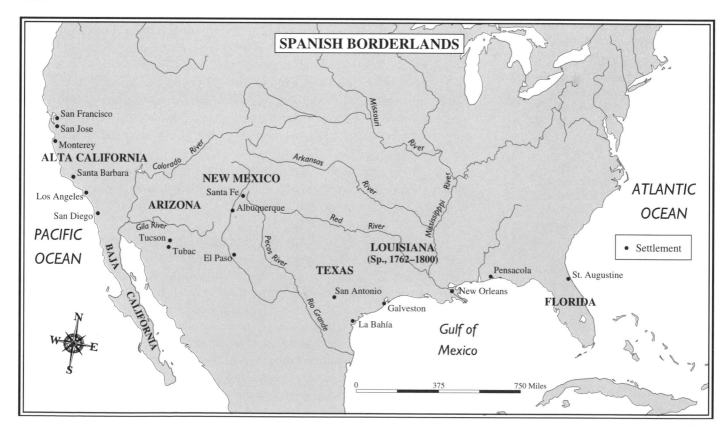

See map in Missions and Missionaries (vol. 3).

* **assimilate** to adopt the customs of a society

* **outpost** frontier settlement or military base

The Spanish Borderlands covered the area now occupied by the states of Florida, Texas, New Mexico, Arizona, and California. Throughout the colonial period, the region was more thinly populated and developed more slowly than the Spanish colonies farther south.

growth. However, the isolation and the small number of people living in the Borderlands created unique regional economies and cultures.

Borderland Institutions. To help colonize and settle the Borderlands, the Spanish established MISSIONS, PRESIDIOS (forts), and towns. Controlled by the Spanish crown, these institutions were developed in a certain sequence, and each of them had specific goals.

In Spanish frontier regions, the missions came first. They allowed Spain to stake a claim to an area and to gain control over Native Americans. Founded primarily to spread Christianity, the missions also introduced the Indians to European ways and helped assimilate* them into Spanish culture. The frontier missions became major landowners, and many developed profitable agricultural and RANCHING activities.

Once a mission community had been established, the Spanish crown sent soldiers to defend it. At first only a small military outpost* would be built near a mission. These outposts gradually expanded into large presidios with anywhere from 50 to 100 soldiers. The presidios enforced Spain's territorial claims and defended mission communities against Indian attack. Over time they also attracted civilian settlers, who made a living providing products such as food and clothing to the military. After retiring from the army, many soldiers settled in the communities that grew up around the presidios.

The establishment of a civilian settlement was usually the last step of the colonization process in the Spanish Borderlands. Only a few of them developed

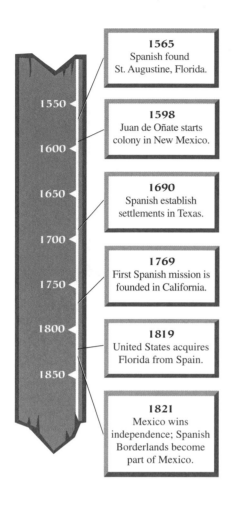

1565
Spanish found
St. Augustine, Florida.

1550

1598
Juan de Oñate starts
colony in New Mexico.

1600

1650

1690
Spanish establish
settlements in Texas.

1700

1769
First Spanish mission is
founded in California.

1750

1800

1819
United States acquires
Florida from Spain.

1850

1821
Mexico wins
independence; Spanish
Borderlands become
part of Mexico.

* *tribute* payment made to a dominant power
* *aristocracy* people of the highest social class, often nobility

before the late 1600s. Spanish authorities divided these communities into three categories: *lugares* (villages), *villas* (towns), and *ciudades* (cities). Each had its own type of administration and government. During the colonial period, only towns and villages existed in the Borderlands.

Spanish Rule. Spain had a highly centralized system of government to administer its empire in the Americas. Royal officials in Spain shaped all government policies, and colonial officials in Mexico City made most of the decisions affecting the Borderland provinces. But the isolation of the Borderlands regions allowed them to develop without much interference from colonial authorities. The task of enforcing official policies fell to provincial governors and various local officials, who often took matters into their own hands.

In the late 1700s, Spain grew increasingly concerned about defending the Borderlands from Indians, the British, and the Americans, leading it to strengthen its authority over the region. The Borderlands were reorganized into a new administrative unit called the Interior Provinces of the North, which had greater independence than in the past.

The ROMAN CATHOLIC CHURCH—the official church of Spain and its empire—played a vital role in Spanish America. The government and the church were closely linked. Catholic missionaries administered religious affairs in the Spanish Borderlands and often tried to influence or dominate political institutions. The missionaries saw themselves as the Native Americans' protectors and expected to control their lives and labor. Colonists, however, wanted to use the Indians' labor for their own purposes. The competition for this labor became a source of conflict between the church and the government. In the 1700s, the Spanish crown greatly limited the power of the church and removed the Indians from direct church control.

Under Spanish rule, the Borderlands never developed strong and diverse economies. In the early colonial period, Spanish officials attempted to promote economic development by granting ENCOMIENDAS, which entitled colonists to labor and tribute* from the Indians. Fearful that this would create a wealthy aristocracy* that might challenge the government, Spanish authorities introduced regulations in the mid-1500s to restrict the *encomienda.* As a result, it declined in importance. The Spanish colonial economy was based primarily on agriculture. Few industries developed, though the production of handicrafts became an important economic activity throughout the Borderlands.

The Borderlands were linked to the trading network of the Spanish empire through military and missionary supply systems and some civilian traders. Strict regulations on imports, exports, and shipping prohibited trade with anyone outside of the Spanish empire. However, Borderland settlers smuggled goods from French, English, and Dutch merchants. Until the end of the colonial period, they relied on commerce with foreign countries and colonies to obtain all but the most basic goods.

Life in the Borderlands. In general, life in the Borderlands was very difficult. Settlers lived with the continual threat of Indian attack, crop failure, and disease. Relatively few products and manufactured goods were imported, so colonists had to provide for themselves. Many people lived or worked on

Spanish Borderlands

The first mission the Spanish built at Pecos, New Mexico, in 1625 was destroyed during the Pueblo Revolt of 1680. The remains of the church shown here date from 1717.

* *artisan* skilled crafts worker

* *mestizo* person of mixed Spanish and Indian ancestry

* *mulatto* person of mixed black and white ancestry

ranches and farms, and rural communities sprang up throughout the region. Most artisans* lived in towns, which served as the focus of political and economic activity. There were no public schools or colleges in the Spanish Borderlands until the very end of the colonial period. As a result, few children received a formal education other than what their parents could provide at home.

Spanish colonial society was divided into groups based largely on race. The major social categories were Spaniard, mestizo*, mulatto*, black, and Indian. European-born Spaniards, known as *peninsulares,* were rare in the Spanish Borderlands. American-born Spaniards, known as *criollos* or CREOLES, made up a majority of the population and generally held the most important positions in society. However, because of the small population of the Borderlands, class distinctions were not as rigid as in other parts of Spanish America, and the gap between rich and poor was smaller. People in these colonies—even free blacks and Indians—found it much easier to gain wealth and to move up in social rank.

End of the Colonial Era. The Spanish Borderlands remained under Spanish rule until the early 1800s. The first region lost was Florida, which the United States acquired in 1819. Three years later, the remaining Borderland colonies became part of Mexico after it won its independence from Spain.

* *cede* to yield or surrender

After 1821 American settlers began streaming into the Borderland regions. Americans in Texas rebelled against Mexican rule and won their independence in 1836. Mexico ceded* most of the remaining territory to the United States in 1848, after suffering defeat in the Mexican War. Although Spanish rule ended, the Borderland region continued to reflect Spanish culture long after the colonial period. (*See also* **Agriculture; Class Structure in European Colonies; Colonial Administration; Economic Systems; European Empires; Exploration, Age of; Frontier; Government, Provincial; Land Ownership; Laws and Legal Systems; Military Forces; Pueblo Revolt; Trade and Commerce.**)

| Spanish Succession, War of |

See *Queen Anne's War.*

| Sports |

See *Recreation and Sports.*

Squanto

ca. 1590–1622
Indian translator and guide

Squanto was a WAMPANOAG INDIAN who helped a group of English settlers establish their colony at PLYMOUTH, Massachusetts. The extraordinary events of his life forced him to adapt to two widely different cultures—Native American and English.

As a young man, Squanto—also known as Tisquantum—lived in Patuxet, a Wampanoag village on Plymouth Bay. At that time, European explorers were beginning to search the New England coast for settlement sites. In 1615 an English sea captain lured Squanto and some other Wampanoag aboard his ship and kidnapped them. The captain took the Indians to Spain, where he sold some of them into slavery. Squanto later managed to reach England. For a few years, he lived in London and learned to speak English.

Acting as a guide and interpreter for an English expedition to New England, Squanto was able to return to North America in 1619. When he found his way back to Patuxet, however, he discovered that nearly all the inhabitants had died of disease during his absence. In 1621 Squanto met the PILGRIMS, who had settled on Plymouth Bay. He served as interpreter in treaty negotiations between the settlers and the Wampanoag chief, Massasoit. Having lived in England, Squanto took a special interest in the struggling colonists. He taught them how to plant corn and how to use fish as fertilizer for their crops. Knowing local agricultural methods helped the newcomers survive the harsh New England climate.

Squanto attempted to become a political leader among the Wampanoag, but his friendship with the English made the other Indians uneasy. As a result, he lived under the protection of Plymouth colony during the last years of his life. Squanto died of smallpox in 1622. (*See also* **Thanksgiving Celebrations.**)

Stamp Act Crisis (1765)

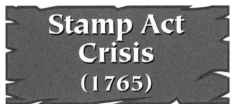

In 1765 the British PARLIAMENT passed the Stamp Act, which imposed a tax on documents and paper goods used by American colonists. The act caused a furor, setting off widespread protests and rioting in the colonies. Although the crisis over the Stamp Act was eventually resolved, the bad feelings it created between Great Britain and the colonists remained, contributing to the movement for independence.

Paying for Colonial Defense. With their victory over the French in the FRENCH AND INDIAN WAR in 1763, the British gained control of a vast amount of territory in North America. They realized that to defend these lands, they would have to strengthen their forces along the frontier and to station British troops permanently in the colonies. These measures would require large sums

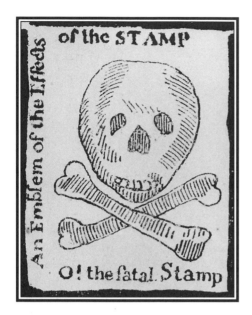

Many colonists protested the Stamp Act after it passed. This political cartoon appeared in the *Pennsylvania Journal* in 1765. The caption surrounding the skull and crossbones bemoans the damaging effects of the "fatal stamp."

* *effigy* dummy of a person

* *resolution* formal statement adopted by a legislature or other organization

of money—but Britain was already heavily in debt because of its expenses from the war.

Parliament decided that the colonies should share the cost of their own defense. In the past, Parliament had not taxed the colonists to raise revenue but had asked them to contribute voluntarily to colonial defense. However, such contributions often fell far short of what was needed, and Parliament believed the Americans could afford to pay more. The government now decided to tax them directly.

The Stamp Act and the Colonies' Response.

In early 1765, Parliament passed the Stamp Act. The act required all newspapers, pamphlets, legal and commercial documents, advertisements, and other papers issued in the colonies to bear official government stamps, which had to be purchased. Even almanacs, playing cards, and dice needed stamps. The act also provided for the creation of a Stamp Office in London and inspectors and stamp distributors in each colony. Because the revenue from the stamps was expected to cover less than half the cost of colonial defense, Parliament believed the law to be fair. Moreover, though the Stamp Act affected everyone, it would fall most heavily on lawyers, printers, merchants, and other prosperous people.

American colonists quickly and loudly protested the Stamp Act. They were outraged by Parliament's attempt to tax them without their consent, which they considered a violation of their rights as British citizens. They insisted that there should be "no taxation without representation." The colonists also argued that Parliament, by giving itself the authority to tax the colonies, threatened the power of colonial assemblies. They declared that only their assemblies had the right to tax them.

Growing Crisis and the Stamp Act Congress.

Colonists reacted at first with a flood of articles in pamphlets and newspapers, as well as with petitions passed by colonial assemblies. By the summer of 1765, opposition to the act had erupted into public protests and violence.

A Stamp Act "riot" occurred in Boston, where colonists hanged an effigy* of the local stamp distributor, then paraded it through the town and burned it. The rioters also destroyed a building they believed to be a future stamp office and attacked the home of the stamp distributor. Similar events took place in other colonies, including a riot in New York City, during which a mob threatened Cadwallader COLDEN, the lieutenant governor.

Meanwhile, in October 1765, 27 representatives from nine colonies met in New York City to discuss the growing crisis. The delegates to this meeting, which came to be known as the Stamp Act Congress, adopted a resolution* called the Declaration of Rights. This document, intended as a petition to Parliament, declared that free men could be taxed only with their consent. It argued that the stamp tax was illegal because the colonists were not represented in Parliament. Parliament refused to consider any petitions from the colonies. In response several colonial assemblies passed resolutions giving themselves the exclusive right to tax.

Organized Protest and Repeal of the Stamp Act.

At about the time the Stamp Act Congress was meeting, some colonists started to form secret

associations known as SONS OF LIBERTY. These groups tried to organize opposition to the Stamp Act. First formed in New York City, Sons of Liberty chapters quickly sprang up throughout the colonies.

Determined to prevent the Stamp Act from being enforced, the Sons of Liberty rallied opposition to it. They continued the protests, but they also circulated petitions, published anti-British pamphlets, and helped organize boycotts* of British goods. In addition, the group worked to focus the public's attention on the issue of greater rights for colonists.

* *boycott* refusal to buy goods as a means of protest

Colonial opposition made it impossible for the British to enforce the Stamp Act. Shocked by the violent reaction of the colonists and faced with a loss of trade, Parliament repealed* the law in 1766. At the same time, however, it passed the DECLARATORY ACT, which proclaimed that Parliament had the right to make laws for the colonies on all matters. This act did not specifically mention the right to tax, but the language of the law clearly seemed to include it. The repeal of the Stamp Act quieted colonial protests for a time, but it left the colonists with feelings of resentment that contributed to their continued opposition to British policies. (*See also* **Independence Movements.**)

* *repeal* to undo a law

Standish, Miles

ca. 1584–1656
English colonist and soldier

* *militia* army of citizens who may be called into action in a time of emergency

Miles Standish was one of the leaders of PLYMOUTH COLONY. Originally an employee of the PILGRIMS who founded the colony, Standish eventually became a member of their community and played a significant role in Plymouth's development.

The Pilgrims hired Standish, an Englishman who had been a professional soldier in the Netherlands, to train and lead their militia*. He sailed with the Pilgrims on the *Mayflower* in 1620, then helped them explore the Cape Cod area in present-day Massachusetts and choose the site for Plymouth colony. As the only person in the group with camping experience, Standish showed the Pilgrims how to survive in the wilderness. When nearly everyone in the colony became sick during the first winter, he took care of them.

During Plymouth's early years, Standish became an expert in dealing with the Native Americans. He learned Indian dialects and protected the colony against threatened Indian attacks. Standish designed, built, and managed the colony's fort and devised other means of defense. He did such a good job of making the colony secure that after 1623 the Pilgrims faced no serious dangers for the next 50 years.

After going through so many difficult times with the Pilgrims, Standish formed close ties with them. In 1625 he went back to England to negotiate a charter* for the colony and to obtain much-needed loans and supplies for the community. Returning to Plymouth, he became active in the colony's government, holding several important positions.

* *charter* written grant from a ruler conferring certain rights and privileges

Standish and his Pilgrim friend John Alden founded the town of Duxbury, Massachusetts, in 1631. The popular story that Alden courted a young Pilgrim woman named Priscilla Mullens on Standish's behalf is probably not true. Standish's first wife died during the sickness of the colony's first winter. He and his second wife, Barbara, had six children and made their home in Duxbury. (*See also* **Military Forces.**)

Stono Rebellion

See *Slave Resistance.*

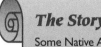

Storytelling

* *narrative* story or description
* *supernatural* related to forces beyond the normal world; miraculous
* *ritual* ceremony that follows a set pattern

The Story of Sedna

Some Native American myths tried to explain the origin of things found in nature. The story of Sedna, told by Native Americans in what are now Canada and Alaska, dealt with the beginning of sea life. The story involves a young girl named Sedna who turns down human suitors to marry a dog (or bird) who promises her happiness. When the new husband fails to fulfill this promise, Sedna's father kills him and escapes with her in a boat. A wild storm arises and Sedna's father throws her overboard to save himself. As Sedna clings to the boat, her father cuts off her fingers, which change into various kinds of fish. The fish destroy the girl's father, and Sedna becomes queen of the lower world.

People living in North America during colonial times enjoyed hearing a good story. In those days before the invention of radio and television and when many people could not read, storytelling served a variety of purposes besides entertainment. Mainly, it was an important means of passing a group's religious and social values on to its children and adults. Storytelling also helped preserve the history of African Americans and Native Americans, who had no tradition of written literature. Immigrants from Europe brought the folk stories of their homeland with them to the new land. Retelling these stories helped them feel close to each other and to their cultural heritage.

Native Americans. Native Americans possessed a rich oral tradition that included myths, historical legends, and personal narratives*. Creation myths attempted to explain the origin of the world. In one story common to many Native American groups, the union of the sky and the earth begins the creation process. In another, the universe develops from the body of a dead giant. A being known as Earth Diver, who plunges to the bottom of the ocean and brings up dirt to form land, appears in Indian creation stories throughout North America.

Cultural myths sometimes featured heroes who embodied the values and attitudes of the group. Others concerned a "trickster," who by his evil or foolish actions illustrated the opposite of what the group believed. Manibozho and Coyote are just two of the names for the trickster character in these myths.

Native Americans used historical legends to tell the story of their ancestors' wanderings before arriving in the present homeland. These legends also offered explanations of special objects, such as strange stone formations left behind by previous inhabitants, or they might describe how a group of Indians became the ally or enemy of another group. Some told the story of the Native Americans' first contact with Europeans.

Personal experience narratives related the remarkable hunting and fishing adventures, supernatural* encounters, dreams, and military heroics of an individual, perhaps those of the storyteller. These tales were sometimes told in a formal setting, such as a tribal council or a religious ritual*, or they might be part of an everyday conversation.

Among Native Americans, the performance of a story was as important as the words, and good storytellers were honored for their skill. With no written text, narrators could vary the details of a story to make it more interesting or suitable to the audience. Their tone of voice, facial expression, and body language also played a role in the interpretation. Storytellers were artists, and each time they told a traditional tale it was a different experience.

African Americans. Blacks in slave communities gathered around campfires and told stories after a long day of hard work. To preserve their African heritage, they repeated the folktales that they or their ancestors had

Storytelling played an important role in the cultural life of many Native American peoples. This plate, presenting a storyteller and his listeners, comes from the early Mogollan culture of the Southwest.

* *oppression* unjust or cruel exercise of authority

* *satire* humor that makes fun of something bad or foolish

* *metaphor* figurative language, a kind of literary comparison

brought across the ocean. To the traditional tales, they added stories of being kidnapped and sold into slavery. Slaves also retold Bible stories they had learned in America, especially stories that dealt with deliverance from oppression*.

African American storytellers often used humor and satire*, rather than anger and sorrow, to express their feelings about their situation. They skillfully employed metaphors* to make comments about their white masters. Benjamin FRANKLIN recalled this example of African American humor:

> White men make the black man work, make the horse work, make the ox work, make everything work except the hog. He, the hog, doesn't work; he eats, drinks, walks about, goes to sleep when he pleases. He lives like a gentleman.

Using a metaphor—hog—to express disapproval of the white man's work habits was much less dangerous than direct criticism.

One type of story that developed in North America was the slave narrative, in which the narrator related his or her own experiences as a slave. Slave narratives included descriptions of brutal mistreatment and generally concluded with a plea for freedom. In time many slave narratives were written down, forming the beginning of African American written literature.

European Americans. Settlers in the French colony of NEW FRANCE enjoyed a rich tradition of oral stories and songs. Most of these originated in the

Middle Ages, a period when storytelling was at its height in Europe. At that time, troupes of storytellers and singers traveled from town to town entertaining royalty and common folk alike. Some of their popular stories of love and romance later appeared in New France.

Telling *cuentos,* or stories, was a common practice in the settlements of Spanish America. The colonists knew hundreds of *cuentos,* covering a variety of topics. They had brought most of these stories from Spain and adapted them to life in North America. Tales of enchantment—featuring witches, ghosts, magic spells, and talking animals—formed one large group. Another group, known as *cuentos morales* (moralistic stories), reminded the settlers to behave properly. (*See also* **African American Culture; Literature.**)

Stuyvesant, Peter

ca. 1610–1672
Dutch colonial governor

* *autocratic* ruling with absolute power and authority

Peter Stuyvesant was the fourth and last director general of the Dutch colony of NEW NETHERLAND. A capable administrator, he enacted many reforms that improved conditions in the colony. But his autocratic* rule and violent temper made him widely unpopular among the colonists.

Born in a region of the Netherlands known as Friesland, Stuyvesant was the son of a pastor in the Dutch Reformed Church. He left his university studies to pursue a career in the military, serving both in the Netherlands and in its overseas colonies.

In about 1635, Stuyvesant began working for the DUTCH WEST INDIA COMPANY, the trading company responsible for colonial activities in the Americas. Stuyvesant held various positions in the company's colonies in Brazil and the West Indies. In 1642 he was appointed governor of the island colony of Curaçao in the Caribbean. As governor, Stuyvesant mounted an aggressive campaign against enemies in the region. While leading an attack on the island of St. Martin in 1644, he was hit by a cannonball. His right leg had to be amputated, and Stuyvesant returned to the Netherlands to recuperate. There he acquired a wooden leg decorated with silver.

The loss of a leg did nothing to hinder Stuyvesant's career. In 1646 the Dutch West India Company appointed him director general of New Netherland. When Stuyvesant arrived in the colony in the spring of 1647, he found it in great disorder as a result of incompetent government. Stuyvesant immediately set out to restore order. He imposed laws to curb public drunkenness and loitering and had the church and other public buildings repaired. He also took steps to stop the colonists' SMUGGLING. Only the West India Company had the right to engage in trade. The new governor's swift measures helped save the colony from political and economic collapse.

Stuyvesant governed New Netherland for 17 years, the longest term of any Dutch director general. During that time, he did much to strengthen the colony. Fighting a series of Indian wars, he overpowered Native American tribes that threatened the colony's survival. He also conquered SWEDISH SETTLEMENTS on the Delaware River and gained control of the FUR TRADE along that river. In addition, Stuyvesant constructed a defensive wall—along what is now Wall Street—to protect NEW AMSTERDAM, the colonial capital, and he

See map in New Netherland (vol. 3).

* **toleration** acceptance of the right of individuals to follow their own religious beliefs

helped establish boundaries between New Netherland and the English colonies.

Despite such accomplishments, Stuyvesant's harsh, inflexible style of governing angered many colonists. Believing that people should submit to the will of their rulers, he rejected cooperative efforts in favor of autocratic rule. His actions against colonists who did not follow the Dutch Reformed Church proved to be especially controversial. The Dutch had a reputation for religious toleration*, and New Netherland had attracted colonists of many different faiths, including JEWS, QUAKERS, and Lutherans.

Stuyvesant's rule ended in 1664, when an English war fleet captured New Amsterdam and took control of the entire colony. The Dutch West India Company recalled Stuyvesant to the Netherlands to explain his failure to defend the colony. He later returned to New Netherland (renamed NEW YORK by the English) and retired to his farm outside the city. (*See also* **Colonial Administration; Governors, Colonial.**)

Suffrage

See *Voting Rights.*

Sugar Act of 1764

Passed by the British Parliament in 1764, the Sugar Act sought to end the SMUGGLING of sugar and molasses between the West Indies and the British colonies. It was also enacted to raise tax revenue from the colonies to help pay for colonial defense.

In 1733 Parliament had passed the MOLASSES ACT, which placed a high duty on any foreign molasses imported in the British colonies. Most colonial merchants opposed this tax, arguing that it would harm trade. However, few colonists openly resisted the law. They simply avoided the duty by smuggling the molasses into their ports, and British officials made little effort to stop them.

In 1764 George GRENVILLE, the British prime minister, ordered a detailed investigation of colonial methods of getting around the Molasses Act and other British trade laws. In response to the findings, Parliament enacted and planned to enforce the American Duties Act of 1764, better known as the Sugar Act. Although the new law halved the import tax on molasses, it added duties on iron, lumber, silk, wine, and other products.

To aid in enforcing the Sugar Act, Parliament created a special vice admiralty court at Halifax, Nova Scotia. A judge, with no jury, would hear cases concerning violations of the law or failures to pay the import duties. In the past, maritime* courts in the colonies had handled such cases, but those courts had juries that could be swayed by local pressures from colonists. The location of the new court in remote Nova Scotia, with authority over cases arising in all the colonies, ensured that the colonists would not be able to influence its decisions.

* **maritime** related to the sea or shipping

Another provision of the Sugar Act required shipowners to post bond—supply money or property as a kind of insurance—for all cargoes before they could be loaded. Any ship found with products not covered by a bond could be seized, along with its cargo, by government authorities.

* *monopoly* exclusive right to engage in a certain kind of business

The American colonists vigorously opposed the Sugar Act. The law gave British sugar planters in the West Indies an almost complete monopoly* on the sugar market. The colonists also resented the complications on shipping introduced by the bonding provision. Most troubling, however, was the fact that the Sugar Act seemed to be a deliberate attempt by Parliament to tax the colonies. Unlike the Molasses Act, which merely attempted to regulate trade, the Sugar Act was designed to raise money for the British treasury. The government intended to use these funds to pay for defending the colonies. The American colonists criticized this attempt to tax them without their consent. Some considered it a threat to their basic rights.

The colonists protested strongly at first. But after Parliament lowered the duties, the opposition died down. Nevertheless, the Sugar Act was another in a chain of laws that threatened the relationship between Britain and its North American colonies. The colonists soon would be protesting more forcefully against "taxation without representation." (*See also* **Navigation Acts; Taxation; Trade and Commerce.**)

Surveyors

*A*s Europeans came to North America and settled the land, surveyors played an essential role in establishing property lines. Surveyors also helped resolve boundary disputes, which arose frequently. The detailed notes of these early officials contributed a great deal to knowledge of the continent's geography, plants, and soil.

Arriving after explorers, trappers, and traders, surveyors were among the first white men to enter a wilderness area. When Indians spotted a surveyor in their territory, they knew that settlers would soon follow. The appearance of surveyors often led to conflicts between Native Americans and colonists.

In venturing into frontier areas, far from established settlements, surveyors faced many dangers and hardships. Heavy snow in the winter made walking and finding food difficult. Mosquitoes and intense heat caused misery in the summer. No matter what the season, there was always the risk of attack from Indians or wild animals.

Surveyors worked for governments or for private land developers. In the New England colonies, government surveyors measured off rectangular towns and divided them into lots. Settlement in the southern colonies was not quite so orderly. Individuals often staked out their own land claims. Later, surveyors followed the settlers' property lines to establish official boundaries. Most of the instruments used in modern surveying, such as the magnetic compass, portable quadrant, bubble level, telescopic sight, and chain, were in use by 1750. People taking measurements on the FRONTIER, however, usually had only primitive versions of these tools.

Several important figures in colonial history possessed experience in this field. George WASHINGTON worked as surveyor of Culpeper County, Virginia, in the 1740s. The astronomer and mathematician David RITTEN-HOUSE used his surveying skills to help establish the boundaries of more than half of the 13 British colonies, including the famous Mason-Dixon Line that separated Maryland from Pennsylvania. (*See also* **Land Ownership.**)

Susquehannock Indians

See second map in Native Americans (vol. 3).

*T*he Susquehannock Indians lived in the Susquehanna River valley of Pennsylvania at the beginning of the colonial period. Attacks from other Native Americans and clashes with colonists caused them to migrate several times. These conflicts and moves devastated the tribe.

Like other northeastern Indians, the Susquehannock lived by farming, hunting, and gathering. They resided in large multifamily dwellings called longhouses and spoke an Iroquoian language. During the 1600s, the tribe became involved in the FUR TRADE with Dutch colonists in New Netherland.

The Susquehannock were bitter rivals of the IROQUOIS CONFEDERACY and engaged in almost constant warfare with its tribes. Following a serious defeat by the Iroquois in 1675, the Susquehannock left their homeland in Pennsylvania and moved south into the Chesapeake region.

The next year the Susquehannock were attacked during BACON'S REBELLION, an uprising of Virginia frontier settlers against colonial authorities. The rebels were protesting the lack of defense by government forces against Indian raids. Disobeying the government, they attacked any Indian tribes they encountered. The Susquehannock responded by joining other Indians in assaults on white settlements.

Bacon's Rebellion almost wiped out the Susquehannock tribe, which had also suffered losses from diseases introduced by European colonists. Some of the surviving Susquehannock fled north. There they eventually converted to Christianity and settled with other Christian Indians at the Conestoga Mission in southeastern Pennsylvania. In 1763 a mob of Pennsylvania colonists, angered by frontier raids by other Indian tribes, attacked the mission and killed several Indians. The rest of the Indians from the mission took refuge in a nearby jail. However, the angry mob soon broke into the jail and killed this group as well. With this massacre, the Susquehannock tribe ceased to exist, though scattered members may have continued to live among other Indian groups. (*See also* **Native Americans.**)

Swedish Settlements

*T*he Swedes, latecomers to North America, founded their first and only colony on the continent in 1638—long after England, France, and Spain had begun establishing settlements. Sweden was also the first European country to abandon its efforts to build an empire in North America. Located in the present state of DELAWARE, the colony of New Sweden lasted only 17 years.

The Founding of New Sweden. The New South Company, a private group of Swedish and Dutch investors organized in 1633, established the colony of New Sweden five years later. The company took its name from the South River—now called the Delaware—which ran along the proposed site of settlement.

The members of the New South Company chose Peter Minuit to lead the first expedition. Minuit, a former director general of the Dutch colony of NEW NETHERLAND, had explored the Delaware River valley and knew it well.

Swedish Settlements

Under his leadership, a small group of Swedes and Finns arrived in the region in March 1638. With Minuit's help, they chose a site for their settlement—near present-day Wilmington—on a small river that flowed into the Delaware. Minuit purchased the land from local Indians, and the colonists began building their first fort, which they named Fort Christina in honor of the Swedish queen.

The site selected proved to be ideal. Located at the entrance to a major fur-trading route, Fort Christina was popular with trappers. They found it more convenient to do business there than to cross the river to Fort Nassau, the Dutch fort on the east side. In 1642 the Swedish government bought out the Dutch investors and took over the colony. The company was renamed the New Sweden Company.

Growth of New Sweden. During the first few years of its existence, New Sweden thrived. More colonists arrived, eventually boosting the population to 400. They cleared forests and cultivated land for farms. A village was laid out behind Fort Christina. Johan Printz, the colony's second governor, strengthened relations with the Indians and expanded Sweden's monopoly* on the fur-trading business in the region. A strict ruler, Printz added to New Sweden's territory, establishing several smaller forts in parts of present-day Pennsylvania and New Jersey.

* *monopoly* exclusive right to engage in a certain kind of business

During its brief existence, the Swedish colony on the Delaware River became a major fur-trading center. This sketch by Peter Lindestrom from the late 1600s shows the Swedes trading with local Indians. Meanwhile, in the background, Native Americans engage in wars and other activities.

Log Cabins

Although New Sweden lasted for only a short time, Swedish and Finnish settlers made an important contribution to American culture. Along with immigrants from other areas, such as Germany, they brought with them the log cabin style of housing construction. Rectangular in shape, a typical log cabin had a center door and windows on either side of the door. Easy and inexpensive to build, log cabins provided the poorest colonists with a basic but cozy place to live. Later, log cabins similar to those of the Swedes became popular with hundreds of thousands of pioneers settling the western frontiers.

Relations With New Netherland. The Dutch had claimed ownership of the Delaware River since the early 1600s, when Henry HUDSON had explored the region for the Netherlands. The Dutch colonists resented the presence of the Swedes and Finns in the valley. However, weakened from a long war against Indians, they needed New Sweden's help in preventing English settlers from Connecticut from settling the area.

The cooperation between the Dutch and Swedish colonies ended in 1647, when Peter STUYVESANT became director general of New Netherland. Determined to regain control of fur trading and river traffic, Stuyvesant built the stronghold of Fort Casimir, a few miles south of Fort Christina. But Stuyvesant was unable to maintain enough soldiers and gunpowder at the fort because of threats from the English in other parts of New Netherland. In 1654 the commander of a Swedish ship bringing supplies and colonists to New Sweden easily forced the surrender of Fort Casimir. The Swedes once again controlled the Delaware River valley.

The loss of Fort Casimir greatly embarrassed the DUTCH WEST INDIA COMPANY, which governed New Netherland. The company's directors ordered Stuyvesant to recapture the territory along the Delaware and drive all Swedes from the river. The Dutch government in Amsterdam sent a large warship to assist Stuyvesant. Leading 300 soldiers, Stuyvesant retook Fort Casimir and quickly destroyed Fort Christina and all other Swedish possessions.

In 1655 New Sweden ceased to exist as a colony. Although some of the colonists returned to Sweden after the surrender, the majority remained in North America. Rather than scattering the Swedes among the Dutch population, Stuyvesant allowed them to remain together and form their own villages. His decision was unusual for the time, but he believed that the Swedes would be more loyal to the Dutch government if they could maintain their identity as a people. The "Swedish nation" thus joined the growing population of New Netherland. Less than ten years later, however, the Dutch colony was captured by the English and became NEW YORK. (*See also* **New Amsterdam.**)

Taverns

After a tiring day's journey on bumpy colonial roads, travelers by horseback and stagecoach looked forward to stopping for the night at a tavern. Though almost all colonial taverns sold liquor, they operated primarily as inns, the forerunners of modern hotels and motels. At a well-run tavern, travelers could relax in front of a fire, eat a warm meal, and fall asleep in a clean bed.

Importance of Colonial Taverns. Taverns and travel went together in colonial times. An expanding system of ROADS encouraged people to travel. But because most journeys took longer than a day, wayfarers needed a place to stay at night. Before taverns became widespread, travelers had to seek food and lodging at homes along the way or else eat and sleep outside. Taverns made taking a trip easier and more convenient.

Although the official function of a colonial tavern was to provide a rest stop for travelers, it also served as a community center or village club. Taverns were gathering places where local residents could relax and enjoy themselves

Taverns

Colonists used taverns for social gatherings and political meetings. In the 1770s, the Green Dragon Inn in Boston became the gathering place of many rebels who went on to become leaders of the American Revolution. Paul Revere wrote in his diary about meeting at the inn to discuss the movements of the British soldiers.

* *Spanish Borderlands* northern part of New Spain, area now occupied by Florida, Texas, New Mexico, Arizona, and California

away from home. Patrons—primarily men—could drink, smoke their pipes, gossip with friends, read the newspaper, gamble on horse races and cockfights, and play cards and dice. They might conduct business over dinner. Taverns also provided a place where people could meet to discuss current events. During the American Revolution, taverns became a popular site for political meetings.

Taverns abounded in colonial America. They could be found everywhere in the French colonies. Boston boasted one tavern for every 25 adult males in 1737. Peter STUYVESANT, the director general of New Netherland, complained about the number of "brandy shops, Tobacco or Beer houses" in New Amsterdam. Only in the Spanish Borderlands*, a thinly settled region with few travelers, were taverns rare. Those who did travel looked for accommodations in private homes or camped outdoors.

Characteristics of Colonial Taverns. Colonial taverns varied widely in size and quality. In cities some taverns consisted of several buildings with large meeting rooms and many small, elegantly furnished apartments for sleeping. Backwoods taverns, off the main roads, tended to be smaller and simpler. At good taverns in either town or country, travelers could expect to find a large room with a fireplace, a bar, and furniture such as benches, chairs, and tables. Some taverns contained a separate ladies' lounge. Rooms in the back or upstairs were available for overnight guests.

Taverns provided a range of services. Some sold a wide variety of alcoholic beverages, including beer, wine, rum, and brandy, as well as toddy and grog—mixed drinks usually served hot. Others offered only a few kinds of drinks. Some taverns specialized in a certain type of food, such as seafood. Those in rural areas often functioned as small shops, selling beef, butter, eggs, and other farm products. A few taverns served as credit houses, lending small amounts of money to customers.

The regular patrons of taverns also varied. In large cities, wealthy, well-educated colonists gathered at certain taverns. Taverns in colonial capitals

often provided accommodations to the legislators when the assembly was in session. Waterfront establishments might serve mostly sailors and unskilled laborers. In the British colonies, blacks, apprentices*, servants, and sailors were not allowed inside taverns without permission from their masters or captains. In the French colonies, particular taverns were set aside for Native Americans.

* **apprentice** person placed in the care of a merchant or crafts worker to learn a profession

Regulation of Colonial Taverns.

All colonies passed laws that regulated taverns. In fact, taverns were also called "ordinaries" in the British colonies because they were governed by ordinances, or laws. The laws specified what the tavern keepers could sell, the prices they could charge, the customers to whom they could sell and in what quantity, and the days and hours on which they could be open for business. The main purpose of these laws was to prevent excessive drinking and rowdy behavior.

Local governments also controlled the tavern business through the granting of licenses to sell alcoholic beverages. Because the tavern keeper was responsible for maintaining order, a person with a questionable reputation seldom received a license to operate a tavern. Besides examining character, local governments considered a number of other factors. Applicants living on high-traffic roads were likely to receive licenses. People who were already overrun by travelers would usually be allowed to turn their homes into taverns. Often widowed women were given permission to open taverns as a means of supporting themselves and their children. Likewise, a person who had been injured and could find no other work might be allowed to go into the tavern business. (*See also* **Food and Drink; Transportation and Travel.**)

Taxation

* **barter** exchange of goods and services without using money

For the colonists of North America, the burden of taxation was relatively light, especially compared to the taxes paid by Europeans at that time. Today governments raise most of their revenue through income taxes and sales taxes. In colonial America, however, these forms of taxation were impractical. Most colonists had little cash. Their incomes consisted mainly of farm produce that they raised and consumed at home. In addition, exchanges of goods and services with people outside the family often involved barter* rather than cash, and few people kept records of such arrangements or of the income received from them. As a result, colonial governments had no reliable information about sales or income on which to base a tax. Instead, they used a variety of other methods of taxation to collect revenue, and each colony developed its own mix of taxes.

British Colonies

The colonial governments needed revenue for such purposes as constructing and maintaining roads and public buildings, providing relief for the poor, supporting public schools and churches, paying elected and appointed officials, and fighting wars. Government expenses in the British colonies were usually relatively low, though. Representatives to colonial ASSEMBLIES received money for travel, food, and lodging while the assembly was in session, but only a few public officials—such as governors and judges—were paid fixed salaries.

To finance their activities, local and provincial governments in the British colonies imposed taxes. But the tax burden on the colonists was quite light—generally less than 5 percent of their income. Moreover, colonists often provided labor to work out taxes rather than paying them in cash. Land and poll taxes were the most important.

Property Taxes.

Taxes on property, especially land, were the simplest and easiest form of taxation. In the course of their duties, assessors, or tax officials, could look over a piece of land and estimate its value as the basis for a tax. Furthermore, colonists were accustomed to land taxes, a common form of tax in Europe, and land was the main source of income and wealth in the colonies.

Disputes often arose over what types of land should be taxed and the appropriate level of taxation. Quitrents, the earliest land taxes, were extremely unpopular. These yearly payments on land reminded colonists of the burdensome system of rents and tenant farming* practiced in Europe. Quitrents assessed* a small amount for each acre of land and taxed all land at the same rate, regardless of its quality.

* **tenant farming** farming land owned by another and paying rent with a share of the produce or in cash

* **assess** to set the amount to pay

Small landholders believed that land should be taxed according to its productive value. A landowner who held rich land near a navigable river, for example, should pay a higher rate than a farmer with less fertile fields. Wealthy landowners opposed taxing all land at the same rate because they often possessed large tracts of undeveloped land, which they believed should not be taxed. Most colonies did not collect taxes on undeveloped land, but they generally taxed other land according to its productive value.

Land taxes were not restricted to the value of the land. They included all income-producing items on the property except food. The government often taxed livestock because oxen and horses could pull plows to work the soil, making it more productive and increasing its value. From cows, farmers obtained milk, cheese, and hides, which added to the income of a household. In addition to land taxes, colonial governments frequently imposed a separate personal property tax. This covered items such as mills and the tools and shops of artisans* because they created income for their owners. The tax also was applied to shopkeepers and merchants for their ships and stocks of goods.

* **artisan** skilled crafts worker

Poll Taxes and Faculty Taxes.

Because labor helped produce income, colonial governments usually imposed a poll tax, or head tax, on all adult males. People who employed others had to pay a poll tax on their workers, and slaveholders paid the tax on their slaves. Fathers paid a poll tax for their sons until the sons became independent. Most colonists considered this tax fair because it fell equally on all productive individuals and was common in Europe. The very poor were generally excused from the tax, as were ministers and older men who no longer worked.

The poll tax was not without problems. Artisans and professionals often worked alone but might produce as much income as a farmer with several hired hands. To equalize the tax burden, some communities replaced the poll tax with a "faculty tax" based on a person's earning capacity. The amount charged varied according to the individual's ability and training. This tax applied mostly to doctors, lawyers, and other skilled workers. It never became as common as poll taxes or property taxes.

Other Sources of Revenue. Colonial governments raised revenue through import and export duties as well. This form of taxation was most common in the southern colonies and, to some extent, in the middle colonies. Because the colonies could not charge a tax on goods imported from England, most duties fell on products from the WEST INDIES and from other countries of Europe. These typically included luxury items, such as liquor and slaves. The colonies imposed export duties on a range of products sent overseas, including tobacco, rice, and furs. In addition, they charged excise taxes on items sold within and between the colonies themselves. The most common of these, a tax on the sale of liquor, was collected from tavern keepers, who also had to pay annual license fees for their taverns.

Taxation was affected in some colonies by the creation of "land banks," which lent money to property owners for the improvement of their land. The interest, or fees, the banks charged for lending the money helped cover the costs of running the colony. Land banks were most popular in the middle and southern colonies, where economies were based primarily on agriculture. In the early 1700s, the land bank in New York covered half of the colony's expenses, and the land bank of Pennsylvania produced a large budget surplus. Delaware and New Jersey also established successful land banks. In New England, however, only Rhode Island had an effective land bank.

Another way for colonies to meet their expenses was by issuing paper money. The government would print up bills, or IOUs, promising to pay a certain amount to the holder and then sell them for that amount. At the same time, it would pass a tax law to ensure that there would be enough money in the treasury to pay off the bills when their holders chose to collect. When funds were urgently needed, as in wartime, a colony might issue paper money without raising tax revenue, waiting until peacetime to pay off the bills.

Taxation as a Political Issue. On the whole, British colonists paid little in the way of taxes. In New England, government expenses were kept low because most town officials served without pay and towns required citizens to provide free labor for many public works. In the middle colonies, the success of land banks helped reduce the burden of taxation, and revenue from import, export, and excise taxes allowed governments to assess lower land and poll taxes. The southern colonies had higher expenses because of the cost of supporting royal governors and other officials. Even in the southern colonies, however, the tax burden was comparatively light.

The British colonists had few problems with taxation until the mid-1760s, when Parliament passed legislation—such as the SUGAR ACT OF 1764 and the STAMP ACT in 1765—that attempted to impose taxes. Designed to raise revenue for colonial defense, the new laws aroused anger and opposition. Thereafter, taxation became a serious issue in the British colonies and contributed to the movement for independence.

Dutch Colony

Neither land taxes nor poll taxes ever took hold in the Dutch colony of NEW NETHERLAND. In 1638 government officials imposed land taxes on colonists, but these went largely uncollected. The colony had little settled land, apart

See color plate 6, vol. 4.

from a few farming plantations, because the Dutch focused their efforts on developing trade rather than agriculture. For this reason, the land tax failed to produce significant revenue. In 1655 colonial authorities attempted to tax real estate in the town of New Amsterdam (present-day New York City). This tax, which was voluntary, raised little money and was assessed only once.

Import and export duties on commercial goods, first collected by the DUTCH WEST INDIA COMPANY in 1621, became the main source of tax revenue for New Netherland. While claiming a commitment to free trade, the company, Dutch traders, and colonial authorities supported import and export duties. The taxes were used to pay for defense and development of the colony, to control colonial commerce, and to eliminate foreign competition in trade.

Import duties covered a wide range of items and varied according to the source of the goods. After 1638 a tax of 15 percent was imposed on all imports from foreign countries and colonies. Duties on articles from the Netherlands or Dutch colonies were much lower. Authorities collected export taxes on articles such as furs, codfish, tobacco, and liquor and on any goods leaving the colony on foreign ships. To encourage trade, they eventually lifted duties on exports to areas such as New England and Virginia.

Import and export duties drew protests, and many colonists tried to avoid paying them. This was difficult to do with import duties because the goods concerned generally arrived by ship. New Netherland had strict port procedures, including the inspection and recording of all articles as they were unloaded from ships. Export duties were easier to get around because merchants could conceal and transport goods overland to neighboring British colonies. SMUGGLING became a common way to avoid such duties. Despite protests, the system of taxation in New Netherland remained focused on international trade, with various tax rates for imports and exports.

French Colonies

To encourage the settlement of New France*, colonial authorities collected few taxes and kept them very low. The colonists were asked to give a small amount to support the Catholic Church. Under the SEIGNEURIAL SYSTEM, tenant farmers paid seigneurs—landholders—an annual rent as well as a small land tax. They sometimes also paid a *corvée,* which involved providing one or two days of required labor. Seigneurs could charge small fees for fishing or grazing livestock on common land and for the use of their flour mills. In addition, they collected a sales tax on land sold by a tenant. Seigneurial rents and fees generally could be paid in either currency or agricultural produce.

As in New Netherland, most tax revenue in New France came from import and export duties. Such taxes affected traders and merchants more than farmers. Import and export duties were collected by enterprises, such as the COMPANY OF ONE HUNDRED ASSOCIATES and FRENCH WEST INDIES COMPANY, that held a monopoly* on trade. These companies taxed furs, moose hides, and various other products. They often sold the right to collect the taxes to individuals in France, who grew very wealthy from the system of trade and taxation.

Duties were imposed on colonial shipping as well. Every ship entering or leaving a port in France and New France had to pay a variety of taxes for

* **New France** French colony centered in the St. Lawrence River valley, an area known as Canada; included the Great Lakes region and, until 1713, Acadia (present-day Nova Scotia)

* **monopoly** exclusive right to engage in a certain kind of business

inspections, registrations, licenses, and passports. This policy was aimed at preventing ships from visiting foreign ports without official permission. The cost of these shipping duties was passed on to consumers on both sides of the Atlantic in the form of higher prices on goods.

Most of the colonial taxes were collected by private companies that paid the French crown for collection rights. In return, the companies had to provide certain government services. In 1725, for example, colonial officials made arrangements with a company to build a wall around Montreal. The funds for the project were raised by a tax on the townspeople, which the company collected. Another private company supplied the colonial army with provisions and charged a small tax on the soldiers' pay to meet the cost of clothing and other supplies.

Spanish Colonies

* **tribute** payment made to a dominant power

When Spain began colonizing the "New World," the Spanish crown believed that revenue would come from duties on trade as well as from tribute* delivered by its new subjects in the Americas. This idea changed when the Spanish discovered rich silver mines in Mexico and Peru. Thereafter, the main focus of colonial taxation shifted to the payment of the *quinta real* (royal fifth)—a 20-percent tax on the ore from the silver mines. The amount was later reduced to 10 percent. Revenue from this tax filled the Spanish treasury, making Spain the richest and most powerful nation in Europe. The funds also reduced the need for taxes on Spanish colonists.

* **Spanish Borderlands** northern part of New Spain, area now occupied by Florida, Texas, New Mexico, Arizona, and California

The Spanish Borderlands* proved to be an exception to the pattern of taxation followed in most of Spanish America. Despite stories of fabulous wealth in a place known as the SEVEN CITIES OF CÍBOLA, the Spanish failed to find any significant amount of gold or silver in the Borderlands. The lack of mines and the isolation of the region discouraged settlement, which affected the way the Spanish collected taxes.

Tax revenues in the thinly settled Borderlands were, understandably, quite small and insufficient to cover the cost of defending the region. Beginning in the mid-1700s, Spanish royal officials decided to do something about this situation. They reasoned that greater economic development would lead to population growth and better security along the frontiers. To improve the economy, colonial authorities organized monopolies on certain products, such as tobacco, gunpowder, stamped paper, and playing cards. The *alcabala,* or sales tax, placed on these and other products became a major source of revenue for the Borderlands and Mexico as well. Because of a shortage of currency, most payments were made in goods or through barter.

When Mexico gained its independence from Spain in 1821, the new government relied increasingly on duties on foreign trade in the Borderlands. The colonists resented these taxes, complaining that the Mexican government also expected them to pay a larger share of their own defense and other needs. Many settlers smuggled goods across the border into the United States to avoid the duties. The residents of the Borderlands never suffered from heavy taxation, but their anger over taxes on foreign trade gradually unraveled their ties with Mexico. (*See also* **Economic Systems; Money and Finance; Trade and Commerce.**)

Tea Act of 1773

*P*assed by the British PARLIAMENT in 1773, the Tea Act enabled the BRITISH EAST INDIA COMPANY to sell tea in the American colonies at lower prices than Dutch smugglers and other tea importers charged. Angry colonists resisted this interference in colonial commerce, adding to the tensions that fueled the movement for independence.

The price of tea and Britain's right to tax tea imports in the American colonies had caused conflict for several years. In 1767 Parliament had placed an import duty, or tax, on tea through the TOWNSHEND ACTS. Many colonists protested, claiming that Britain had no right to tax them. They avoided the tax by buying smuggled—and cheaper—tea, primarily from the Dutch.

By the 1770s, the East India Company faced serious financial problems, partly because the sale of smuggled tea in the colonies hurt the company's business. Parliament introduced the Tea Act in 1773 to help the company resolve its crisis. The act eliminated some of the export fees paid on tea by the East India Company and allowed the company to sell tea in the colonies through its own agents. These measures made the price of the company's tea—even with the Townshend tax—lower than that of smuggled tea.

Parliament hoped that the lower price would tempt Americans to buy British tea. But that did not happen, largely because the colonists feared that the arrangement would establish Britain's right to tax them. Instead, the colonists pressured the company's agents not to sell the British tea and tried to prevent company tea ships from unloading their cargoes. Resistance to the Tea Act included the BOSTON TEA PARTY, in which colonists raided British tea ships and dumped tea in Boston harbor. Similar protests took place in other colonies. Parliament responded to this defiance of its authority by passing the INTOLERABLE ACTS (1774), which only aroused further opposition in the colonies. (*See also* **Independence Movements; Smuggling; Taxation; Trade and Commerce.**)

See color plate 6, vol. 4.

Technology

*I*n colonial times, technology—the development of useful and practical tools, products, and ways of doing things—was not closely connected to science. Most people thought of science as something remote from everyday life, a hobby for educated gentlemen. Ordinary folk, by contrast, could practice "the mechanical arts," a form of technology.

Many advances in technology came from the workshops of colonial artisans* meeting the needs of settlers in a new environment. The ax is a good example. The ax was an important tool in North America because colonists had to have large quantities of wood for fuel and construction. They also wanted to clear the forests so they could use the land for farming. Gradually, colonial toolmakers began making axes with longer handles and broader, sharper blades—changes that allowed people to cut down large trees more quickly and easily. As colonists made such changes and invented new devices, they came to think of themselves as having their own distinctive technology.

* *artisan* skilled crafts worker

Native Americans

Long before Europeans arrived in North America, Native Americans had reached high levels of technological skill. Unlike Europeans, the Indians did

Native Americans in northern regions used snowshoes and toboggans to travel across snow and ice. These methods of transportation were adopted by European colonists. Peter Rindisbacher painted this scene of Saulteaux Indians near Lake Winnipeg, Canada, about 1825.

* **artifact** ornament, tool, weapon, or other object made by humans

not use the wheel in transportation or heat for separating metal from ores. They did, however, employ natural materials in many imaginative ways that improved the quality of their lives.

Stoneworking and Basketry. One of the most important Native American technologies was stoneworking. Indians employed various methods to transform pieces of stone into the size and shape needed for a particular application. One basic technique was knapping, or flaking—a delicate process requiring considerable skill and experience, in which small pieces of stone were chipped away from a larger piece. Indians used knapping to produce projectile points—those sharp stone artifacts* commonly called arrowheads.

Each Indian culture had its own way of making projectile points. The different sizes and styles were so distinct that modern scientists studying these artifacts can tell when they were made and by which Indians. Scholars have learned that Indians went to considerable trouble to obtain the best stone for knapping, often digging trenches and quarries when they could not find good stone on the surface of the ground.

Some technologies involved animal products. Native Americans used animal brains and livers, which contain powerful chemicals, to tan the hides of animals—that is, to turn them into leather. They fashioned the leather into moccasins and clothing, and some PLAINS INDIANS used it for the well-designed portable shelter known as the tepee. The Indians used strips of rawhide—cleaned but untanned animal skin—as cord, and they made containers for storage out of sheets of rawhide.

Almost all Native American peoples possessed the technology to make baskets with bark or other plant material. Some Indian baskets were so tightly joined that they could hold water. In terms of both beauty and technological skill, North American Indian basketry ranks among the finest in the world.

Most Indians south of the Great Lakes, as well as some in eastern Canada and the western Arctic, made pottery by forming vessels of clay and then baking them in fire to make them hard and waterproof. Weaving, another important Indian technology, was well established in the southwestern and southeastern parts of the continent, where people wove cloth from various plant and animal fibers. Indians in other regions did not weave cloth, but they made fabrics out of natural fibers using twining—a technique employed in basket making—and other methods.

Technological Exchange.   The meeting of Europeans and Indians led to technological exchanges. European colonists adopted many useful Indian products, such as birchbark and dugout CANOES, snowshoes, moccasins, and the toboggan. In turn Indians found applications for European materials. They covered leather and cloth garments with European-made glass beads and used the beads for necklaces and other jewelry. They made clothing out of European fabrics and substituted lightweight European canvas for leather in their tepees, wigwams, and other dwellings. Indians in the Great Lakes region developed a new art form called ribbonwork, which involved embroidering garments with overlapping layers of European ribbon. Northern tribes began using European woolen yarn instead of plant and animal fibers for braiding ropes and fabrics.

Another technological exchange involved metalworking. Indians in the northeastern part of the continent learned how to make silver ornaments by employing various European techniques. In the Southwest, Spanish blacksmiths taught Native Americans how to work with melted metal, and the Indians soon developed distinctive styles of jewelry making.

European Colonies

In the European colonies, technology helped shape more than everyday life. It also promoted the growth of industries such as mining, milling, and shipbuilding. American colonists brought basic technological knowledge from their homelands in Europe and expanded it by borrowing from the Indians and by experimenting with new materials, methods, and ideas. The result often combined elements of both European and Native American traditions to produce a new technology well suited to the needs of a new environment.

* *Spanish Borderlands* northern part of New Spain, area now occupied by Florida, Texas, New Mexico, Arizona, and California

Spanish Colonies.   Technology in the Spanish Borderlands* was at a low level compared with that in other parts of Spanish America. The Borderlands had few well-educated people, and imported tools and goods were very costly. Most developments in technology on the frontier came about as people applied practical experience and knowledge to local materials. For example, they made armor and shields from thick leather instead of costly, hard-to-replace steel. Crafts workers and builders in the Borderlands learned to substitute strips of rawhide for metal nails and hinges. They also used scraped and oiled hides for windows in place of rare and expensive glass.

The Spanish brought various forms of technology to the Borderlands from Europe. Among these were surveying, silversmithing, candle making, and cart making. Because the region lacked both metal and skilled crafts

Developing technology promoted the growth of colonial industries. G.A. Boeckler's 1662 engraving shows some of the processes involved in making paper.

workers, the colonists fashioned simple wheels from solid rounds of wood. Squeaking and grating with every turn despite frequent greasing, these wheels carried *carretas* (freight carts) throughout the Borderlands.

One form of Spanish technology that became strongly identified with the Southwest was the manufacture and use of adobe—a sun-dried brick made of earth that was bound together with straw, grass, pine needles, or weeds. Colonists brought the technique from Spain, but the PUEBLO INDIANS who

 Acadian Dikes

Settlers living along the Atlantic coast of the French province of Acadia (now Nova Scotia) used technology to turn tidal marshlands into farmland. First they built earthen dikes around the areas to be drained. Covered with grasses and strengthened with timbers, the dikes ranged from 5 to 20 feet high. Then the colonists opened the sluices—gates or valves—in the dikes just long enough to allow water from the marshes to drain out. The closer to the sea and its mighty tides, the higher they built the dikes.

* *New France* French colony centered in the St. Lawrence River valley, an area known as Canada; included the Great Lakes region and, until 1713, Acadia (present-day Nova Scotia)

* *scythe* farm cutting tool with a long, curving blade

lived in the Borderlands had been making adobe for centuries. The Spaniards used the bricks to build homes, forts, and European-style churches.

Dutch Colony. Technology in New Netherland centered on building. One of the first people to arrive in the settlement in the 1620s was Cryn Fredericksz, an engineer and surveyor, who laid out the fort and the streets of New Amsterdam. In the 1650s, the Dutch constructed a large wall to seal the town off from the rest of Manhattan Island. This major building project took seven years to complete.

The people of the Netherlands were famed for their skill in constructing dikes and dams to control water. Much of the Netherlands consisted of low-lying land, once covered by the sea, that was reclaimed for human use by Dutch technology. The Dutch brought this land-shaping technology to North America, where they built dikes and drained marshes. The diking of marshes continued after the English conquered New Netherland in 1664, though much of the work was done by the Dutch settlers who remained in the colony.

French Colonies. French military engineers designed and built some of the most elaborate forts and buildings in North America. Surveyors in New France* laid out well-planned towns and created a distinctive pattern of agricultural property along the St. Lawrence River. A thriving shipbuilding industry emerged. A wide variety of colonial artisans practiced virtually every craft and used an impressive array of tools.

French colonists made significant contributions to several technologies. In food production, they borrowed the Indian technique of making maple sugar from tree sap and turned this traditional practice into a large-scale industry through the use of metal tools and boiling vessels. Mills to grind flour or saw wood were an important part of life in New France, and colonists developed windmills and waterwheels to power these mills. The colony's biggest mill rose three stories high and had four pairs of waterpowered millstones.

New France saw many advances in transportation technology. Colonial boatbuilders adopted the Indian birchbark canoe, and by the mid-1700s, they were producing the largest canoes on the continent—up to 36 feet long. French settlers met the challenge of Canada's snowy winters by building the *carriole,* a sleigh that could glide over 80 miles of deep snow in a single day without exhausting the horse that pulled it. After the snows left, they used a light, horse-drawn carriage called the *calèche* that could travel at remarkable speeds.

British Colonies. The early English settlers in North America took European and Native American technology and adapted it to their needs. Colonists also invented new machines, devices, or ways of doing things. In the mid-1600s, for example, Joseph Jenkes of Massachusetts developed a new kind of scythe* that became a popular farm tool. Inventors such as Jenkes designed and created countless gadgets and devices that helped improve people's lives. Yet many colonial inventors failed to win support for their work. The most successful inventions were those that did not require immediate, costly, large-scale changes in the way tools were made or used.

By the early 1600s, England had developed patent laws—laws that let inventors register their creations and receive profits from their use. Some English

Conflict

CONQVISTA DE MEXICO POR CORTES. Nº 7

Plate 1
Spanish explorer Hernando Cortés conquered the powerful Aztec empire of Mexico in 1521. This painting from the 1600s shows the Spaniards and their Indian allies preparing to attack the Aztec capital of Tenochtitlán.

Plate 2

In 1564 a group of French Protestants made an attempt to settle in Florida, near present-day Jacksonville. They built Fort Caroline, shown in this engraving by Jacques Le Moyne, an artist who accompanied the French expedition. The Spanish destroyed the fort the following year, beginning two centuries of Spanish domination in Florida.

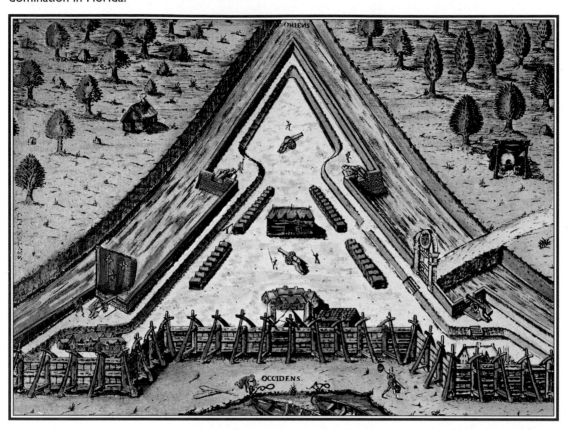

Plate 3

In the late 1600s, Puritan communities in New England were torn apart by witch-hunts. Crafted in wood, this 1800s copy of an earlier work shows the accusation of a witch and the heightened emotions of the time.

Plate 4

Angered by the invasion of Indian lands, the Wampanoag chief Metacom waged a bloody battle against New England colonists in 1675. The conflict—known as King Philip's War—lasted for more than a year, but the Indians were defeated. Ninigret, the Niantic Indian chief pictured here, kept his people out of the war and earned the gratitude of the English.

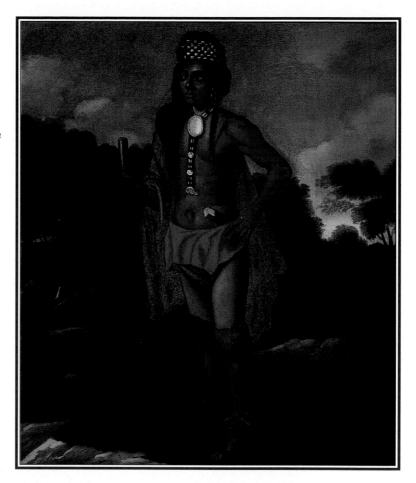

Plate 5

Many immigrants came to North America seeking freedom or economic opportunity. But others—slaves from Africa—were literally dragged to the "New World" in chains. After the British captured a Spanish slave ship in the early 1800s, a young British officer named Francis Meynell made this painting of the brutal conditions he saw below deck on the Spanish vessel.

Plate 6

Massachusetts colonists played a leading role in resisting British efforts to control and tax colonial trade. They resented the Tea Act of 1773 because it allowed the British East India Company to sell its tea in the colonies very cheaply. Dressed as Indians, angry Bostonians dumped 342 chests of tea in the city's harbor. Their bold challenge to British authority came to be known as the Boston Tea Party.

Plate 7

This 1775 engraving by Amos Doolittle presents one of the opening scenes of the American Revolution. As British troops marched through the town of Concord, Massachusetts, on April 19, 1775, two British officers reviewed the military situation. The battles that took place that day at Lexington and Concord launched the American War of Independence.

colonies also had patent laws, but they were difficult to enforce. Inventors could not be sure that their patents would be honored in their own colonies, much less in other colonies. As a result, many inventors did not apply for patents but turned their energies to winning awards offered to individuals who improved agriculture or industry. In the 1770s, the Virginia Assembly gave a cash prize to John Hobday and his brother for inventing a threshing machine that could process 120 bushels of grain a day.

Interest in inventions was limited to a fairly small number of American colonists, but some of them were quite prominent. Philadelphia scientist David RITTENHOUSE created highly accurate clocks and measuring tools, such as thermometers, compasses, and barometers. Thomas JEFFERSON developed various gadgets that he built into his Virginia home, including a dumbwaiter, or small elevator, for carrying bottles up from the wine cellar and a weather-vane that could be read from inside the house. The most technology-minded colonist was probably Benjamin FRANKLIN, who invented the lightning rod and a wood-burning stove that is still known as the Franklin stove. The attention that Franklin paid to technology in his newspapers and other writings, together with his efforts to establish the AMERICAN PHILOSOPHICAL SOCIETY, helped bring invention to public notice in the colonies. He led the way in showing the links between science and technology and their benefits to industry, agriculture, and the general economy.

By the end of the colonial period, Britain and western Europe were approaching what historians call the Industrial Revolution, an era when machines driven by waterpower or steam replaced hand workers and when goods were made in factories rather than in homes. The British colonists were just as interested in machinery as were people in Europe—and sometimes more willing to accept change. For example, British sawmill operators resisted new inventions and techniques that threatened the traditional use of hand tools. However, faced with a shortage of skilled sawmill operators, colonists eagerly adopted the mechanized sawmill.

Americans came to understand the power of technology. They realized that better machines and improved techniques could make an enormous difference in their everyday lives and in the shape of society itself. (*See also* **Agriculture; Architecture; Artisans; Construction and Building Techniques; Crafts; Industries; Native Americans; Ships and Shipbuilding; Transportation and Travel; Water Systems; Weapons.**)

Texas

See map in Spanish Borderlands (vol. 4).

See second map in Native Americans (vol. 3).

*I*n colonial times, Texas was part of the SPANISH BORDERLANDS, the northern reaches of Spain's empire in North America. Spanish Texas covered only half the area of the modern state of Texas. Its territory extended inland from the Gulf of Mexico between the Nueces River and the Red River (in present-day LOUISIANA). Texas's population remained small and scattered during the colonial period. Spanish missionaries and soldiers built few missions and presidios*, and the hot, dry climate and presence of hostile Indians discouraged Spanish settlers. Among the Native Americans of the region were the APACHE and the COMANCHE INDIANS, who roamed the Texas plains.

Texas

* **presidio** Spanish fort built to protect mission settlements
* **conquistador** Spanish explorer and conqueror

See first map in Exploration, Age of (vol. 2).

Early Exploration and Settlement. The Spanish conquistadors* Alvar Núñez CABEZA DE VACA and Francisco Vásquez de CORONADO explored western Texas in the 1530s and 1540s while searching for the SEVEN CITIES OF CÍBOLA. Instead of discovering those fabled cities, with streets of gold and silver, the explorers found only mile after mile of barren landscape. Survivors of an expedition led by Hernando DE SOTO crossed eastern Texas in 1542.

Reports by these early expeditions—filled with descriptions of unfriendly Indians and desolate wilderness—discouraged colonization in Texas. For many years, Spain showed little interest in establishing permanent settlements there. One Spanish community established in Texas, Ysleta—near present-day El Paso—was founded in 1682 by colonists fleeing NEW MEXICO after the revolt of the PUEBLO INDIANS. Many of these settlers returned to New Mexico when Spain reconquered the region.

The Spanish attitude toward Texas changed in 1685, after a group of French soldiers led by René-Robert Cavelier de LA SALLE erected a fort near Matagorda Bay on the Gulf of Mexico (between present-day Corpus Christi and Galveston). The French settlement failed, largely because of poor organization and Indian attacks. Nevertheless, the Spanish realized that they needed to occupy Texas in order to protect their territorial claim to the region.

In 1690 Spanish colonial authorities sent a combined military and missionary expedition to establish settlements in East Texas. The next year, Spain declared Texas a province and appointed a governor. Meanwhile, the threat of French intruders from Louisiana seemed to diminish. After three years, the Spanish decided to abandon their settlements in East Texas to save money. Contributing to the decision were warnings missionaries received from local Indians to leave or be killed.

Permanent Settlement and Colonial Life. About 20 years passed before Spain attempted further colonization of Texas. But once again, the threat of French expansion into Texas prompted the Spanish to act. Between 1716 and 1722, they built a series of missions and presidios along the Gulf coast and the border with French Louisiana, helping to strengthen Spain's hold on East Texas.

The most significant colonization effort at this time occurred in 1718, when the Spanish founded the presidio of San Antonio de Béxar and the mission of San Antonio de Valero in southern Texas. Later relocated, the mission gained a place in history as the Alamo—the site of a battle between Americans and Mexicans in 1836, during the Texas struggle for independence from Mexico. In 1731 the Spanish established the town of San Fernando de Béxar, which with its neighboring presidio and missions became San Antonio, the capital of the province of Texas.

In the early days of colonization, most settlers in Texas earned a living as small-scale farmers. In addition to corn and other basic food crops, they raised sugarcane and cotton, primarily for local use. Eventually RANCHING became more important, as cattle, horses, sheep, and other livestock were brought to the region from Mexico. By 1750 Texas ranchers were exporting beef to French Louisiana in exchange for manufactured goods. Texans also

Renegades

While Spanish missionaries and military authorities tried to convert the Native Americans of Texas to Christianity and European ways, some Spanish soldiers deserted the military to live among the Indians. Many of these soldiers, known as renegades, may have been fleeing from military discipline. Others may simply have been attracted to the open frontier and Indian lifestyle. Other members of Spanish society, such as the mulattoes, joined the Indians as well. These individuals of mixed black and white ancestry, scorned by Spanish society, hoped to find freedom and acceptance in Indian communities.

supplied beef to American troops during the American Revolution. Over time Texas developed a distinct ranching culture identified with the vaquero, or cowboy.

For most Texas colonists, life tended to be lonely, drab, and dangerous. Settlements and ranches were scattered and isolated, and colonists had to work hard to survive. Unlike missions in New Mexico and CALIFORNIA, the missions of Texas failed to attract and assimilate* Native American populations. As a result, Indian labor was not available to colonists, and hostile Indians remained a serious threat. Because of such conditions, there was little to attract new settlers. In 1790 the colonial population of Texas numbered only about 3,000.

Texas After the Mid-1700s.
Throughout the 1700s, Spain and France argued over the border between Spanish Texas and French Louisiana. These disputes ended in 1762, when France ceded* Louisiana to Spain during the FRENCH AND INDIAN WAR. Because Spain no longer needed to defend the border between the two regions, authorities decided to abandon the missions and presidios of East Texas. Several hundred colonists left that region and relocated in San Antonio. In 1779 a number of these settlers, who had been forced to move against their will, returned to East Texas. They founded the town of Nacogdoches, which became the major Spanish community in that part of Texas.

Spain returned the Louisiana Territory to France in 1800. Three years later, the United States bought it in the Louisiana Purchase. Boundary disputes now arose with the Americans. In 1806 Spain and the United States signed a treaty that established a buffer zone* between Texas and Louisiana. Then in 1819, the two nations signed the Adams-Onís Treaty, which fixed the northeastern boundary of Spanish Texas at the Sabine River. This river marks the present-day border between the states of Texas and Louisiana.

In the early 1800s, Texas became a battleground during Mexico's struggle for independence from Spain. Many Americans came to Texas from the United States to support the Mexicans. When Mexico won its independence in 1821, Texas became part of the Republic of Mexico.

The new Mexican government tried to increase settlement in Texas through a special land grant plan. The plan provided huge tracts of land to *empresarios,* or contractors, who would recruit colonists, distribute the land, and impose various regulations. The *empresario* system was very successful, but it drew more Americans than Mexicans to Texas. One contractor, Stephen Austin, brought 300 American families to the region. By 1830 American settlers formed a majority of the population.

The Mexican government viewed the growing American presence in Texas with alarm and attempted to tighten its control over the region. Its actions led to a revolt by the American settlers, who declared their independence in March 1836. Unable to put down the revolution, Mexico was forced to recognize Texas independence after some fighting, including the famous battle at the Alamo in San Antonio. Texas remained an independent republic until 1845, when it joined the United States as the twenty-eighth state. (*See also* **Colonial Administration; Frontier; Independence Movements; Mexican Independence; Missions and Missionaries.**)

* ***assimilate*** to adopt the customs of a society

* ***cede*** to yield or surrender

See second map in European Empires (vol. 2).

* ***buffer zone*** neutral area between two enemy areas

Thanksgiving Celebrations

The early English settlers brought with them a tradition of thanksgiving celebrations—prayers and feasts in appreciation for good fortune. English colonists in North America held the first festivals of this kind for specific occasions. Later a general thanksgiving celebration became an annual event.

Although colonial thanksgiving days were usually connected with a successful harvest, they took place for other reasons as well—perhaps for safe arrival after a difficult ocean voyage or for rainfall after a long drought. At the end of the Revolutionary War, the Continental Congress declared a special thanksgiving celebration for the return of peace.

Lammas Day, the British wheat harvest festival, provided a model for the Plymouth colony's first thanksgiving in the autumn of 1621. Although almost half of the settlers had died during the first grim year in New England, the survivors still felt great relief and a sense of gratitude to God. They had harvested their first crops, they had timber for shipment to England, and they had begun to trade with Native Americans for furs. They also were grateful for SQUANTO, an English-speaking Indian, who had helped them plant corn and communicate with the local tribes.

Plymouth's first thanksgiving celebration was a three-day festival of prayers and feasting. The colonists invited approximately 90 of their Wampanoag Indian neighbors as guests. The menu included wild turkey, deer, fish, corn bread, and other foods that had saved the colonists from starvation. After 1630 the Plymouth colonists held a similar event every year following the harvest. The custom spread to other communities in New England and elsewhere, becoming the basis for the Thanksgiving holiday observed today. (*See also* **Festivals; Pilgrims; Plymouth Colony; Wampanoag Indians.**)

Theater

See *Drama.*

Timucua Indians

* *Franciscan* member of the Order of Friars Minor, a religious brotherhood

The Timucua Indians lived in northern FLORIDA before the arrival of Europeans. Contact with the Spanish during the 1500s and 1600s had a devastating effect on the Timucua, reducing the tribe to a fraction of its former size and eventually destroying its traditional culture.

In 1565 the Spanish established the town of ST. AUGUSTINE in the midst of Timucua lands. The Indians lived in villages surrounded by large cornfields. Gradually Spanish settlers and Franciscan* missionaries spread out across the tribe's territory, setting up villages and founding MISSIONS. Later some of the Timucua moved into the missions.

The missionaries insisted that the Indians adopt Catholic beliefs and forms of worship and discouraged their traditional religious and cultural practices. Many Timucua were forced to work for the missionaries or sold into slavery in the West Indies. Large numbers of Indians living in the missions were struck by European diseases, such as smallpox and measles. Epidemics of the late 1500s and early 1600s may have wiped out more than 90 percent of the tribe. In 1656 the Timucua attempted to put an end to their oppression* by organizing a revolt against the Spanish. Their attempt failed.

* *oppression* unjust or cruel exercise of authority

Artist Jacques Le Moyne made sketches of the Timucua Indians when he visited Florida in 1564 and 1565. In this painting, Le Moyne shows a Timucua chief with some European visitors and a column the French gave to the tribe.

See second map in Native Americans (vol. 3).

Conflicts between the Spanish in Florida and the British colonies to the north also brought hardship to the Timucua Indians. In 1702 a group of English settlers from Charleston, South Carolina, and their Indian allies destroyed most of the missions where the Timucua lived. When Spain lost Florida to the British in 1763, the remaining Florida missions were moved to Cuba and Mexico. The Timucua who survived probably joined the SEMINOLE INDIANS or other tribes in the area.

Tituba

See *Salem Witchcraft Trials.*

Tlingit Indians

See second map in Native Americans (vol. 3).

* *clan* related families

When European explorers first arrived on the southeastern coast of present-day Alaska, the Tlingit Indians occupied the area. During the late 1700s and 1800s, Russian traders established a colony in the middle of Tlingit territory and greatly influenced the tribe's culture.

The islands and shore regions of the Tlingit homeland were rich in timber, fish, shellfish, and waterbirds. The Indians obtained much of their food from the sea. Members of the tribe were divided into two large groups—the Ravens and the Eagles, or Wolves. Each group contained many clans*, and related families lived together in large houses.

Skillful artists, the Tlingit made ceremonial objects and jewelry as well as wood carvings, especially symbolic totem poles. They also used cedar bark and wool to weave blankets. The Indians often decorated their work with clan crests or images from nature.

Tlingit life began to change when the Russian traders arrived. In 1799 members of the Russian-American Company settled on Baranof Island, near

See second map in European Empires (vol. 2).

* **shaman** person with spiritual and healing powers

what is now Sitka, Alaska. The Tlingit began to trade with the newcomers, who were eager to obtain sea otter skins. However, the Russians sometimes took over Tlingit villages, angering the Indians.

The Russians also introduced smallpox and other diseases to the area. A great many Tlingit died during smallpox epidemics in the 1830s. As a result, the Indians began to doubt the powers of their shamans*, who could not cure smallpox. This led some of the Tlingit to abandon their traditional beliefs and adopt the Russian Orthodox religion practiced by the Europeans.

While the Russian colony in Alaska grew, Americans also traveled there to trade with the Tlingit. In 1867 the United States purchased Alaska from Russia. The Tlingit remained in the region and maintained many of their traditions. (*See also* **Russian Settlements.**)

Tobacco

* **cash crop** crop grown primarily for profit
* **commodity** article of trade

* **hallucination** vision; imagined image, sound, or smell

*E*ven before the arrival of Europeans, tobacco was one of the most widely grown crops in North America. For centuries NATIVE AMERICANS had smoked, eaten, and drunk the plant in many forms. It was used both for pleasure and for ceremonial and religious purposes. In the early 1600s, English settlers in the southern colonies began to plant tobacco, and it soon became a major cash crop*. By the end of the colonial period, tobacco had emerged as the most important commodity* exported from the colonies.

More than a dozen varieties of tobacco exist, all of which are native to the Americas. However, the plant commonly used today was not the kind favored by early Indians. The variety they preferred could cause intoxication—even hallucinations*—if inhaled deeply and held in the lungs. This tobacco, brought back to Europe by the early explorers of the Americas, quickly gained popularity. Doctors even prescribed it as a treatment for various diseases.

Governments, however, were less enthusiastic about its use. In 1604 King JAMES I of England called smoking "loathsome to the eye, hatefull to the Nose, harmfull to the brain, dangerous to the Lungs." During the 1600s, the Russians fined, imprisoned, and even tortured tobacco users. In the Middle East, the Ottoman Empire declared smoking punishable by death. Despite such risks, tobacco use spread rapidly throughout Europe and into Asia.

In 1612 the Virginia planter John ROLFE conducted experiments to develop a new variety of tobacco that would be suitable for export. The following year Rolfe shipped his first crop to England. This variety, which was milder and did not cause hallucinations, quickly gained popularity with the English public. By 1620 tobacco had become the leading export of Virginia, Maryland, and North Carolina, and by 1760 colonial planters had produced 80 million pounds of the crop. Tobacco made up almost 45 percent of all exports from the British colonies.

See map in Trade and Commerce (vol. 4).

Tobacco was also grown in NEW NETHERLAND and in the Spanish Borderlands*. In the 1700s, the Spanish colonial government attempted to gain a monopoly* on the production and sale of tobacco in the region. The efforts succeeded in most areas, but the government was not able to stop colonists and PUEBLO INDIANS in New Mexico from growing a local variety of tobacco called *punche*. Even so, the near monopoly on tobacco brought substantial income to the Spanish crown between 1765 and 1809.

* **Spanish Borderlands** northern part of New Spain, area now occupied by Florida, Texas, New Mexico, Arizona, and California
* **monopoly** exclusive right to engage in a certain kind of business

Tobacco, the most important crop of the Chesapeake region, was hung in sheds to dry and then packed in barrels. As shown in the picture from William Tatham's book, *Culture and Commerce of Tobacco,* barges often carried the tobacco from the plantation to markets or ports.

* *clergy* ministers, priests, and other church officials

Because of the shortage of coins in North America and the high value of tobacco, the plant was used as currency in the Chesapeake colonies throughout the colonial period. Virginia made it legal currency in 1642, and Marylanders began using it as money soon after the colony's founding. Nearly all business deals were conducted in tobacco rather than cash, and people generally accepted tobacco more readily than cash. In Virginia even the salaries of the clergy* were paid in tobacco. Because handing over large quantities of the crop for payment was impractical, Virginia adopted a system of "tobacco notes" in 1727. These were certificates, issued to planters by inspectors at government warehouses, that could serve as currency in place of the tobacco. The use of tobacco as money was very important in developing the economies of Virginia and Maryland.

The growth of the tobacco industry created a number of problems. Because the crop exhausted the soil very quickly, planters needed more land every few years. Pushing west in search of new areas to plant, they moved into territory occupied by Native Americans. Their expansion increased the friction between colonists and Indians.

Tobacco also led to an increase in the number of slaves imported into North America. Planting, harvesting, and curing the crop required large numbers of workers. Planters turned to slaves to meet this demand. (*See also* **Agriculture; Money and Finance; Plantations; Slavery; Trade and Commerce.**)

Tohono O'odham Indians

See map in Missions and Missionaries (vol. 3).

The Tohono O'odham Indians, also known as the Papago Indians, lived in the southern part of present-day Arizona and the northern part of the Mexican state of Sonora. Like their neighbors, the PIMA INDIANS, the Tohono were desert farmers and hunters.

Although the homeland of the Tohono is dry and barren, they managed to make it fruitful. Each of their villages had two locations. In the summer, they lived near an arroyo—a creek or gully—where flash floods provided water to irrigate corn, beans, and squash. In the winter, they moved to the mountains, where they could collect water from mountain springs. The tribe supplemented its crops by hunting game and gathering edible wild plants.

The Spanish were the first Europeans to encounter the Tohono O'odham. In the 1690s, Father Eusebio KINO, a Jesuit missionary, established MISSIONS in the region. San Xavier del Bac—a mission located in present-day Tucson, Arizona—became a religious center for the Tohono. Members of the tribe mixed Catholicism with their native faith. As might be expected in the desert, ceremonies and prayers for rain formed an important part of Tohono culture.

See second map in Native Americans (vol. 3).

In addition to Christianity, the Spanish brought new farming techniques and crops, such as wheat, to the region. They also introduced livestock, including cattle and HORSES. The new settlers often took Indian land, causing several Tohono revolts against Spanish rule. But when the Spanish built forts alongside the missions, the Tohono decided to stop fighting the Spanish and to join them against their common enemy, the APACHE INDIANS.

Toleration Act

See *Acts of Toleration.*

Tories

See *Loyalists.*

Toussaint L'Ouverture

See *Hispaniola.*

Town Meetings in British Colonies

* status social position

*T*he town meeting lay at the heart of local government in Britain's New England colonies. Eligible residents gathered together to make decisions about local affairs. The town meeting was one of the first democratic institutions in colonial America.

Every New England town held such meetings. Although procedures and forms varied slightly from community to community, all town meetings were based on the idea that every adult white male could participate in government and hold office regardless of wealth, status*, or the amount of property owned.

Town meetings occurred at least once a year. At this annual gathering, elections were held for local officials, such as constables to maintain the peace, town clerks to keep local records, and tax collectors. The citizens also voted for selectmen, who had responsibility for administering the community's day-to-day affairs.

Besides this annual election meeting, towns could call as many meetings as necessary to deal with local issues or resolve problems. They held them in convenient, central locations such as a church, TAVERN, or private home. By law all meetings had to be announced well in advance, allowing citizens to make arrangements to attend. The gatherings usually ended an hour before sundown to give people who lived in rural areas time to get home before dark.

The frequency of town meetings and number of elected officials depended on the size of the town. Small towns generally held meetings more frequently than large towns and elected fewer officials. Because of the small size of these meetings, it was possible for most citizens to be directly involved in discussing issues and making decisions. Larger towns tended to rely on elected officials to make the everyday decisions needed for the well-being of the community.

An elected chairman presided over each town meeting. The citizens who attended discussed matters under consideration and usually voted orally to

reach decisions. Most meetings tried to settle controversial issues through compromise rather than a majority vote, which would leave some voters dissatisfied with the outcome. In this way, the town meeting helped unify the community as well as govern the town.

The British viewed town meetings as hotbeds of resistance to royal authority and eventually tried to limit them. The Massachusetts Government Act, passed by the British PARLIAMENT in 1774, declared that town meetings could not be held unless approved in advance by the royal governor. However, attempts to restrict these meetings had little effect and only increased opposition to Britain. Throughout the Revolutionary period and after, town meetings remained the basic institution of local government in New England. (*See also* **Cities and Towns; Colonial Administration; Government, Provincial.**)

Townshend Acts (1767)

* *boycott* refusal to buy goods as a means of protest

*T*he Townshend Acts were a series of laws passed by the British PARLIAMENT in 1767. Named after Charles Townshend, a leading member of the British government at the time, the acts were aimed at establishing Britain's right to govern and tax its North American colonies. Parliament planned to use the revenue raised by the laws to pay for colonial administration. The colonists vigorously opposed the Townshend Acts, and attempts to enforce them led to boycotts* and violent protests.

The Revenue Act. The first Townshend Act, known as the Revenue Act, required colonists to pay an import duty on paints, paper, glass, china, and tea. Through this act, Parliament intended to raise money to pay the salaries of royal governors and other colonial officials. However, the use of trade laws to collect revenue went against long-standing British policy. In the past, such laws had been used to regulate trade or to protect British industries from competition. The only exception was the SUGAR ACT OF 1764, which had faced strong opposition in the colonies. For this reason, many prominent British leaders—including Sir William PITT—opposed the Revenue Act.

As for the colonists, they saw the Revenue Act as a serious threat to their political liberty. Until this time, all royal officials in the colonies had been paid with funds raised by colonial assemblies. This arrangement gave the colonists considerable control over local government. They could reduce or refuse to pay the salary of any official who dealt with them unfairly. The Revenue Act took away that power and transferred it to Parliament.

* *tyranny* unjust use of power

Declaring the Revenue Act a major step toward tyranny*, many colonists rose up in protest. They organized public demonstrations, refused to pay the duties, boycotted goods, and supported the creation of colonial industries to make items covered by the law. They also harassed officials responsible for enforcing the act. Early in 1768, the Massachusetts Assembly issued a "circular letter" attacking the act as unjust taxation. This was sent to other colonial assemblies, which heartily supported it.

The American Customs Board Act. The second Townshend Act created a Board of Customs Commissioners with broad powers to collect import duties and enforce the law. One of the most unpopular means of enforcement involved the power of officials to obtain "writs of assistance"—legal documents that authorized them to search buildings for smuggled goods. The writs were to be issued by local courts, which led to an ongoing dispute. These courts consistently refused to issue writs except when customs officials could show good cause for searching a particular building.

The colonists directed much of their resentment of the Townshend Acts against the Board of Customs Commissioners. Stationed in Boston—which the British considered the center of colonial resistance—the commissioners fled the city in June 1768 because of angry mobs. They returned in September, accompanied by British troops. In March 1770, some of these troops were involved in the BOSTON MASSACRE, which erupted when colonists taunted soldiers guarding the British customs house. The event forced the customs commissioners to flee Boston once again. However, they returned later in the year and remained until the beginning of the American Revolution.

Repeal of the Townshend Acts.

repeal to undo a law

The colonial protests had the desired effect. By 1770 Parliament had repealed* all the import duties imposed by the Townshend Acts—except for the tax on tea. By retaining the tea duty, Parliament continued to assert its right to tax the colonies.

Repeal of most of the Townshend duties did not quiet the unrest in the colonies, however. Colonists continued to protest the increasingly strict enforcement of the NAVIGATION ACTS—which protected British shipping—and the actions of the customs officials. In June 1772, frustration flared into violence when angry colonists in Rhode Island raided and burned the *Gaspée,* a British ship sent to crack down on smuggling in the region.

More resistance followed. To American colonists, the Townshend Acts were proof of how little Parliament respected their rights. From this point on, new British legislation—the TEA ACT OF 1773 and the INTOLERABLE ACTS (1774), in particular—met with colonial protests and acts of resistance. The growing tensions contributed to the American INDEPENDENCE MOVEMENT. (*See also* **American Revolution; Boston Tea Party; Quartering Acts; Smuggling; Taxation; Trade and Commerce.**)

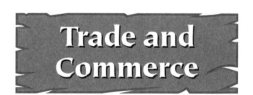

Trade and Commerce

capital wealth or property invested to create more wealth

*N*orth American colonies provided countries in Europe with resources and agricultural products as well as new markets for their manufactured goods. Some colonial areas had certain assets—such as natural resources, mild climate and good soil, or an ample supply of labor and capital*—that made them especially valuable to their parent country. However, European colonial powers had different ideas about the role of their colonies and how they should be managed, and this led to great variation in trade policies.

British Colonies

From the first, trade and commerce in the English colonies revolved around exports and imports. Because of the small size of local markets, colonial planters and manufacturers tended to produce items that were in demand in

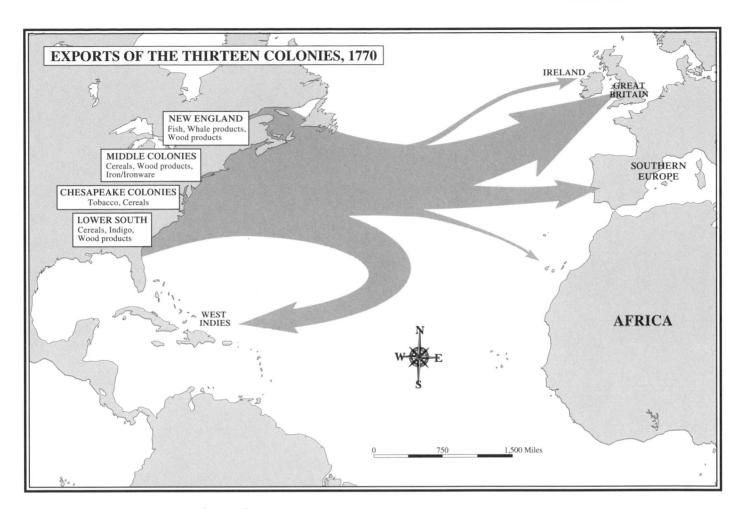

EXPORTS OF THE THIRTEEN COLONIES, 1770

NEW ENGLAND
Fish, Whale products,
Wood products

MIDDLE COLONIES
Cereals, Wood products,
Iron/Ironware

CHESAPEAKE COLONIES
Tobacco, Cereals

LOWER SOUTH
Cereals, Indigo,
Wood products

IRELAND

GREAT BRITAIN

SOUTHERN EUROPE

AFRICA

WEST INDIES

0   750   1,500 Miles

Although grain was a major export of many of the British colonies, some products were specific to one region. New England shipped large quantities of fish abroad, the Chesapeake region specialized in tobacco, and the southern colonies exported indigo.

* **cash crop** crop grown primarily for profit
* **commodity** article of trade

* **indigo** plant used to make a blue dye

England or in other markets in Europe and the WEST INDIES. Early colonial commerce centered largely on furs, fish, and cash crops* such as TOBACCO. Only by exporting these commodities* to larger markets overseas could colonists obtain the money or credit they needed to buy goods imported from Europe and elsewhere. Over time the colonies themselves became an increasingly important market for colonial and foreign goods. Yet for the most part, providing products for export continued to fuel the colonial economy.

Colonial Exports. Exports from British North America consisted overwhelmingly of raw materials and agricultural products. The colonies had little manufacturing and produced few finished goods. In 1770 the major colonial exports included tobacco, rice, wheat and other grains, indigo*, furs, fish, beef and pork, and various wood products such as lumber, tar, and turpentine. Of these, grains and tobacco made up more than 55 percent of all exports.

Market conditions and British trade regulations determined the destinations of colonial exports. Naturally, products could be sold more easily and profitably in places where they were most needed. For example, the colonies found a ready market for their grain and wood products in the West Indies, which did not produce those goods. At the same time, however, the English NAVIGATION ACTS (1651–1696) limited the markets to which the colonists could sell their goods. The acts listed certain products—known as "enumerated goods"—that could be exported only to England or to another English colony.

The Navigation Acts regulated colonial trade in ways that were meant to benefit England and strengthen its empire. Little consideration was given to the economic needs of the colonists. The original list of enumerated goods included sugar, tobacco, cotton, and indigo. By the mid-1700s, the list had expanded to cover a much wider range of products.

As a result of the Navigation Acts, a significant amount of colonial exports—about 53 percent by 1770—went to Britain. Many of these products, however, were not consumed in Britain but were reexported elsewhere. In 1700 about 65 percent of tobacco exports to Britain were reexported to other markets; by the 1770s, this figure had risen to 85 percent.

Commodities not on the list of enumerated goods generally had little or no market in Britain. For example, Britain had abundant supplies of fish and, for the most part, of wheat and other grains. As a result, colonists could send large quantities of these products to the West Indies and southern Europe.

The West Indies became one of the most important markets in colonial trade, especially for the northern colonies. Merchants from New England, New York, and Philadelphia exchanged fish, wheat and other grains, and forest products in the West Indies for such goods as sugar, molasses, and coffee. Traders often brought back more of these goods than they needed and tried to sell the surplus in other colonies or in European markets. In this commerce, buyers generally paid part of the cost with bills of exchange—paper notes that gave the holder credit toward the purchase of goods in England. These bills of exchange were often applied to the purchase of manufactured products such as tools, clothing, or furniture.

Tobacco was a leading export of the British colonies. In this 1784 illustration by Matthew Albert and George Frederick Lotter, barrels of tobacco are being loaded onto ships at a Virginia dock.

Colonial Imports.   Colonists imported many items from Europe for a variety of reasons, including the price, quality, and availability. Locally manufactured goods often cost more than those shipped from abroad because the colonies lacked skilled workers. Imported luxury items were expensive but usually superior in quality to anything found in the colonies. Of course, many luxury items were not produced in the colonies at all and had to be imported. Furthermore, English trade laws banned the manufacture of some items, such as hats, in the colonies. Finally, colonists devoted their energies to agriculture and trade rather than manufacturing because they could make profits and find markets readily.

With labor in short supply, the colonies depended greatly on imported workers. Until the mid-1600s, this demand was met largely by indentured servants* who traveled to North America in search of economic opportunity. By the early 1700s, however, the flow of indentured servants to the colonies had begun to decline as population growth in Britain slowed and economic conditions improved. Thereafter, slaves from Africa became a more important source of colonial labor, particularly in the southern colonies. At first the British crown granted a monopoly* on the SLAVE TRADE to some British companies. When these companies could not meet the growing demand, independent traders, many of them based in the colonies, took over the commerce in slaves.

Under the Navigation Acts, indentured servants and slaves were among the few articles of trade that could be imported directly by the colonies. Most non-British goods had to be shipped first to England and then sent on to North America. Two other products could be imported directly by the colonies: salt, used to dry and preserve fish and meat, and wine from the Portuguese islands of Madeira and the Azores.

British goods dominated colonial imports. The leading commodities shipped from Britain were cloth and wrought iron—a tough, purified form that was easy to shape. Woolen cloth accounted for between 30 and 35 percent of imports from Britain by the 1770s. The colonists also bought large quantities of linen from Britain, much of it made in France and Ireland.

The colonies imported various products from the British West Indies as well. The most important of these were sugar, molasses, and rum, although rum was also produced in the colonies. In 1733 Britain passed the MOLASSES ACT, requiring colonists to purchase these items only from the British West Indies and not from islands belonging to other countries. But colonists got around the law by SMUGGLING. Efforts by Britain to stop this illegal trade—such as the SUGAR ACT OF 1764—angered colonists and aroused opposition to British policies.

Shipping and the Conduct of Trade.   The large volume of trade goods carried into and out of the colonies involved a great deal of shipping. Towns such as Boston, Newport, New York, and Philadelphia grew into significant port cities. Shipbuilding also developed in the colonies. The Navigation Acts required that all commerce with Britain be carried on ships built in Britain or its colonies. By the mid-1700s, the British were turning to colonial shipbuilders for vessels. As a result, colonial shipping and shipbuilding flourished, mostly in New England and the middle colonies. By the 1770s, one-third of all the ships engaged in British trade were built in the colonies.

* ***indentured servant*** person who agreed to work a certain length of time in return for passage on a ship to the colonies

* ***monopoly*** exclusive right to engage in a certain kind of business

 See map in Slave Trade (vol. 4).

Colonial Manufacturing

During the 1700s, increasing numbers of British colonists began producing manufactured goods to compete with British imports. The New England and middle colonies led the way. Because money and labor were limited, most colonial manufacturing was carried on by small enterprises. Glassworks, potteries, paper mills, textile mills, gristmills (for grinding grain), sugar refineries, saltworks, and distilleries, as well as silversmiths and furniture makers, were among the early small-scale industries. Along with the highly successful iron industry, they helped lay the groundwork for the development of American manufacturing after the colonial period.

Much of the commerce in the colonies was conducted on the basis of credit, often provided by English merchants. Individual traders and merchants often used bills of exchange in making purchases. Commercial transactions typically consisted of a chain of credit that involved colonial farmers or producers, traders, and merchants, as well as their business partners in Britain or elsewhere. This network of credit helped support colonial trade and commerce, providing colonists with the labor, tools, and other items required to meet their needs and expand production.

Dutch Colonies

Dutch commerce in the Americas was controlled by the DUTCH WEST INDIA COMPANY, a trading company owned by private investors. Much of the company's early profits came from sugar plantations and slave trading in the Brazilian colony of New Holland, which the Dutch had seized from Portugal in 1630. After New Holland fell to a Portuguese rebellion in 1654, the company devoted more attention to its North American colony of NEW NETHERLAND.

The most important business of New Netherland's early years was the FUR TRADE. At its height, this trade involved as many as 46,000 animal pelts being shipped to Europe a year. By the 1650s, however, the fur trade was in decline, and timber and grain became more valuable commodities for export. Colonial merchants shipped these products primarily to the Dutch islands of Curaçao and Bonaire in the Caribbean Sea. In exchange they received salt, which they sold to New England fisheries for use in drying and preserving fish. The English continued this valuable trade after conquering New Netherland in 1664.

In the early years, cloth goods and liquor led the list of products imported by New Netherland. Firearms and iron goods were also major imports. As the colonial population of New Netherland grew, so did the demand for European luxury products such as French soap, fine porcelain, spices, books, and furniture. Some merchants in the Dutch colony specialized in this trade, which may have become even more profitable than the fur trade.

The Dutch West India Company developed a lively trade in WAMPUM— shells made into beads that Native Americans used in ceremonies and as currency. The company came to control the sources of the most highly valued wampum and distributed it to areas where it was in short supply. This monopoly in wampum allowed Dutch merchants to increase their profits in trading with the Indians. But by rapidly increasing the Indians' "money supply," the Dutch also caused inflation—a rise in prices—that hurt local Indian economies.

Traders in New Netherland tended to send their ships to a variety of ports rather than relying on one or two trade routes. They developed a strong coastal trade with the English colonies as well as overseas trade with the West Indies. They also remained on the lookout for new trade opportunities. When the fur trade declined, Dutch traders turned to the slave trade. When demand for food grew in the West Indies, they entered the fish and grain trade between the mainland colonies and the Caribbean. The result was a trade system that followed the markets and often ignored the boundaries between colonial empires.

The loss of New Netherland to the English in 1664 redirected Dutch commercial efforts to the Caribbean and Africa, where they dominated the sugar and slave trade for more than 50 years. Their former colony, now called New York, became part of the English trading system. Although commercial exchanges between New York and the Netherlands almost disappeared, English colonists continued other trade patterns established during the period of Dutch rule.

French Colonies

French colonial activity was driven primarily by the desire to counter Britain and Spain, France's rivals for empire. Building and maintaining a colonial empire required a great deal of money, and the French government saw colonies mainly as a source of revenue for the state. This attitude did not encourage settlement. Moreover, it gave French merchants little reason to invest in colonial trade or commerce. As a result, the French colonies in North America grew slowly, and trade and commerce failed to develop to any significant extent.

Early Commercial Activity. The earliest French commercial interests in the Americas involved piracy and fishing. Throughout the 1500s, French privateers* raided and plundered Portuguese and Spanish ships sailing between their American colonies and Europe. But the French failed to establish any colonies or commercial bases of their own in the Americas at this time. French merchants, looking for a quick profit without a great deal of risk, preferred to trade with Spanish and Portuguese colonial markets rather than to make their own colonial investments.

While French privateers roamed the Caribbean, French fishermen flocked to the rich fishing grounds off the northeastern coast of North America. France had begun fishing this area—the Great Banks—soon after Christopher COLUMBUS made his first voyage to America. This fishing industry became very important to the French economy. But like privateering, it failed to encourage colonization or the development of colonial trade.

The Fur Trade. The leading commercial activity in France's North American territory was the fur trade. Trading began in the 1530s, when French fishermen exchanged European goods for furs with Native Americans living along the Atlantic coast. But it was not until the early 1600s that the fur trade became firmly established in New France*.

The colonial fur trade led to some unusual arrangements. First, because the acquisition of the furs depended primarily on Native Americans, very few French colonists needed to be involved. Second, the key role of Indians in the fur trade created a unique partnership between them and the French. Some Indians hunted and trapped animals, while others acted as agents between Indians and French traders. For both the French and the Native Americans, the fur trade was more than a commercial activity. It was also a tool of diplomacy that helped bind the two groups together in a political alliance.

As the fur trade grew in importance, French merchants attempted to eliminate competition by obtaining trading monopolies from the French

* *privateer* privately owned ship authorized by the government to attack and capture enemy vessels; also the ship's master

* *New France* French colony centered in the St. Lawrence River valley, an area known as Canada; included the Great Lakes region and, until 1713, Acadia (present-day Nova Scotia)

In an effort to attract settlers and trade to Louisiana, the French Company of the West had artists create scenes of a prosperous and idyllic land. This 1720 painting of the bustling "Port of Mississippi" is the work of François Gerard Jollain.

crown. The merchants were interested only in increasing their profits, not in promoting colonization. French authorities eventually realized that these individually controlled monopolies were discouraging colonization in New France and hindering the development of other commercial activities. In 1627 government officials established the COMPANY OF ONE HUNDRED ASSOCIATES, a trading company backed by the king. The company received political power over New France and a monopoly on all trade except for fishing.

Promoting Colonization and Commerce. Only partially successful in encouraging settlement and trade, the Company of One Hundred Associates was dissolved in 1663 because of financial difficulties. The French crown took over the administration of New France, giving control of colonial trade to the FRENCH WEST INDIA COMPANY. This company also failed in its efforts to promote colonization or commerce, and it was dissolved in 1674. Meanwhile, French authorities began taking steps to reduce dependence on the fur trade and to make the colonial economy more diverse.

In the late 1600s, officials tried to encourage agriculture and industry in New France. One step was to introduce trade laws similar to England's Navigation Acts. Their goal was to make the colony more self-sufficient and a participant in the growing colonial trading system. Not until the mid-1700s, however, did French Canada have enough settlers to develop agriculture on any significant scale. Even then, its growth was limited by the lack of a market for its surplus goods. The French colonists could not compete in trade with the cheaper farm products produced by the British colonies. Without a ready market for their commodities, French colonists produced little beyond what they needed to feed themselves.

Attempts to promote the growth of industry suffered a similar fate. In the 1720s and 1730s, the port of LOUISBOURG developed a vigorous trade based on the fishing industry. But the efforts of French officials to establish large-scale iron and shipbuilding industries left New France with costly, unprofitable ventures that damaged efforts to build other local industries.

Trade and Commerce in Louisiana. The French had no more success in promoting trade and commerce in LOUISIANA than they had in New France. Founded in 1700 primarily for political and military reasons, Louisiana quickly became an economic burden to France. French officials considered tobacco a possible cash crop for the colony. However, the need for revenue led the French government to create a state monopoly on the purchase of all tobacco for sale in France. The prices that the government was willing to pay for tobacco were too low to make tobacco growing profitable in Louisiana. Instead, men called "tax farmers" bought cheaper, better-quality tobacco from the British colonies of Virginia and Maryland and sold it to the French government. After a while, French authorities discouraged tobacco growing in Louisiana.

Other commercial activities in Louisiana fared no better than tobacco did. The creation of fur-trading monopolies hindered the development of the fur trade. The lack of capital and labor in Louisiana made large-scale agriculture impossible. For the most part, the colony's settlers survived by raising a few crops and trading with Indians for deerskins, which could be exchanged for imported goods. A small trade in food crops and forest products developed between Louisiana and the French West Indies. But it was carried on chiefly by French rather than colonial merchants and thus did little to stimulate local commerce. Commercial ties between France and Louisiana remained weak throughout the colonial period, and French policies continued to discourage the growth of trade and commerce in the colony.

Spanish Colonies

The SPANISH BORDERLANDS—the northern reaches of Spanish territory in North America—experienced little development of trade and commerce during the colonial period. Several factors contributed to this, including the scattered population, the vast distances between settlements, and the threat of Indian attack. The policies of the Spanish crown played a major role as well. Like France, Spain was more concerned with the military and political importance of its colonies than with the development of trade and commerce.

The Commercial Structure of Spanish America. The Spanish crown wanted to make sure that its American colonies were linked securely with Spain. For that reason, they set up a highly centralized system in which agents of the crown controlled all commercial activity in the colonies.

In 1503 the Spanish crown established the Casa de Contratación (House of Trade) to manage the country's overseas empire. The Casa controlled colonial immigration, enforced maritime* laws, and collected customs duties on colonial imports and exports. It even trained the pilots who guided Spanish ships across the Atlantic. Through the activities of the Casa, the crown was able to regulate all aspects of colonial trade and commerce.

* maritime related to the sea or shipping

Trade and Commerce

The *consulado,* an organization of Spanish merchants, received a monopoly from the crown on trade between Spain and its colonies. *Consulado* agents in colonial ports set prices for all goods being imported to or exported from the colonies. This practice ensured high profits for members of the *consulado,* but it drove up the cost of Spanish goods. As prices rose, *consulado* agents began to work with foreign merchants, primarily from France and Italy, seeking better goods for less money. As a result, much of what was imported by Spanish colonists came from places other than Spain.

Within the colonies, trade and commerce were conducted by a variety of individuals. Among the most important were the *comerciantes,* members of the *consulado* who provided trade goods to local merchants and other traders. Many *comerciantes* also acted as bankers and often invested in various enterprises. The activities of the *consulado, comerciantes,* local merchants, shopkeepers, and others tied all parts of Spanish America into a vast network of trade and commerce.

Borderland Trade and Commerce. The Borderlands were linked to the commercial network of the Spanish empire primarily through military and missionary systems. Trade with the civilian population was limited.

* **buffer zone** neutral area between two enemy areas

Spain maintained a strong military presence in the Borderlands because these frontier areas served as a buffer zone* between the French and British colonies and the heart of NEW SPAIN. The military payroll, or *situado,* formed the backbone of most Borderland economies. Paid in Mexico City, most of this money never reached the frontier, however. Each Borderland presidio, or fort, had agents in Mexico City who used the *situado* to buy goods there and arrange for their transportation to the frontier. Borderland soldiers generally received credit for their salaries rather than cash. Their purchases of goods from the presidio stores would be deducted from that amount. This system led to many abuses. Officers often sold goods to soldiers at very high prices. Because the soldiers rarely received salaries in cash, they had few opportunities to buy goods from other sources.

The missions also played an important role in the Borderland economies. The missions received an annual payment, the *sínodo,* that was used to purchase supplies. Like the *situado,* the *sínodo* was paid in Mexico City, and supplies rather than cash were sent to the missions. This governmental payroll and supply system for the presidios and missions discouraged the development of commercial activity in the Borderlands by limiting the opportunities of local merchants to sell goods.

As the population of the Borderlands grew, commercial opportunities increased for a small number of local merchants. Most of these tradespeople worked on a part-time basis and dealt in a variety of goods rather than specializing in any one type of merchandise. In some instances, these merchants traveled from place to place, picking up and distributing goods as they went along. Because there was a scarcity of currency on the frontier, many of their transactions were based on barter*. Among the items they traded were Indian goods—such as animal hides, pottery, and blankets—and Spanish products—such as wool, soap, candles, and dried beef.

* **barter** exchange of goods and services without using money

Full-time merchants remained rare in the Borderlands. For one thing, there were few items produced in the region that were valuable enough to attract

them. Agricultural goods, the bulk of frontier production, offered little profit for traders. In addition, all commodities exported to Spain had to pass through ports in Mexico or Cuba. The expense of shipping, plus the danger of losing goods to hostile Indians while en route to ports, discouraged the development of any large-scale commerce on the frontier. The scarcity of currency and the reliance on barter and credit also hindered the development of trade. Another problem was the continuing competition from presidios and missions.

Because of the scarcity and expense of Spanish goods, illegal trade with Spain's European rivals became a common feature of frontier commerce. English and French merchants exchanged guns, textiles, tools, and luxury items for animal hides, grain, livestock, and sometimes Spanish SILVER. In the late 1700s and early 1800s, American traders replaced the British and French in smuggling goods to the Borderlands.

Eventually, Borderland commerce suffered from a lack of valuable goods that could attract investment and a population that remained too small to take full advantage of the region's natural resources. The missions and presidios, with a ready supply of Indian labor, were the only institutions able to produce an agricultural surplus they could trade. Perhaps most important, Spain's colonial policies made it impossible to overcome the difficulties of establishing commerce in a vast and undeveloped land. (*See also* **Agriculture; Economic Systems; Fish and Fishing; Industries; Labor; Mercantilism; Merchants; Money and Finance; Ranching; Rum Trade; Ships and Shipbuilding; Taxation; Trading Posts.**)

Trading Posts

* *outpost* frontier settlement or military base

Frontier trading posts provided a marketplace for Native Americans and white traders. At these colorful places of business, Indians exchanged beaver pelts, deerskins, and other furs for guns, ammunition, tools, and household goods. Because much of the contact between Indians and colonists took place at trading posts, they were extremely important in developing friendly relations and goodwill.

In NEW NETHERLAND, the DUTCH WEST INDIA COMPANY set up three outposts* at the far ends of the colony: one in the Hudson River valley, another in the Connecticut River valley, and still another in the Delaware River valley. Eventually New Netherland's highly profitable trade was centered at Beverwyck, a market town next to Fort Orange. When the English took over New Netherland in 1664, Fort Orange—renamed ALBANY—remained a major trade center. Along with Fort Oswego, Albany provided a base for the fur trade between the English and the IROQUOIS and other tribes in northwestern New York.

The French understood the value of using trading posts to form alliances with Indians. In their attempt to curb British expansion into the interior of North America, the French established a chain of trading stations that extended from the St. Lawrence River valley to the lower Mississippi River valley. They portrayed these outposts, most of which were also military forts, as places where Indians could go for a fair exchange of goods and for support in times of danger. Becoming familiar with Native American customs, such as exchanging gifts or smoking the peace pipe, helped the French establish good trading relations.

The French created three levels of trading posts. Major bases, including those at MONTREAL and NEW ORLEANS, served as transfer points for furs and trade goods. At the next level were district outposts such as Detroit, Mobile, and St. Louis. Smaller trading stations opened and closed depending on relations with the Indians and the demand for goods. The French government authorized all posts, but trade was usually carried out by private companies and individuals.

In the Spanish Borderlands* in the 1600s, MISSIONS functioned as trading posts. The Franciscans* and Jesuits* who ran the missions also handled the exchange of goods between the Native Americans who worked on the missions and the Spanish. Instead of trading furs, the missionaries exchanged food grown on mission farms and products made in their workshops by Indians for cloth, tobacco, tools, medicine, and other items. They frequently demanded cash for Indian goods. The missionaries' control of the Indian trade led to friction with settlers.

In the 1700s, Spanish authorities began imitating the French and British system of trading posts, which they considered more effective than the mission system. Spain hoped to secure the benefits France and Britain did from the Indian trade: furs, alliances, and warriors to fight in colonial conflicts. Because the Spanish had few traders skilled at dealing with Native Americans, the government brought in foreign agents and companies to conduct its trade. Many of these were Scottish merchants, who had experience with Indians in Britain's southern colonies and access to the English goods the Indians wanted. Panton, Leslie and Company, the most influential and widespread of the Scottish companies operating on behalf of Spain, established trading posts along the Gulf of Mexico and in Florida in the late 1700s. (*See also* **Fur Trade; Trade and Commerce.**)

* **Spanish Borderlands** northern part of New Spain, area now occupied by Florida, Texas, New Mexico, Arizona, and California
* **Franciscan** member of the Order of Friars Minor, a religious brotherhood
* **Jesuit** member of Roman Catholic religious order

Transportation and Travel

Transportation and travel in colonial North America began on water with the voyages that carried people and goods across the Atlantic Ocean. Water remained the primary route of transportation within many colonies for some time, but gradually a network of ROADS emerged, linking neighbor to neighbor and later colony to colony.

Although colonists rarely traveled far from home, people needed transportation routes to move goods to market, to carry communications, and to open new areas for settlement. Most journeys were related to work. Peddlers and traders moved about selling or exchanging goods, judges traveled around to the different courts in their district, and colonial representatives and government authorities had to attend assemblies and official functions in various places in the colonies. By the late 1700s, most settlers in the North American colonies lived within reach of reliable—though often slow and uncomfortable—means of transportation.

* **New France** French colony centered in the St. Lawrence River valley, an area known as Canada; included the Great Lakes region and, until 1713, Acadia (present-day Nova Scotia)

River Travel. The best, and sometimes the only, transportation available to early colonists was by river. This was especially true along the Atlantic coast, where numerous rivers provided routes into the interior, and in New France*, where the combination of the St. Lawrence River and the Great

The first public transportation in British North America was provided by the stagecoach lines of the 1750s. This print of a carriage leaving a tavern appeared in Isaac Weld's *Travels Through the States of North America* (1799).

Lakes gave French settlers a 2,000-mile waterway into the center of the continent. Cargo ships bound for the sea could enter large rivers such as the Delaware, Hudson, and St. Lawrence.

Colonists used several types of small boats for river voyages. Pirogues—vessels made of long, hollowed-out logs—were common in the southeast and along the Mississippi River. For moving large cargoes, colonists relied on a flat-bottomed boat called a bateau, which had a sail and carried a crew of four to eight to pole the boat upstream. French settlers adopted the birchbark CANOE of the Native Americans and used it extensively throughout the colonial era. In winter they drove sleighs over the frozen surface of the St. Lawrence River.

Transportation by river could be slow and difficult. Sandbars, rapids, currents, fog, floods, floating logs, low water, and ice could interfere with travel. But in the early, roadless years of colonial North America, many settlers depended on rivers and streams for transportation. Most did not own boats, however. They used commercial shipping and hired boatmen to haul their goods to market and to deliver supplies. For local travel, they moved about on foot.

Road Travel. The first colonists followed Indian trails. Originally little more than slight ruts in the ground, these trails grew wider and deeper with

The Camino Real

The longest road in colonial North America was the Camino Real (Royal Road), which ran north from Mexico City into Spain's frontier territory. In the late 1500s, Juan de Oñate, the founder of New Mexico, extended the road past deserts and over mountains to Santa Fe. For more than 200 years, the 1,800-mile Camino Real remained the principal link between dozens of forts, missions, mining towns, and ranches. Missionaries, troops, traders, and colonists traveled its dusty length—a six-month journey. For protection from Indians, most people made the trip in large wagon trains.

* **Spanish Borderlands** northern part of New Spain, area now occupied by Florida, Texas, New Mexico, Arizona, and California

use by colonists and their horses and cattle. The regularly traveled routes eventually became broad enough for carts and wagons.

Road construction in the colonies began in 1639 with the Coast Path, which linked the New England settlements of Boston and Plymouth. Other roads followed, but progress was slow and uneven because each colony went at its own pace. By 1700 Maryland, Connecticut, and eastern Massachusetts boasted extensive road networks, but New York had few roads. Georgia had almost no roads as late as 1750.

Legislative assemblies or courts organized the building of many roads. In 1703 the New York Assembly passed a law for "Laying out, Regulateing, Clearing and preserving Publick Comon highways thro' out this Colony." After a roadway was completed, local settlers might ask the county courts to build bridges over the smaller streams and establish ferry service across the larger ones.

Wagons and Carriages.   Most colonists traveling by land walked or rode horseback. Throughout North America, farmers and workers used two-wheeled wooden carts to carry stones, crops, and other materials over short distances. For longer hauling, they used pack animals. Sure-footed pack mules remained the favored form of transportation in New Mexico's rocky terrain into the 1800s. These animals could carry up to 400 pounds and could go where horses and wagons could not. In other regions, wagons came into use by the early 1700s. Most popular were the Conestoga wagons preferred by German settlers in the backcountry of Pennsylvania and Virginia. These canvas-topped, boat-shaped vehicles could haul more cargo than any other wagon in the colonies.

Other forms of land transportation were available to passengers who could afford them. Especially in bad weather, wealthy city dwellers used sedan chairs—covered seats carried by servants or pulled by horses. Owning a private carriage or coach was a sign of high social standing. Regular public stagecoach lines began operating during the 1750s, offering travelers in the British colonies the first reliable transportation system.

As stagecoach travel became more common, roads improved and TAVERNS sprang up along them. These establishments, generally spaced about three or four miles apart along public roads, provided food and lodging for both travelers and their horses. In addition to filling the needs of the traveler, taverns also became centers of community life for local residents. The French and British colonies had numerous taverns. In the Spanish Borderlands*, inns, forts, and missions served some travelers. But because most roads in the Southwest covered long stretches of almost uninhabited countryside, travelers often had to camp under the stars or sleep in their wagons.

Nowhere in the colonies was travel swift or very comfortable, but it improved greatly during the 1700s. Sarah Kemble KNIGHT's account of her 1704 journey from Boston to New York City is filled with references to broken bridges, rocky roads, and other disasters, dangers, and discomforts. Forty years later a Maryland physician traveled to Maine and back and expressed a high opinion of most of the roads, ferries, and taverns he used. Travel within the colonies continued to improve in the years that followed. (*See also* **Ships and Shipbuilding; Trade and Commerce.**)

Treaty of Paris (1763)

*T*he Treaty of Paris ended the FRENCH AND INDIAN WAR, the last in a series of struggles between Britain and France for control of North America. The treaty confirmed Britain's victory in the war and established its dominance of lands east of the Mississippi River. France lost nearly all of its colonial territory.

Part of a European conflict known as the Seven Years' War, the French and Indian War lasted from 1754 to 1763 and spread across a wide area of North America. Despite help from various Indian groups and an alliance with Spain, France was defeated. Britain's decisive victory changed the balance of power on the continent, setting the stage for a growing conflict between Britain and the American colonists.

Terms of the Treaty.   The Treaty of Paris was signed by Britain, France, and Spain on February 10, 1763. Under its terms, France agreed to transfer all of New France* and the part of its LOUISIANA territory east of the Mississippi River to Britain. France kept only the islands of St. Pierre and Miquelon near NEWFOUNDLAND and the sugar-producing islands of St. Lucia, Martinique, and Guadeloupe in the WEST INDIES. France also retained fishing privileges along the northern and western coasts of Newfoundland. Despite huge territorial losses, the French were able to continue to profit from the sugar and fishing industries they had developed in the Americas.

Though it had been France's ally in the war, Spain came away from the treaty negotiations with its American empire largely intact. It ceded* FLORIDA to Britain but regained possession of Cuba, which the British had seized during the war. Spain also kept the portion of Louisiana west of the Mississippi River, including the port of NEW ORLEANS, which it had acquired from France under a secret agreement in 1762.

Britain gained the most under the Treaty of Paris. In addition to taking control of an unbroken expanse of territory between the Atlantic Ocean and the Mississippi River, it received the islands of St. Vincent, Tobago, and Dominica in the West Indies. Britain also acquired the right to sail freely on the Mississippi River, which now served as the border between British and Spanish territory. With the defeat of the French, Spain and Britain became the dominant powers on the continent.

Effects of the Treaty.   After signing the Treaty of Paris, Britain faced the task of governing an expanded colonial empire and the problem of heavy war debts. In trying to meet these challenges, Britain sowed the seeds of conflict between itself and American colonists.

Britain's new territories contained thousands of Native Americans who were accustomed to dealing with the French. Many Indians in the Great Lakes and Ohio Valley regions feared the spread of British settlers into their land. In the months following the signing of the treaty, they attacked several British forts in those areas. To establish peace and calm Indian fears, the British issued the PROCLAMATION OF 1763, which prohibited white settlement beyond the Appalachian Mountains. However, the policy angered American colonists eager to settle in the new territories.

Britain's expanded empire also included French settlers in Canada and Spanish colonists in Florida. Most of Florida's Spanish residents fled when

* **New France** French colony centered in the St. Lawrence River valley, an area known as Canada; included the Great Lakes region and, until 1713, Acadia (present-day Nova Scotia)

* **cede** to yield or surrender

See second map in European Empires (vol. 2).

See map in British Colonies (vol. 1).

141

* *civil law* body of law that regulates and protects the rights of individuals

Britain took control, so the British had little trouble governing that area. However, many French-speaking inhabitants remained in Canada. In an effort to lessen their resistance to British rule, Parliament passed the QUEBEC ACT in 1774. The act created a centralized government, restored French civil law*, gave Catholic French Canadians full religious freedom, and extended the boundaries of Quebec to include the lands of the Ohio Valley. The Quebec Act infuriated American colonists and contributed to the opposition that had already formed over Britain's economic policies.

After Britain signed the Treaty of Paris, it began taking steps to reduce its enormous war debts. Part of its solution was to tax the colonists to help pay for colonial defense. New tax laws, such as the SUGAR ACT OF 1764 and the STAMP ACT (1765), and various trade regulations passed by Parliament angered the colonists and deepened the growing conflict with Britain.

British policies after the Treaty of Paris created crises that eventually led to the American Revolution. During the Revolutionary War, Britain paid a price for its victory over France and the territories it gained under the Treaty of Paris. The American Revolution gave the French a new opportunity to challenge their old rival. With financial and military support, France helped the American rebels win their independence from Britain. (*See also* **American Revolution; European Empires; Independence Movements.**)

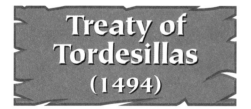

Treaty of Tordesillas (1494)

*T*he Treaty of Tordesillas was an agreement between SPAIN and PORTUGAL that determined the two countries' rights to claim land across the Atlantic Ocean. Through negotiations that involved Pope Alexander VI, Spain and Portugal established a line separating their areas of exploration.

The need for such an agreement arose after the first voyage of Christopher COLUMBUS in 1492–1493. King Ferdinand and Queen Isabella of Spain were eager to follow up the success of this expedition with further voyages. They asked Pope Alexander to grant them the right to lands in the western Atlantic Ocean. In 1493 the pope issued a series of decrees—known as "bulls"—establishing a north-south line in the Atlantic, 100 leagues (about 300 miles) west of the Cape Verde Islands. The pope gave Spain the right to explore lands not already claimed by Christians west of this line. Portugal received the same rights east of the line.

Wanting the opportunity to explore the Americas, the Portuguese were unhappy with the arrangement. King John II of Portugal asked the Spanish rulers to consider moving the line westward. Representatives from the two nations met at Tordesillas, Spain, to discuss the issue. On June 7, 1494, in the Treaty of Tordesillas, they agreed to move the boundary to a line 370 leagues (about 1,100 miles) west of the Cape Verde Islands. The new line gave Portugal the right to claim Brazil.

At the time, little was known about the size of the Americas, so the parties involved did not realize that Spain received rights to a much larger territory than Portugal did. Moreover, the treaty failed to take into account other European countries, such as England and France, that had an interest in exploring the Americas. In the years that followed, these nations sponsored voyages of their own, largely ignoring the Treaty of Tordesillas. (*See also* **Exploration, Age of.**)

Treaty of Utrecht (1713)

* *succession* transferring authority on the death of a ruler to the next ruler
* *cede* to yield or surrender

he Treaty of Utrecht consisted of a series of agreements between Great Britain, France, Spain, and several other European countries that had been involved in the War of the Spanish Succession*— known in the British colonies as QUEEN ANNE'S WAR. The treaty greatly increased the amount of North American territory controlled by Britain and reduced the lands held by France.

The nations that had taken part in the War of the Spanish Succession met at Utrecht, a city in the Netherlands, to negotiate a peace settlement. Many of the treaty's points concerned matters in Europe, but others involved the colonies. On April 11, 1713, France and Britain signed a treaty that ceded* several parts of NEW FRANCE to Great Britain. These included ACADIA, NEW-FOUNDLAND, and the land around the Hudson Strait and Hudson Bay, which had been a disputed area. The British promised to allow French colonists in these regions to practice the Roman Catholic religion. The French also gave up the Caribbean island of St. Christopher (also known as St. Kitt) and recognized British authority over the IROQUOIS Indians. France retained the right to use the north shore of Newfoundland during fishing expeditions.

The treaty between Britain and Spain, signed on July 13, 1713, did not alter the boundaries of their North American colonies. Spain pledged not to transfer any of its American possessions to any other country. An earlier agreement, signed on March 13, had given Britain a 30-year contract to sell slaves in Spain's American colonies and some trading rights there.

Overall, Britain gained the most territory under the Treaty of Utrecht, and France lost the most. However, the long struggle between these nations for land in North America was far from over. Throughout the long peace that followed the treaty, they continued to compete for trade and territory, and eventually they came to blows again in 1744 in KING GEORGE'S WAR. (*See also* **European Empires; French and Indian War.**)

Triangular Trade

See *Trade and Commerce: British.*

Tuscarora Indians

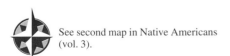

See second map in Native Americans (vol. 3).

he Tuscarora were related to the Iroquois tribes of New York but had separated from them some time before Europeans arrived in North America. They settled in Virginia and North Carolina, where they came into violent conflict with English settlers in the early 1700s.

For the first 200 years of European colonization, relations between the Tuscarora and the settlers were fairly peaceful. The Tuscarora engaged in trade with the English, sometimes selling the rum and other goods they acquired to other Indians. However, white settlers eventually began to take over the tribe's lands, and traders kidnapped and sold the Indians' children for slaves. Members of the southern branch of the Tuscarora took their revenge in the Tuscarora War. Led by Chief Hencock and joined by members of several other tribes, these Indians attacked several North Carolina settlements in the fall of 1711.

North Carolina asked the other colonies for help. New York persuaded the Seneca—one of the Iroquois tribes—not to assist the Tuscarora, and Virginia

prevented the northern Tuscarora from helping their kinfolk. South Carolina sent a military force, composed mostly of Indians who were allies of the British, to attack the Tuscarora in early 1712. This campaign led to a brief truce that was frequently broken.

In March 1713, a second expedition from South Carolina attacked the Tuscarora at Fort Nohoroco in eastern North Carolina. After a three-day battle, the Indians surrendered and accepted a peace treaty. Following the war, most of the Tuscarora migrated northward to join the five-nation IROQUOIS CONFEDERACY of New York. They were formally adopted as the confederacy's sixth nation in 1722. A few survivors of the Tuscarora War became part of the MAROON COMMUNITY formed by escaped slaves in the Great Dismal Swamp, near the Virginia border. (*See also* **North Carolina; Warfare and Diplomacy.**)

United States of America

Relations With European
Colonial Powers, 1781–1848

* *cede* to yield or surrender

The Liberty Bell became a symbol of the United States after it rang to announce the reading of the Declaration of Independence in Philadelphia in July 1776. But contrary to legend, it was not until 1835 that the bell developed its famous crack.

With the end of the AMERICAN REVOLUTION, the 13 BRITISH COLONIES along the Atlantic coast became the United States of America. Free from British rule, the new nation faced many challenges throughout the remainder of the colonial period. These included strengthening and reorganizing its government and handling conflicts with Britain, France, and Spain.

The first American constitution, the Articles of Confederation, created a weak national government that proved unable to deal with the problems facing the new nation and the individual states. One important accomplishment of the Confederation government, however, was the Northwest Ordinance of 1787. This law paved the way for settlement of the Northwest Territory—a region between the Ohio River and the Great Lakes that Britain had ceded* to the United States—and established a procedure for admitting new states to the Union. In the summer of 1787, delegates from 12 of the 13 existing states met in Philadelphia and created a plan for a stronger central government, the Constitution of the United States.

During the late 1700s, Great Britain angered the United States by refusing to surrender forts in the Great Lakes area and supporting Indian attacks on settlers there. Americans also resented British attempts to restrict U.S. trade with other countries. When Britain and France went to war in 1793, the United States remained officially neutral. But attacks by both countries on American shipping hurt their relations with the United States.

Problems with Spain arose in the 1780s after the Spanish closed the lower Mississippi River and the port of NEW ORLEANS to American shipping. The two nations later reached an agreement, known as Pinckney's Treaty (1795), which opened the river to American trade. Five years later, Spain ceded LOUISIANA to France. Concerned about French control of the area, the United States purchased the Louisiana Territory from France in 1803. The addition of this vast region brought the nation into direct contact with Spain and its possessions in the Southwest.

In 1812 the United States went to war with Britain, largely because British ships had been harassing U.S. merchant vessels and some Americans wanted to gain control of CANADA. The War of 1812 settled no issues

and resulted in no territorial changes, but it did confirm the independence of the United States and its growing power.

Soon after independence, the United States had begun to expand westward. In the 1790s, three new states—Vermont, Kentucky, and Tennessee—joined the Union, and others were added in the early 1800s.

In the following years, many Americans came to believe that it was the "manifest destiny"—a future event regarded as inevitable—of the United States to expand all the way to the Pacific Ocean. Most of the territory in the West, however, was controlled by Britain and Spain. In the mid-1840s, conflict erupted between the United States and Britain over the Oregon Territory in the northwest. In 1846 the two nations reached an agreement that gave the United States control over a large part of that region.

That same year, a dispute with MEXICO over the border of Texas—which the United States had annexed* in 1845—led to the outbreak of the Mexican War. At the end of the war in 1848, Mexico ceded California and most of its territory in the southwest to the United States. In the 67 years since winning its independence, the United States had expanded its territory across the continent from the Atlantic Ocean to the Pacific Ocean.

* **annex** to add a territory to an existing state or nation

Urban Life

See *Cities and Towns.*

Ute Indians

See *Great Basin Indians.*

Van Cortlandt Family

*T*he Van Cortlandt family, one of the wealthiest and most prominent families in the Dutch colony of NEW NETHERLAND, maintained their position in society after the English took over the colony. The family adapted well to changes in colonial rule, with several members distinguishing themselves in public service.

Oloff Van Cortlandt (1600–1684), the founder of the family, arrived in New Netherland in 1638 as a soldier for the DUTCH WEST INDIA COMPANY. He soon left the military to become a merchant. He began acquiring land and developing various businesses, including a brewery. Van Cortlandt's leadership skills led to positions in the colonial government. He also served as mayor of NEW AMSTERDAM (later New York City). A determined businessman, Van Cortlandt was not afraid to challenge powerful individuals, such as Governor Peter STUYVESANT. In 1664 the English took over the colony, renaming it New York. But Van Cortlandt continued to be active in community affairs, serving several terms on the city council. He also became one of the richest men in the colony.

Stephanus Van Cortlandt (1643–1700), Oloff's eldest son, had a long and notable public career as well. As a young man, he began trading beaver skins from the Hudson River valley for wine from the Netherlands. Recognizing his talents, New York's royal governors appointed him to various administrative

and judicial posts. He became a trusted adviser to Governor Edmund AN-DROS, who named him mayor of New York City in 1677. During LEISLER'S REBELLION against the government, Van Cortlandt was forced to flee the colony. But when he returned, he helped convict Jacob Leisler of treason. His influence in government enabled Van Cortlandt to purchase a huge piece of land along the Hudson River. This property became the Van Cortlandt family estate at Croton-on-Hudson. Stephanus also helped his sister Maria VAN RENSSELAER in the management of her estate, Rensselaerswyck.

Pierre Van Cortlandt (1721–1814), grandson of Stephanus, also rose to prominence in the colony. Like earlier family members, Pierre held several offices in colonial government, but he abandoned the British to help the patriots* during the American Revolution. Following the war, Van Cortlandt presided over the convention that drafted the constitution for the state of New York and became the state's first lieutenant governor. His son, Philip (1749–1831), an officer in the Continental Army, was promoted to brigadier general for his bravery in the Battle of Yorktown. In later years, he served in the New York Assembly and Senate and in the United States House of Representatives.

* **patriot** American colonists who supported independence from Britain

1645–1689
Estate manager

See map in New Netherland (vol. 3).

* **tenant farmer** person who farms land owned by another and pays rent with a share of the produce or in cash
* **gristmill** mill for grinding grain

Following the death of her husband, Maria Van Rensselaer took control of the family estate of Rensselaerswyck. A capable businesswoman, she helped make the Van Rensselaers one of the most important families in early New York.

Born in New Amsterdam (now New York City), Maria was the daughter of Oloff and Anna Van Cortlandt. Her father, a wealthy Dutch merchant and city official, founded the VAN CORTLANDT FAMILY. At the age of 16, Maria married Jeremias Van Rensselaer, holder of a patroonship—large land grant—called Rensselaerswyck, near present-day Albany, New York.

In 1674, shortly after the birth of their sixth child, Jeremias died. The children were too young to take over the estate, and none of Jeremias's relatives lived in the colony. The management of Rensselaerswyck fell to Maria. Her brother Stephanus Van Cortlandt was eventually named director, but he lived in New York City and could not help with the daily operations of the estate.

Running Rensselaerswyck was not an easy task. Covering 24 square miles, the estate resembled a small town. Besides raising her six children and managing her household, Van Rensselaer had to deal with the tenant farmers* living on the property. She also supervised Rensselaerswyck's industries, including sawmills and gristmills*.

Maria Van Rensselaer faced other problems. The change from Dutch to English rule of the colony in 1664 left the legal ownership of the estate in doubt, and she spent many years corresponding with English authorities, trying to convince them of her family's right to the property. She also quarreled with members of her late husband's family in the Netherlands, who demanded a share of the estate's profits.

Maria Van Rensselaer formed alliances with other influential families through the marriages of her children. The family finally gained clear title to the estate in 1685. (*See also* **Land Ownership; New Netherland; Women, Roles of.**)

Vassa, Gustavus

See *Equiano, Olaudah.*

Vermont

See map in British Colonies (vol. 1).

* *militia* army of citizens who may be called into action in a time of emergency

V ermont experienced conflict during much of the colonial period. From the late 1600s to the mid-1700s, the area was a battleground in the struggle between the French and British over control of North America. Then, in the mid-1700s, Vermont became the focus of a dispute between the colonies of NEW YORK and NEW HAMPSHIRE, both of which laid claim to the region.

The ABENAKI INDIANS lived in what is now Vermont when the French explorer Samuel de CHAMPLAIN arrived there in 1609 and claimed the region for France. In the 1660s, the French built a fort at Isle La Motte, an island in Lake Champlain, which extends along Vermont's western border. In 1724 British colonists from Massachusetts built a fort and settlement near present-day Brattleboro. During the FRENCH AND INDIAN WAR, the British and French clashed in Vermont. Britain's victory in 1763 gave it control of the region.

In 1764 a crisis arose over land disputes in Vermont. The governor of New Hampshire had issued a number of land grants to settlers in Vermont, but New York claimed the same land. British authorities ruled in favor of New York, which then demanded payment from the people living on these New Hampshire Grants. The settlers resisted the demands. Led by Ethan ALLEN, some of them formed a militia* called the GREEN MOUNTAIN BOYS that rebelled against the New Yorkers.

The outbreak of the American Revolution brought a halt to the struggle over land claims, at least temporarily. The Green Mountain Boys fought against the British and helped capture FORT TICONDEROGA. While the Revolution raged in other regions, Vermont settlers formed a new government, declaring an independent republic, in January 1777. Several months later, they adopted a constitution—the first to abolish slavery and give all male citizens the right to vote. Vermont remained independent for 14 years. In March 1791, after resolving its land disputes with New York and New Hampshire, Vermont was admitted to the United States as the fourteenth state.

Verrazano, Giovanni da

See *Exploration, Age of: French.*

Vespucci, Amerigo

See *Exploration, Age of: Spanish.*

Viceroys

T he most powerful officials in Spanish America, viceroys governed vast territories called viceroyalties that contained several provinces. One of these territories—the viceroyalty of NEW SPAIN—included the SPANISH BORDERLANDS, MEXICO, the Spanish WEST INDIES, and most of Central America.

During the early years of colonial rule, Spanish explorers and warriors governed the regions they had conquered. Soon, however, the Spanish crown decided that these governors were becoming too powerful and might pose a threat to royal control. The crown reduced their authority and appointed viceroys to rule Spain's American empire. Only men of proven loyalty—often members of the nobility with military experience—were entrusted with this important office. The king could dismiss viceroys at any time, but most served for three to six years.

As the official representative of the crown, a viceroy lived like a king in a palace with many servants. As head of the colonial government, he presided over the *audiencia,* or high court, and served as commander in chief of the military. He managed colonial finances and was the official guardian of the church. The viceroy's responsibilities also included supervising the settlement and economic development of all the provinces and protecting the Indians from exploitation*.

The viceroy had considerable freedom in interpreting and applying the laws. But all his decisions had to be reviewed by the Council of the Indies—the group of officials who advised the crown on colonial affairs—and approved by the king. This decision-making process helped the crown keep its viceroys from acquiring too much power. However, it also made government in the Spanish colonies a slow and inefficient process. (*See also* **Colonial Administration; Government, Provincial; Laws and Legal Systems.**)

* *exploitation* relationship in which one side benefits at the other's expense

Vikings

See *Norse Settlements.*

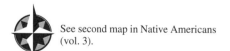

Virginia

See second map in Native Americans (vol. 3).

Expanding from the early settlement of Jamestown, Virginia became one of the most important and prosperous British colonies in North America. Virginia also produced many of the political and military leaders who inspired and organized colonial opposition to British policies in the years before and during the American Revolution.

Early Years. When the first English settlers founded Jamestown in 1607, somewhere between 15,000 and 30,000 Algonquian-speaking Native Americans lived in the region that became Virginia. These Indians, the Powhatan, relied primarily on agriculture for their food. Few of them lived in the Jamestown area because most of the land there was not suitable for farming. For this reason, the first English settlers believed the coast to be uninhabited.

Although the newcomers were largely unaware of the Native Americans, the local tribes were familiar with Europeans. They had traded with explorers and sailors for many years and knew that Europeans could be dangerous, especially those who wanted to settle an area. Therefore, the Powhatan greeted the first English colonists with a mixture of goodwill and caution.

The Founding of Virginia. The Virginia Company of London, a group of English investors, provided the money for establishing a colony in

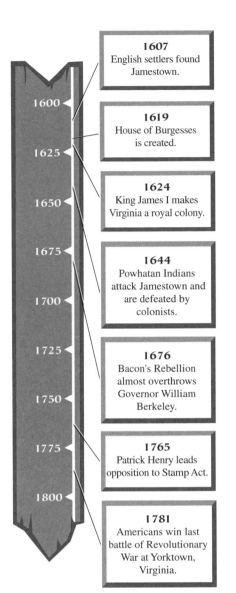

1607
English settlers found Jamestown.

1619
House of Burgesses is created.

1624
King James I makes Virginia a royal colony.

1644
Powhatan Indians attack Jamestown and are defeated by colonists.

1676
Bacon's Rebellion almost overthrows Governor William Berkeley.

1765
Patrick Henry leads opposition to Stamp Act.

1781
Americans win last battle of Revolutionary War at Yorktown, Virginia.

See map in Trade and Commerce (vol. 4).

gentry people of high social position

North America. In 1606 they sent out three ships with 144 settlers. Upon arriving in April 1607, the 105 colonists who had survived the journey began looking for a site for their settlement. They chose a place on a large river that flowed into Chesapeake Bay, calling it Jamestown in honor of England's King JAMES I.

Life in the new colony proved to be very difficult. Jamestown was located in a swampy area that served as a breeding ground for malaria-carrying mosquitoes. During the summer and autumn, many settlers became sick and died. Furthermore, those who survived would not work together to build their community. Many of the men were gentry* who considered physical labor beneath them and had no practical skills. Instead of hunting, fishing, and planting crops, they often went off to search for GOLD. The settlement faced a food shortage. Without help from the Powhatan Indians, it might not have survived.

The settlers also began to quarrel about how the community should be run. Order was finally restored under the firm leadership of Captain John SMITH, a former soldier. He forced the colonists to spend time each day tending crops or working on buildings. Smith was captured and held by the Powhatan for a few weeks. During his absence, his enemies managed to take control of Jamestown. In October 1609, Smith returned to England to be treated for an injury caused by exploding gunpowder.

"The Starving Time."   By this time, the Powhatan chief—known to the colonists as Powhatan—realized that the English had no intention of leaving. The growing conflict between the Indians and the settlers led him to attack Jamestown, burning crops and killing livestock. During this winter, known as "the starving time," most of the English died from malnutrition or from Indian attacks. By June 1610, the survivors had decided to abandon the settlement when relief arrived. Lord De La Warr, the new governor from England, brought supplies and reestablished order. The colony's leaders founded new settlements in the region—at healthier spots than Jamestown—and forced the Indians to accept a truce. In 1611, 200 new English settlers arrived who had the skills and experience needed for the difficult task of building a colony.

For the next two years, the settlement was governed quite strictly. Codes of conduct were enforced with harsh punishments—including the death penalty—for various crimes. The government brought order to the colony. Jamestown also benefited from the work of a planter named John ROLFE, who began growing a new variety of TOBACCO. The crop soon became Virginia's most profitable export. Rolfe married Chief Powhatan's daughter, POCAHONTAS, establishing a temporary peace between the settlers and the Indians.

In 1619 the colony created the VIRGINIA HOUSE OF BURGESSES, an assembly consisting of delegates elected by the settlers. Although the laws it passed could be vetoed by the governor or the directors of the Virginia Company, the House of Burgesses was the first representative assembly in the North American colonies.

Virginia Becomes a Royal Colony.   Conditions in Virginia improved, but the colony remained unprofitable. As the settlement grew, tensions with the Indians increased. Moreover, as tobacco replaced trade with the Powhatan as the settlers' main source of income, the colonists made less of an effort to remain on friendly terms with the Indians. Clashes occurred frequently, and in 1622, after a tribal leader was murdered, the Powhatan

staged an attack. They killed some 350 colonists, leading to fierce counterattacks that severely weakened the Indians.

In 1624 King James I, tired of the mismanagement of the colony, ended the Virginia Company's charter. Virginia became a royal colony ruled by a royal governor and council. For the next 20 years, Virginia prospered under the control of the English crown. Realizing that the colony's future lay in growing tobacco, the government abandoned attempts to develop other crops and industries. New settlers began to flock to Virginia, hoping to make a profit from the growing demand for tobacco. By 1640 the population had swelled to 8,000, including about 200 Africans. The colony's leaders sent out expeditions three times a year to kill Native Americans and seize their lands. In 1644 the Powhatan attacked again. But defeat by the English a few years later forced them to leave the Jamestown area, largely ending the Indian threat and opening new land for expansion.

The English Civil War and Bacon's Rebellion.

During the English Civil War in the mid-1600s, Virginians supported King Charles I and his followers. This faithfulness earned Virginia its nickname, "the Old Dominion." After the king was forced to resign, Parliament took control in England and sent a military expedition to Virginia to enforce loyalty to the new government.

When the English monarchy was restored to power in 1660, Sir William BERKELEY returned as the colony's royal governor, an office he had held with some success earlier. This time, however, Berkeley faced great resentment because of his autocratic* rule, his support of wealthy eastern planters, and his policy on frontier lands. In an attempt to keep peace with the Indians, he

* **autocratic** ruling with absolute power and authority

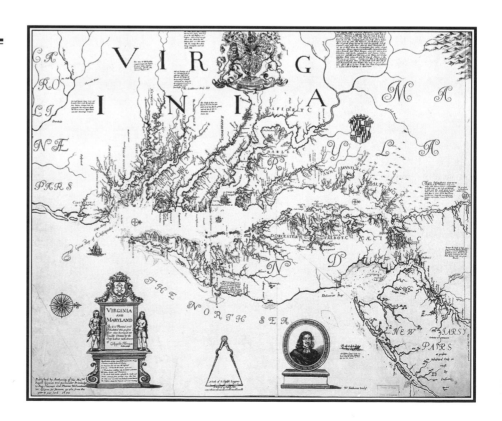

Jamestown, the first settlement in Virginia, was founded in 1607 on a river flowing into Chesapeake Bay. This 1673 map shows that bay, which forms part of the coastlines of Virginia and neighboring Maryland.

From Sea to Shining Sea

Virginia was named in honor of Queen Elizabeth I, the "Virgin Queen." Its original charter defined it as all the territory between 30° and 45° north latitude, stretching inland for 50 miles. Thus, it originally covered the entire Atlantic coast from southern Maine to northern Florida. A new charter in 1609 extended Virginia's boundaries westward to the Pacific Ocean. In 1612 the colony's eastern border was pushed 750 miles eastward to include the Bermuda Islands.

* *indentured servant* person who agreed to work a certain length of time in return for passage on a ship to the colonies

 See map in British Colonies (vol. 1).

* *resolution* formal statement adopted by a legislature or other organization

* *boycott* refusal to buy goods as a means of protest

had promised them certain western regions and banned settlement there by colonists. The governor also failed to defend frontier settlements against Indian attacks. The situation led a western landowner named Nathaniel Bacon to raise an army of angry colonists to fight the Indians. After achieving some victories, Bacon marched on Jamestown to drive out Berkeley. He defeated the governor's forces and burned the town but died of a fever shortly afterward, bringing an end to the uprising. Berkeley regained control and hanged many of Bacon's supporters. Although BACON'S REBELLION failed, it may have provided a model of action for the colonists who rose up against British rule a hundred years later.

Bacon's Rebellion may have also contributed to the dramatic increase of African slaves in Virginia. Bacon's followers were mainly poor white settlers from the frontier who had little or no voice in the colony. Many were indentured servants*. Wealthy planters believed that African slaves would be easier to control than white workers. Other factors also contributed to the rapid rise in the slave population after 1680. The demand for slaves in the Caribbean islands was declining, leading slave traders to look for other markets. In addition, the planters believed that buying slaves to work their fields would be cheaper in the long run than using indentured servants.

Prosperity and Revolution. Over the next 75 years, Virginia developed into a center of colonial culture and politics. The College of William and Mary was founded in 1693. WILLIAMSBURG, the site of the new college, became the state capital in 1699. Governor Alexander Spotswood encouraged the development of industries other than tobacco, promoted peace with the Indians, and ended the threat posed by Edward Teach, the notorious pirate known as Blackbeard. Spotswood also led Virginia's first colonizing mission over the Blue Ridge Mountains into the interior. New immigrants moved into the western portions of the colony, and many of them fought alongside British troops in the FRENCH AND INDIAN WAR (1754–1763).

When the British Parliament passed the STAMP ACT in 1765, Virginia politicians led the opposition to this tax on papers and documents. Patrick HENRY delivered a stirring speech in the House of Burgesses, which passed resolutions* against the act. In 1768 Virginia joined Massachusetts in calling for action by the colonies against British attempts to tax them. The next year, in response to the TOWNSHEND ACTS, Virginia started a boycott* of British goods. In 1773 the colony established a COMMITTEE OF CORRESPONDENCE to exchange information about British policies and to plan the colonists' response. The following year Peyton Randolph, a Virginian, was elected president of the FIRST CONTINENTAL CONGRESS. At the SECOND CONTINENTAL CONGRESS, Richard Henry LEE, a Virginia delegate, proposed the resolution for independence. Another delegate from the colony, Thomas JEFFERSON, wrote the DECLARATION OF INDEPENDENCE.

In the Revolutionary War, Virginia served as a major battlefield and contributed many of the Americans' military leaders, including George WASHINGTON and John Paul Jones. The final battle of the war was fought in 1781 at Yorktown, Virginia, where the British troops surrendered to Washington's forces. (*See also* **Independence Movements; Ohio Company of Virginia; Plantations; Roanoke Island; Slavery.**)

Virginia Company of London

* *charter* written grant from a ruler conveying certain rights and privileges

*I*n the early 1600s, a group of investors in London formed a trading association called the Virginia Company of London. They wanted to establish settlements in North America and profit from goods produced there. Although the company was not a commercial success, it did establish JAMESTOWN COLONY, the first permanent English settlement in North America.

In 1606 King JAMES I of England gave the founders of the Virginia Company of London a charter* granting them the right to create a colony in VIRGINIA and the surrounding region. The colony would be governed by a council in London, under the authority of the English crown.

Months after receiving its charter, the London company sent a group of colonists to Virginia. These immigrants arrived in the spring of 1607 and selected a site on the James River for their settlement. They named it Jamestown after the king. From the start, the colonists faced serious hardships, including disease and food shortages. Although many died, some managed to survive and keep the colony going.

In 1609 and again in 1612, the Virginia company received new charters. These documents gave it greater authority, including the right to appoint the colony's governing council. TOBACCO soon became an important crop in Virginia. As a result, demand for farmworkers grew. The company encouraged settlers to migrate to the colony with offers of land, and communities developed outside the original town.

In spite of the colony's growth, the Virginia Company never became profitable for its investors. In 1622 an Indian uprising devastated the colony, and many settlers were killed. Shortly afterward, disputes about managing the colony arose among the company's directors. King James decided to end the Virginia Company of London and assumed control of the colony in 1624.

Virginia House of Burgesses

*M*ade up of settlers from each of the communities in the English colony of Virginia, the House of Burgesses was the first representative legislature in North America. It played an active role in Virginia's government until the Revolutionary War.

In 1607 the VIRGINIA COMPANY OF LONDON, a trading corporation, established the colony of Virginia. About 11 years later, the company directed the governor to establish a citizens' assembly in the colony. The Virginia House of Burgesses met for the first time in the church at JAMESTOWN on July 30, 1619. Governor George Yeardley presided over the meeting, which also included the members of the governor's council and 22 colonists, 2 from each of Virginia's 11 settlements. The colonists in the assembly were known as burgesses.

Over time the House of Burgesses gained authority in the colony. It acquired the right to pass laws, although the governor and the council had the power to veto them. In 1643 the legislature was divided into two parts—an upper house, made up of the council, and a lower house, consisting of the burgesses—and became known as the General Assembly. In 1699 the legislature moved to Virginia's new capital of WILLIAMSBURG. In the following

years, it often governed the colony with little interference from the British government, which had to deal with conflicts at home.

The House of Burgesses played an important role in colonial politics in the years leading up to the AMERICAN REVOLUTION. Various members of the house, including Patrick HENRY, Thomas JEFFERSON, Richard Henry LEE, and George WASHINGTON, influenced political developments in Virginia and throughout the colonies. In 1765 Henry spoke in the house against the STAMP ACT, which placed taxes on paper and documents. His remarks helped create opposition to the act. Four years later, the governor temporarily suspended the House of Burgesses to prevent its members from opposing the TOWNSHEND ACTS, which attempted to impose new taxes on the colonists. The burgesses responded by holding an unofficial meeting in a tavern and issuing the Virginia Resolves on May 16, 1769, in which they protested the acts.

In 1773 the House of Burgesses established a COMMITTEE OF CORRESPONDENCE to communicate with groups working to resist British rule. The house called on other colonies to do the same. The following year, Britain passed the INTOLERABLE ACTS, partly to punish Massachusetts after the Boston Tea Party. When the Virginia House of Burgesses expressed support for the Massachusetts colonists, Governor Dunmore, Virginia's royal governor, suspended the house again. As the members had done before, they met unofficially. This time they formed the Virginia Convention, which elected delegates to the FIRST CONTINENTAL CONGRESS in Philadelphia. (*See also* **Assemblies.**)

Voting Rights

* *absolute monarchy* rule by a king or queen who possesses unlimited power

Voting rights in the European colonies of North America generally reflected the political practices of the parent countries. Spain and France, both absolute monarchies*, did not allow their citizens a role in selecting the countries' leaders. Neither did the Spanish and French colonies. The Netherlands had a representative government. But the colony of New Netherland was a private enterprise of the DUTCH WEST INDIA COMPANY governed by a small group of officials appointed by the company. In England only male property owners could vote, and the qualifications for voting in its colonies followed this pattern.

* *indentured servant* person who agreed to work a certain length of time in return for passage on a ship to the colonies
* *suffrage* right to vote

Voter Eligibility. Several factors, including property ownership, gender, race, and religion, restricted the number of colonists who could vote in British North America. The most basic qualification for eligibility was the ownership of property, a requirement for voting in England since 1430. Many political writers believed that "people of small substance and no value" should not be allowed to vote because they had no stake in the welfare of society. As a result, indentured servants* and citizens without property were denied suffrage*.

In all the British colonies, citizens had to own land or personal property to gain the right to vote. In some colonies, estates worth a certain amount fulfilled this requirement. This allowed residents of large towns and cities, who generally owned little land, to participate in elections. Most colonies, however, insisted that voters own land. In the northern colonies, especially in New England,

the property requirement was generally quite small. Farther south, where land was cheaper, large landholdings were necessary to qualify a person as a voter.

The exclusion of women, African Americans, and Native Americans from participation in the political process stemmed primarily from custom rather than law. Only four colonies passed laws prohibiting women's suffrage. Although records from New York and New England show some instances of property-owning women voting, this was a rare exception rather than the rule. In general, women were considered too "delicate" for the rough-and-tumble world of politics and government.

Racial minorities participated in elections to a greater extent than women, particularly in early colonial times. Records indicate that some Native Americans voted in Massachusetts, and free blacks occasionally took part in elections in the Carolinas and Virginia in the early 1700s. In fact, only two colonies ever passed laws prohibiting the suffrage of blacks—South Carolina (in 1716) and Virginia (in 1723). But there is little evidence of widespread voting among nonwhites.

Colonies that had an official church often limited suffrage to church members. Those who did not belong to the church were seen as a threat to the harmony of the colony. In Massachusetts only PURITANS could vote, and in most Anglican* colonies, dissenters* were denied suffrage. But most of these restrictions were lifted by 1700. Several colonies passed laws prohibiting Catholics from voting. Catholics even lost the right to vote in Maryland, which they had founded, after Protestants gained control of the colonial assembly in the early 1700s. Jews also faced voting restrictions in the colonies. However, communities did not always enforce such prohibitions against Jews and Catholics strictly.

Other limitations on voting included age, citizenship, and residence. By tradition, the minimum voting age was 21 in most colonies. Generally, only individuals born in Britain or the colonies and those who had been naturalized* were allowed to vote. Although Britain had no residence requirements, several colonies restricted voter eligibility to people who had lived in the area for a period of time ranging from six months to two years.

Anglican of the Church of England

dissenter person who disagrees with the beliefs and practices of the established church

naturalize to grant the privileges of citizenship to a person born in another country

Voting and Elections. Because of the various restrictions and requirements, less than half the colonists qualified as voters. About 50 to 80 percent of white males had the right to vote, but few elections drew more than 20 to 40 percent of eligible voters. Most colonists took no active interest in the election process, and voting places were often located far from their homes. However, colonists were more likely to vote when an important issue was at stake.

Voters generally felt it was important to be personally acquainted with candidates for office. Campaigns rarely lasted more than a week and involved mostly handshaking and talking. Sometimes the candidates would treat the voters to food and drink. Unlike modern elections, there was no fixed time or place for voting. At the polling place, citizens voted either by voice or paper ballot. Voice voting involved stating aloud the names of selected candidates. Many northern colonies, including all of New England, used paper ballots on which voters marked their choices. (*See also* **Elections; Government, Provincial; Political Thought; Town Meetings in British Colonies; Women, Roles of.**)

Wampanoag Indians

See second map in Native Americans (vol. 3).

*A*t the beginning of the colonial period, the Wampanoag Indians lived in southeastern New England, primarily in the coastal areas and islands of present-day Massachusetts and Rhode Island. These Indians—also known as the Pokanokets—helped the early PILGRIMS at PLYMOUTH COLONY. In the mid-1670s, however, many of them turned against New England colonists in KING PHILIP'S WAR.

An Algonquian-speaking people, the Wampanoag were skilled farmers, hunters, and food gatherers. They lived in villages, each ruled by a sachem, or chief. The villages formed a loose alliance that was headed by a grand sachem.

When the Pilgrims arrived in Massachusetts in 1620, they received help from SQUANTO, an Indian who had spent several years in Europe. Massasoit, the grand sachem of the Wampanoag, also developed a friendly relationship with the colonists, and he remained their ally for more than 40 years. Largely because of this friendship, the Wampanoag stayed neutral during the PEQUOT WAR (1636–1637).

As colonial settlement spread, clashes began to occur between the settlers and the Wampanoag, who resented attempts to take over their land. Conflicts increased until 1675, when Massasoit's son METACOM (usually called Philip by the English) led an uprising of several tribes against the colonists and their Indian allies. During what came to be known as King Philip's War, thousands of people on both sides were slain. The Indians were defeated after more than a year of fighting. Although devastated by the defeat, the Wampanoag remained a presence in the region, and several of their communities survive to this day.

Wampum

*W*ampum—a collection of small beads, usually white or dark purple, made from shells—was highly prized among northeastern Indian tribes. They used it in religious and diplomatic ceremonies and as a means of recalling past events. Early European colonists adopted wampum as a type of currency.

The word *wampum* came from the Algonquian word *wampumpeag,* meaning a string of white shell beads. The term later included beads of other colors as well. Indians made wampum from various types of shells, using stone tools to shape the beads into cylinders and to drill tiny holes in them. The Indians used the finished beads, which were about one-quarter inch in length, in necklaces and bracelets and for decorating clothing. Beginning in the early 1600s, they also strung the beads on leather thongs and wove them into belts. Wampum had symbolic and ceremonial value for many Indian tribes. The IROQUOIS often exchanged wampum belts during peace and trade negotiations with other tribes. The Indians saw this giving of wampum—a symbol of truth—as an assurance that treaty decisions would be honored.

When early European traders and colonists recognized the value of wampum to the Native Americans, they adopted it as a form of currency and took steps to control its supply. Eventually, they began to manufacture wampum themselves. Wampum became especially valuable in the FUR TRADE. Dutch traders set up a system that involved trading cloth, guns, and

other European goods to coastal tribes for wampum. They then traded the wampum for furs with tribes in the interior. Europeans also adopted the custom of exchanging gifts of wampum during negotiations with the Indians. (*See also* **Economic Systems; Money and Finance; Pequot Indians; Trade and Commerce.**)

Warfare and Diplomacy

European Colonies and
Native Americans

* *diplomacy* practice of managing relations
between nations without warfare

*T*here were two basic worlds of warfare and diplomacy* in the North American colonies. One involved the relationships between the European colonizers and the Native Americans who inhabited the continent. The other concerned relationships among the European powers attempting to establish colonial empires. These two worlds were often linked. European rivalries and conflicts frequently influenced the way colonial authorities dealt with Indian peoples, and many of the wars and treaties between colonists and Indians resulted from the competing interests of European powers. However, Europeans and Native Americans had very different ideas about the nature and purpose of war and diplomacy. The inability of these two sides to understand each other's attitudes led to much of the conflict between them.

Different Views of War and Diplomacy. Conflicts among European powers during colonial times had political, economic, or religious causes. In terms of the colonies, economic factors such as access to valuable resources or control of trade routes played the most important role. In many cases, the goal of diplomacy was not to stop bloodshed or promote understanding but to gain economic advantages. When diplomacy failed, war followed.

European diplomacy and warfare were in the hands of state institutions such as the monarchy or, in the case of Great Britain in the 1700s, the PARLIAMENT. These central authorities made decisions affecting diplomatic relations between nations and expected the people they ruled to cooperate with them. Within the colonies, leaders were prepared to impose their will on Indians by force if they could not get what they wanted through negotiation.

For Native Americans, diplomacy and warfare were quite different. Most tribal societies were not organized around strong centralized authority. Chiefs and headmen ruled on the basis of kinship, mutual obligation, and moral authority rather than by force. Few Indian leaders had the kind of absolute control exercised by European monarchs and parliaments.

Indian warfare and diplomacy were often initiated by families and individuals in response to actions by members of other tribes. For example, "mourning wars" were fought primarily to seize captives who would replace members of the community killed in tribal conflicts. Emotional satisfaction, rather than economic gain, was frequently the driving force behind Indian warfare and diplomacy. In many cases, diplomacy involved exchanging gifts as a way to establish relations among groups. This created networks of obligation that created ties between tribes and reduced the likelihood of future conflict.

British and Indian Relations. Relations between the British and the Native Americans were often strained during colonial times. These tensions resulted not only from conflicting interests but also from misunderstandings

This engraving, called "The End of the War," shows representatives from France, England, Spain, and the Netherlands signing the Treaty of Ryswick in 1697. The agreement brought an end to King William's War in North America and the War of the League of Augsburg in Europe.

between the two peoples. While Indian leaders focused on establishing a good atmosphere in negotiations with the British, colonial officials pressed for specific advantages concerning trade, land, and other matters. Indian chiefs could not compel tribal members to follow their wishes, but the British misinterpreted this as an unwillingness to enforce agreements. When Native Americans expected an exchange of gifts to symbolize and reinforce diplomatic relations, the English considered such gifts to be bribery or handouts. The British never fully appreciated Indian customs and came to understand them only slowly. The bad feelings caused by this lack of understanding helped poison relations between the British and the Indians.

The British desire to extend colonial settlement was central to their problems with Native American societies. Expansion meant taking land from Indians, who naturally responded with force. The early settlers of Virginia fought three wars with local tribes while establishing trading ties with Indians farther inland. However, the colonists' later expansion along the frontier led to bloody wars with some of their trading partners, setting a pattern for relations with Indians for many years to come.

Early settlers in New England met less organized resistance from Native Americans because Indian populations there had been drastically reduced by disease. Moreover, the colonists adopted a policy of playing one tribe off against another. The strategy of "divide and rule"—forming alliances with some tribes in order to weaken others—became an important feature of British colonial policy. Colonial authorities used such alliances not only to gain advantage over Indians but also to strengthen their position against European rivals.

Warfare and Diplomacy

Contented Captives

Most wars involve the taking of prisoners. Generally, the prisoners want to return to their homes when the war is over. However, European colonists captured by Indians sometimes preferred to stay with their captors. Some of these colonists adopted Indian ways of life. In 1771 José Maria Gonzales, a Spanish settler, was taken prisoner by Apache Indians. Ten years later, he led an Apache raid on a Spanish settlement near his former home. The raiding party killed 53 people and captured 44 others, including Gonzales's two brothers. Gonzales remained with the Apache and had an Indian wife and children.

* **hierarchy** division of a society or an institution into groups with higher and lower ranks

* **Spanish Borderlands** northern part of New Spain, area now occupied by Florida, Texas, New Mexico, Arizona, and California

The British alliance with the IROQUOIS CONFEDERACY, for example, played an important role in the struggle with France for control of North America.

French and Indian Relations. The French enjoyed better relations with Native Americans than did the British. This was partly due to the fact that the French were more interested in developing the FUR TRADE than in establishing agricultural settlements. The Indians became valuable trading partners, and the slow expansion of French settlement posed less of a threat to Indian lands. Moreover, because the French colonists were few in number, they tended to rely more on Indian allies in struggles against European rivals. Unlike the British, the French also made a great effort to learn about Native American customs. For their part, many Indians found French soldiers and weapons of great value in their conflicts with other tribes or with the British.

Many Indian tribes—such as the ABENAKI, the HURON, and the OJIBWA INDIANS—allied themselves firmly with the French and remained allied throughout the colonial period. But others came to see the advantage of maintaining a neutral position, finding that Europeans would compete for their support by offering better trading terms or protection against enemies. The Iroquois often played the British against the French, with some Iroquois tribes favoring the British, others the French, and still others remaining neutral. After years of fighting on both sides, the Iroquois signed treaties with the French and English in the early 1700s, allying with neither.

Spanish and Indian Relations. From the beginning, the Spanish saw Native Americans as obstacles to conquest and colonization, and they pursued a policy of aggressive warfare against Indian peoples. But when necessary, the Spanish would seek alliances with Indians. In the 1520s, Hernando CORTÉS and a small Spanish force defeated the mighty Aztec empire of MEXICO with the help of Indians who hated the Aztecs. The Aztecs had a highly organized society with a strict hierarchy* of leaders. The fall of these leaders marked the end of Aztec resistance to the Spanish.

The Spanish encountered a very different situation in the Spanish Borderlands*. Those frontier regions contained many different Indian tribes spread over a vast and thinly populated area. Most tribes consisted of small bands with little central authority, and the Spanish had to deal with each Indian band separately. Spanish missionaries converted some Native Americans, which helped keep them loyal. Yet incidents such as the PUEBLO REVOLT of 1680 revealed that great tensions remained between Indians and the Spanish. Throughout the Borderlands, Spain built PRESIDIOS, or forts, to defend the frontier. But there were never enough soldiers to eliminate all Indian threats. Groups such as the APACHE INDIANS frequently raided settlements and then disappeared into the vast open spaces. The hit-and-run warfare practiced by Indians in the Borderlands plagued the Spanish during the entire period of their occupation of the Southwest.

Colonial Warfare. When war broke out in the North American colonies, it was very different from the type of fighting known in Europe. Large battles between trained armies fighting in tight formation were rare. Conflicts between Indians and colonists usually consisted of small raids in which women,

children, and the elderly were the most frequent victims. Attackers would strike quickly and unpredictably, destroying crops and other resources needed to support a community.

The British referred to this kind of warfare as "skulking war." The French called it *la petite guerre* and the Spanish called it *guerrilla*—both of which mean "little war." Although Europeans considered this style of fighting cowardly, they adapted to it and sometimes practiced it themselves. The French used it to great advantage in battling the much larger forces of the British.

European armies occasionally faced each other in North America. Most clashes involved only a few hundred men. The largest engagements—such as the battle between British and French troops on the Plains of Abraham in Quebec in 1759—might feature several thousand soldiers on each side. But such battles were rare. Maintaining large permanent armies in the colonies was too expensive, so colonial forces generally included numerous soldiers of the local militia* and Indian allies. During and after the French and Indian War, the British greatly increased the size of the regular army stationed in North America. The cost of supporting that army led to British policies that played a major role in setting off the AMERICAN REVOLUTION. (*See also* **European Empires; Frontier; Military Forces; Native Americans; Weapons.**)

* **militia** army of citizens who may be called into action in a time of emergency

Warren, Mercy Otis

1728–1814
Playwright, poet, and historian

* **patriot** American colonist who supported independence from Great Britain

* **satiric** referring to humor that criticizes or makes fun of something bad or foolish

With her plays, poems, and other works critical of British rule, Mercy Otis Warren played an important role in the revolutionary politics of the American colonies. Her three-volume *History of the Rise, Progress, and Termination of the American Revolution* (1805) remains an important and colorful firsthand account of people and events of the time.

One of 13 children of a prominent Massachusetts colonist, Mercy Otis received an education by sitting in on her brothers' lessons and by reading. Later in life, she argued that more women should be educated and allowed to take part in activities such as politics that were normally limited to men. In 1754 Otis married James Warren of Plymouth, with whom she had five sons.

In the years leading up to the American Revolution, the Warrens became active in politics, and their home often served as a meeting place for colonial patriots* such as John ADAMS, Samuel ADAMS, and Mercy's brother James OTIS. In the early 1770s, Mercy Warren began writing satiric* plays that criticized the royal governor of Massachusetts and other British officials. She completed at least three such works, which were intended to be read rather than performed.

After the Revolution, Warren published a volume of poetry that included two plays on historical topics. At the same time, she continued working on her three-volume history of the Revolution, begun in the late 1770s. By this point, the Warrens had fallen on hard times, and Mercy grew angry with their old friend John Adams, now a powerful figure in the United States government, for not helping the family. She also quarreled with Adams and others over the U.S. Constitution, which she felt gave too much power to the federal government. Mercy Otis Warren stayed active throughout the remainder of her life, maintaining a lively correspondence with political and literary friends. (*See also* **American Revolution.**)

Wars

See individual wars.

Washington, George

1732–1799
Military commander, statesman, and first President of the United States

When Charles Willson Peale painted this portrait of George Washington in 1772, the 40-year-old general was known for his role in the French and Indian War. Later he would gain great fame as the leader of the Continental Army and the first President of the United States.

*A*s commander in chief of the CONTINENTAL ARMY, George Washington played a crucial role in the American victory over Britain in the AMERICAN REVOLUTION. Throughout his life, he devoted himself to the needs of the colonies and of the United States, quietly accepting the roles and duties thrust upon him. Washington's efforts won the admiration of fellow Americans, who elected him the first President of the United States, as well as the esteem of later generations.

Early Years. George Washington was born in Virginia, the son of a prosperous planter. Little is known of his early childhood except that he attended school irregularly and seemed to have a talent for mathematics. Washington's father died when George was only 11 years old. George spent the remainder of his youth with his half brother Lawrence, who cared for him and supervised his education, which included training in surveying.

Washington began his career as a SURVEYOR in 1748, by joining an expedition to survey the lands of Lord Fairfax, a wealthy and prominent Virginian. The next year Washington became the surveyor of Virginia's Culpeper County. This position, which often took him to the colony's western areas, taught him survival skills and also gave him knowledge of the frontier.

In 1751 Washington interrupted his work to accompany his brother Lawrence, who was ill, to BARBADOS in the West Indies. When Lawrence died the following year, George inherited his Virginia estate of Mount Vernon. Throughout his life, Washington lavished great care on Mount Vernon, expanding its acreage, enlarging the main house, adding buildings, and experimenting with crops and livestock. Washington loved the estate, but public duties often took him away from it.

Early Military Career. In 1753 Governor Dinwiddie of Virginia made Washington a military officer and sent him to the Ohio Valley region. The French had begun building FORTS in that area, which Virginia also claimed, and Washington's mission was to warn the French to leave. After a long and difficult journey, Washington arrived at Fort Le Boeuf and delivered his message. But the French refused to heed the warning.

Returning to Virginia, Washington told Dinwiddie about the buildup of French forces in the Ohio region and suggested establishing a fort there to counter French moves. The governor agreed and sent some troops to begin construction. On the way to join them, Washington heard that the French had seized and completed the unfinished fort, calling it FORT DUQUESNE. The Virginians stopped about 40 miles away from Fort Duquesne and began building a camp called Fort Necessity. In May 1754, Washington led a successful surprise attack against the French. The French struck back in July with a larger force, forcing Washington to surrender Fort Necessity. These battles marked the beginning of the FRENCH AND INDIAN WAR (1754–1763).

During the war, Washington served as aide to General Edward BRADDOCK, commander of the British forces. He gained a reputation for bravery

and bold actions, including an ill-fated attack on Fort Duquesne in 1755 in which General Braddock was killed. Later that year, Washington was named commander in chief of all Virginia forces, with the responsibility of defending Virginia's western frontier against the French. In 1758 he led one of the three brigades that captured Fort Duquesne. He retired from the military the next year, returned to Mount Vernon, and married Martha Dandridge Custis, a wealthy young widow with two children.

A Leader in Politics and War.   During this time, Washington became a member of the VIRGINIA HOUSE OF BURGESSES. For the next 15 years, he divided his time between the assembly in Williamsburg and Mount Vernon. He worked hard to improve the agricultural practices at his estate, but he found time to enjoy hunting, fishing, cardplaying, dancing, and other activities. This pleasant life did not last, however. As tensions grew between the colonies and Britain in the 1760s, Washington became increasingly involved in colonial affairs.

Washington served as a delegate to the FIRST CONTINENTAL CONGRESS, at which he supported economic measures against Britain and offered advice on military issues. A member of the SECOND CONTINENTAL CONGRESS as well, he was unanimously chosen to be commander in chief of the new Continental Army. For the next eight years, Washington shouldered the military burden of the American Revolution. His skill, determination, and courage played a vital role in the eventual American victory in the war.

Washington's first task as commander in chief was to end the British occupation of Boston. Arriving outside Boston in July 1775, he found untrained and poorly equipped colonial militias*. He brought discipline to these troops, provided them with guns and ammunition, and eventually forced the British out of the city. Problems with training, organization, and equipment would continue to plague the Continental Army throughout the war. But Washington managed to overcome such difficulties through great persistence.

Washington suffered a number of humiliating setbacks in the Revolution. In 1776 his attempt to defend New York City against the British resulted in a massive retreat of his forces all the way to Pennsylvania. Yet he also achieved brilliant victories, such as his attacks on the British at Trenton and Princeton in New Jersey. One of his most difficult tasks was getting his troops through a severe winter at Valley Forge in 1777 and 1778. Illness and inadequate food and clothing caused terrible suffering among the troops. Many considered desertion, but the example of Washington's courage and determination helped them go on.

The Presidency.   When the Revolution ended in 1781, Washington retired to Mount Vernon. For the next few years, he worked to restore the estate, which had been somewhat neglected during his years at war. In 1787 Washington presided over the Constitutional Convention, a meeting in Philadelphia that produced a plan for a new national government. After the states ratified* the Constitution, Washington was elected the first President of the United States.

During his two terms in office, Washington shaped the office of the presidency. He established a distinguished cabinet of advisers that included people of differing political views. He pursued a neutral foreign policy, refusing to become involved in foreign wars, and worked to strengthen the United

* *militia* army of citizens who may be called into action in a time of emergency

* *ratify* to approve formally

161

States economically and politically. Though he faced increasing opposition from political enemies, Washington remained a popular President.

Weary of public life, Washington refused to be considered for a third term as President. Before retiring once again to Mount Vernon in 1797, he delivered an eloquent Farewell Address, written with the help of James MADISON and Alexander Hamilton. In the speech, he urged the nation to avoid "permanent alliances" with other countries. He also warned that bickering political factions* could weaken the government. His death in December 1799 left the nation in mourning. Congressman Henry Lee of Virginia expressed the feelings of most Americans when he described Washington as "First in war, first in peace, and first in the hearts of his countrymen." (*See also* **Independence Movements; Military Forces.**)

* *faction* group within a larger group

Water Systems

One of the biggest challenges to settlers in North America was obtaining water both for daily use and for agriculture. Natural sources such as lakes and streams usually provided enough water for small settlements and individual farms. However, as the population expanded and more land was cultivated, the demand for water increased. The colonists used wells and cisterns—tanks for storing rainwater—but eventually they needed more elaborate systems. Both Native Americans and European settlers developed new methods to satisfy their requirements for water.

For hundreds of years, the Dutch had been building dikes in their homeland to gain the use of land covered by the sea. The seawater was usually drained into canals built alongside the fields. Dutch settlers applied this technology in their colony of NEW NETHERLAND. They drained marshes and swamps near rivers, producing fields that were very fertile. In the 1670s, one Dutch governor "dyked and cultivated a large piece of meadow or marsh, from which he gathered more grain than from any land which had been made from woodland into tillable land." The French settlers in Acadia (present-day Nova Scotia) also built dikes and dams to control the water supply. At first they used dams to enclose land next to rivers. Later they began to build dams as close to the sea as possible so that they could cultivate land near the coast without the risk of fields flooding at high tide.

Planters in SOUTH CAROLINA used dams not only to drain fields but also to flood them to create rice paddies. A dam at one end of a field allowed water from swamps to flow in, while a dam at the other end released the water. However, this method gradually lowered the level of water in the swamps. Planters then began to cultivate fields closer to the coast. As the tide rose and fell, so did the level of the rivers in the area. Planters built dams along the rivers to control the flooding and drainage of their fields.

In the arid climate of the Southwest, water management was a major concern. Spanish settlers often appointed an overseer to divide the water fairly among the community's residents. This official also resolved disputes among water users and fined those who broke the usage regulations. Irrigation was necessary for agriculture in the region. Entire communities often took part in constructing irrigation ditches and dams. They laid out a main ditch far upstream, with smaller and smaller canals branching out to reach individual plots

of land. Finally, a dam was built to drain off excess water during times of heavy rainfall or flooding. A few of these irrigation systems are still in use today.

Native Americans in the Southwest had been practicing irrigation for many years before the first Spanish arrived. The HOPI and PUEBLO INDIANS usually planted crops in places where the natural features of the land would carry water—at the base of cliffs, for example, or in low-lying areas. The PIMA INDIANS in ARIZONA channeled water from the Gila and Santa Cruz rivers for irrigation. They also built dams and dikes in the arroyos* to prevent flooding and guide rainfall to their fields. Some Indian irrigation systems covered thousands of acres, and the fields they watered were among the most productive in the world.

* **arroyo** gully or riverbed in a dry region

Wealth

In most of the colonies of North America, wealth was connected to land. The richest people had usually started off in the "New World" with large land grants from European or colonial rulers. In NEW FRANCE, such grants were called seigneuries, and their owners held positions of authority in the colony. Some Spaniards received ENCOMIENDAS in NEW SPAIN in reward for service to the Spanish crown. These land grants, which brought great wealth and power, included the right to rule the Native Americans living on the property and use their labor. A few Dutch colonists became wealthy from patroonships, large estates awarded for bringing settlers to NEW NETHERLAND.

In the British colonies, however, the pattern of wealth was more complex. Although many wealthy settlers were large landholders, others had acquired their fortunes through trade. Wealth grew at an impressive rate in the British colonies, though it was not equally distributed. Most settlers arrived in North America with little or no personal wealth. Yet by the mid-1700s, the average colonist was about as well off as the average citizen of Great Britain.

In the years following a colony's founding, its economy expanded rapidly. The value and productivity of land typically rose during this period, as settlers cleared and improved the land. Wilderness became cultivated fields, small farms grew larger, and villages developed into towns and then cities. All these changes increased the economic base of the colony and added to the wealth of its inhabitants. A growing population also created a local market for goods and services. However, economic growth usually slowed as the productivity of the land leveled off.

Most colonies experienced only moderate growth from these early days until about 1740. At that point, a population boom in Europe caused an increased demand for American agricultural products, boosting the colonial economy. At the same time, England's industrial revolution reduced the cost of manufactured goods imported by Americans. More colonists could afford items that in earlier times would have been considered luxuries. This new wealth, however, was concentrated largely in the hands of PLANTATION owners and MERCHANTS along the Atlantic coast.

A regional pattern of wealth emerged. Colonists who lived near the coast had easy access to markets for their goods and could earn higher incomes than colonists who lived inland and had to pay the costs of transporting their goods to market. In addition, southern plantations that specialized in a single

* **aristocracy** people of the highest social class, often nobility

crop, such as TOBACCO or RICE, turned out to be more profitable than northern farms that produced several different crops. The southern agricultural system led to the growth of a planter aristocracy* that dominated both the economic and political life of the region.

Inequalities in wealth were greater in the cities than in the countryside. While land on the frontier remained relatively cheap, urban land prices increased as the cities grew. In addition, the wages of workingmen rose slowly during the late 1700s. Artisans* and laborers found they could not afford to purchase property, and by the time of the American Revolution, most of them had become tenants, not homeowners.

* **artisan** skilled crafts worker

Meanwhile, the business leaders who controlled the export trade in places such as NEW YORK, PHILADELPHIA, and CHARLESTON prospered. In 1700 a merchant with an estate of 2,000 pounds was considered very wealthy. By 1750 the most successful merchants had built personal fortunes five to ten times as great. Like the planters in the South, merchants became the social and political leaders in the northern colonies. Laws passed by the British PARLIAMENT to regulate colonial commerce in the mid-1700s, such as the TOWNSHEND ACTS, particularly affected the merchants and planters. As a result, these two groups would play a leading role in the movement toward American independence. (*See also* **Class Structure in European Colonies; Economic Systems; Land Ownership; Money and Finance; Poverty; Seigneurial System; Taxation.**)

Weapons

*C*hanges in weapons technology had a dramatic effect on European warfare in the century before the "discovery" of the Americas. Until the early 1400s, armored knights played the leading role in warfare. Mounted on horses, they carried heavy swords and axes for use in hand-to-hand combat. Because armor and horses were very expensive, knights came almost exclusively from the ranks of wealthy and noble families. Infantry, or foot soldiers, were peasants typically armed with only farm tools. Military commanders rarely used them effectively in combat. The development of firearms—which could kill from a distance—made heavily armored knights and their style of hand-to-hand combat obsolete*. Trained infantry, armed with muskets, became the most important fighting force in any European army.

* **obsolete** no longer useful

Muskets were the first effective firearms. Muskets resembled rifles, but they had a much shorter range, and loading and firing them was a more complicated process. During early colonial times, the most common musket in use was the matchlock musket. To fire the weapon, the shooter held a lighted match to the gunlock, a compartment containing gunpowder and a ball or bullet. The match ignited the gunpowder, which discharged the bullet.

Although matchlock muskets had an effective firing range of about 300 feet, loading and firing them was a complex and time-consuming process. In the mid-1600s, Prince Maurice of the Netherlands, a leading firearms expert of the day, broke the process down into a number of distinct steps and drilled soldiers in carrying these out efficiently. Because of the time required to load and shoot, not all musketeers in a group would fire at once. One row of soldiers would fire while others behind them cleaned and loaded their

Large and heavy, cannons were typically used in the colonial period to defend forts and ships. This etching of several cannons by John Norman appeared in Muller's *A Treatise of Artillery* in 1779.

weapons. After the front row fired, those musketeers moved to the back of the formation to reload while another row moved forward to shoot. This procedure increased the frequency of fire and the effectiveness of armed troops.

Soldiers in colonial times used other types of muskets as well. The arquebus, or heavy musket, was employed primarily as a defensive weapon in forts because of its weight. Wheel lock and flintlock muskets, developed in the 1500s and 1600s, required much less time to load and had fewer problems with misfiring than matchlock muskets. All muskets were handmade, and parts that broke had to be repaired by trained gunsmiths. After an extended period of use, muskets could no longer be repaired and were discarded.

Most armies used cannons, but primarily as stationary weapons at forts and on ships. Because of their size and weight, cannons were difficult to transport, especially across rough terrain. Before the 1750s, they were rarely used in the field anywhere in North America.

Despite the availability of firearms, swords and other bladed weapons remained important in situations that required hand-to-hand combat. Most soldiers carried a sword in addition to a musket. Daggerlike blades called bayonets were attached to muskets for use as a stabbing weapon in close combat. Another important bladed weapon was the pike, a long pole with a large

pointed blade at the end. Pikes were used mostly to create a barrier that would keep the enemy away from musketeers while they reloaded. As the range and accuracy of muskets increased, pikes gradually became obsolete.

NATIVE AMERICANS initially fought Europeans using weapons such as tomahawks, war clubs, and bows and arrows. However, they quickly recognized the superiority of European weapons and traded to obtain guns, especially flintlock muskets. Most conflicts between Europeans and Indians were fought with such weapons on both sides. (*See also* **Military Forces; Warfare and Diplomacy.**)

West, Benjamin

1738–1820
Artist

* *patron* person of wealth and influence who supports an artist, writer, or scholar; protector

Benjamin West spent most of his adult life in England and achieved his greatest success as an artist there. Yet he is sometimes called the "father of American painting" because he influenced many important American artists of the 1700s and early 1800s.

Born in rural Pennsylvania near Philadelphia, West showed artistic talent at an early age and began painting portraits while in his teens. West's family encouraged him to become an artist and sent him to Philadelphia to study painting. In 1760, with money raised from supporters, West traveled to Italy. He studied there for three years and then moved to England. Many wealthy people in England greatly admired West's work, including King GEORGE III, who became his patron*. Though a supporter of the American movement for independence, the artist remained popular in England and maintained his friendship with George III. He lived in that country for the rest of his life, never returning to the United States.

Most of West's paintings are of historical subjects, often reflecting American themes. One of the best known, *The Death of General Wolfe* (1771), portrays the death of a British general during the FRENCH AND INDIAN WAR. The painting created a controversy at the time because it was the first to show historical figures wearing clothes of the proper time and place rather than traditional costumes of earlier periods. This work and others that followed helped introduce a new era of realism in historical painting.

Many young American painters, including John Singleton COPLEY and Gilbert Stuart, came to London to study with West. The influence West had on these artists helped shape American painting for a generation after his death. (*See also* **Art.**)

West Indies

* *outpost* frontier settlement or military base

During the colonial period, the term *West Indies* referred to the crescent of islands that stretches across the Caribbean Sea between Florida and South America. After crossing the Atlantic Ocean in 1492 on his first voyage of exploration, Christopher COLUMBUS landed on a Caribbean island. He named it San Salvador. For many of the Europeans who came to explore, conquer, or settle the Americas in the years that followed, the West Indies served as the starting point. The islands soon became outposts* of colonial empires and sources of rivalry among European powers. European settlers established immensely profitable PLANTATIONS on some of the islands. In addition, a close network of trading relationships developed between the American colonies and the West Indies, including the SLAVE TRADE.

Claims and Colonies.   The European colonization of the West Indies began with Spain and Christopher Columbus. He established a settlement on HISPANIOLA in 1492 before returning to Spain to report on the lands he had discovered. That first settlement failed, but Columbus and his followers soon founded another on the island. By the end of the 1490s, Hispaniola's capital, Santo Domingo, was an important center of Spanish activities in the Americas.

Within a very short time, the Spanish had removed all of Hispaniola's gold and killed most of its Indians. Seeking new worlds to conquer, the Spaniards fanned out in all directions. By 1511 they had laid claim to JAMAICA, PUERTO RICO, Cuba, and a number of the smaller West Indian islands near the coast of South America. Although Spain valued its West Indian possessions, it soon focused its efforts on MEXICO and Peru. In those wealthy mainland provinces, the Spanish could exploit* sources of gold and silver and establish large estates.

Soon other European powers arrived in the Caribbean. At first they claimed and settled islands that Spain had neglected. Before long, however, these powers were competing with each other and with Spain for control of various islands. Like the colonies of mainland North America, the Caribbean islands were prizes in the contest to build empires, and possession sometimes changed as a result of war or diplomatic agreements.

France was the first European power to challenge Spanish claims in the Americas. In the mid-1500s, the French tried to establish colonies in what is now Canada and in Florida and South America. Although these early French attempts at colonization failed, they made Spain realize that its American empire needed protection—particularly its ships loaded with gold and silver that passed through the Caribbean on the way back to Europe. For this reason, the Spanish built a chain of fortresses at ports throughout the Caribbean. During the 1600s, France established a number of colonies in the West Indies, including Guadeloupe and Martinique (1635), Grenada and St. Croix (1650), and St. Lucia (1667). Its most important West Indian possession was the western part of Hispaniola, ceded* by Spain in 1697. The French called it St. Domingue.

England's activity in the West Indies has often been overshadowed in colonial history by the story of its mainland colonies. Yet in the early years, the English paid as much attention to the islands as to the American colonies, sometimes more. After settling the tiny mid-Atlantic island of Bermuda in 1610, the English established colonies on the Caribbean islands of St. Kitts in 1625, BARBADOS in 1626, and Montserrat in 1632. In 1655 they also gained control of Jamaica. Many planters and indentured servants* who left England headed for the West Indies. Until about 1670, the islands had as many English settlers as the mainland colonies.

The Dutch shared some early ventures in the West Indies with the English. Privateers* and adventurers from the Netherlands and England often combined forces against Spain and Portugal, and Dutch financial support and skill helped the English establish some West Indian colonies, especially Barbados. The Dutch also claimed a number of small Caribbean islands not already taken by Spain, France, or England. But in a series of wars with England, the

* **exploit** to use for selfish reasons without regard to the consequences

See first map in European Empires (vol. 2).

* **cede** to yield or surrender

* **indentured servant** person who agreed to work a certain length of time in return for passage on a ship to the colonies

* **privateer** privately owned ship authorized by the government to attack and capture enemy vessels; also the ship's master

The West Indies was the first part of North America to be colonized by Europeans. This engraving from the 1600s shows some of the region's exotic animals and plants, including the iguana, armadillo, and fig tree.

See second map in European Empires (vol. 2).

Dutch lost many of their American possessions in the mid-1600s. They held on only to the islands of Aruba, Bonaire, and Curaçao near South America, part of St. Martin, and the tiny isles of Saba and St. Eustasius.

Many West Indian colonies changed ownership during the colonial period, sometimes more than once. When Britain emerged victorious from the FRENCH AND INDIAN WAR with France in 1763, it won not only Canada but also some French West Indian possessions, including the island of St. Vincent. Spain explored St. Croix in the Virgin Islands, but the island was later claimed in turn by the Netherlands, England, Spain, and France. Denmark bought several of the larger Virgin Islands in 1753 and held them until long after the colonial period had ended. England acquired the smaller Virgin Islands in 1666.

Pirates, Plantations, and Trade. The West Indies offered a variety of opportunities to Europeans who hoped to make their fortunes in the Americas. From the earliest years of exploration, the hundreds of harbors and isolated beaches scattered through the islands provided shelter to PIRATES who preyed not just on shipping but also on island and mainland settlements. Some places in the West Indies became known as pirate haunts. Among these were remote and wild stretches of coast on Hispaniola, the island of Tortuga off the northeastern coast of Hispaniola, the Bahamas, the town of Port Royal on Jamaica, and the southern coast of Cuba.

Like the pirates, privateers found good hunting and hiding places in the West Indies. Whenever any two European nations were at war—a common

event in colonial times—adventurous captains from one nation attacked ships or even colonies belonging to the other. Prosperous towns in the Spanish West Indies and Spanish fleets of treasure ships were frequent targets. In 1595, for example, the English privateer Francis DRAKE tried to raid the Puerto Rican port of San Juan.

After the first century of exploration and colonization, Europeans found a new use for the West Indies. By the 1640s, the Dutch had established profitable sugar plantations in Brazil on the mainland of South America. But after losing Brazil to Portugal, the Dutch brought the idea of large-scale sugar planting to Barbados. The island was first colonized by the Courteen Company, an enterprise owned and operated jointly by the Dutch and the English. From Barbados the plantation system spread in the 1660s to other colonies in the West Indies.

The West Indian plantations were astonishingly profitable. Each acre planted in sugar earned five times more than an acre planted with other food crops. But because raising sugar required large quantities of both land and labor, only wealthy planters could afford to grow this crop. Many of these so-called sugar barons became very powerful. They had enough influence in Britain to persuade PARLIAMENT to protect their interests by passing the MOLASSES ACT in 1733 and the SUGAR ACT OF 1764.

The growth of the sugar plantations had several lasting effects in the West Indies. It created a huge workforce of African slaves, who formed the basis of the black heritage of the modern West Indies. It also forced out most small landholders. At first the English viewed Jamaica as a refuge for small property owners displaced by the spread of plantations on other islands. But by 1770, Jamaica had replaced Barbados as the most productive of the British sugar colonies, with 800 plantations and a force of black slave laborers that outnumbered the white population ten to one. The French colony of St. Domingue (present-day Haiti) eventually became one of the most profitable colonies of slave-worked plantations in history.

St. Domingue and other French West Indian colonies depended for trade and supplies on the parent country rather than on France's mainland colonies, which had too few settlers to provide a profitable market. In contrast, a thriving trade relationship developed between the British West Indies and Britain's American colonies. By 1770, for example, New England was exporting nearly two-thirds of all the dried fish it produced to the islands.

See map in Trade and Commerce (vol. 4).

indigo plant used to make a blue dye

From Boston, New York, Philadelphia, Charleston, Savannah, and many smaller English mainland ports, ships carried goods such as butter, cheese, vegetables, beans, corn, flour, rice, cattle, horses, sheep, pigs, poultry, lumber, barrels, bricks, and leather to the West Indies. They returned with cargoes of cotton, indigo*, coffee, and slaves. Even more important, they brought sugar and molasses, which were used in the production of rum. By 1770 the New England and middle colonies had at least 25 sugar refineries and 127 rum distilleries to process the sugar and molasses imported from the West Indies. The RUM TRADE formed an important part of the so-called triangular trade, in which goods and slaves moved between Europe, Africa, and the American colonies. Over all, trade between the mainland colonies and the West Indies was so important that one historian has claimed that without it "the sugar colonies could not have existed and the North American colonies could not have developed."

Merchants in the American colonies traded not only with the British West Indies but also with the Caribbean colonies of other nations. Although such trade was prohibited by the NAVIGATION ACTS, Britain did little to enforce these laws. After 1765, however, the British government introduced new, stricter trade laws and made a greater effort to enforce them. These new regulations, which attempted to limit and control trade between the mainland colonies and the West Indies, fueled the resentment of the American colonists against British policies and contributed to their movement for independence. (*See also* **European Empires; Exploration, Age of; Privateers; Slavery; Trade and Commerce.**)

Whaling

maritime related to the sea or shipping

Whaling was one of the leading maritime* industries of the British colonies. Centered in New England, it contributed to the colonial economy in a number of ways, but its significance went beyond economics. Regarded as a heroic enterprise, whaling became the subject of folklore, songs, and art.

The first whalers in North America were coastal Indians. When they found whales washed up on beaches or grounded in shallow water along the shore, they cut up the bodies and took the whale's meat, bones, and oil. Some tribes also hunted whales at sea in canoes. When the huge animals surfaced to breathe, the Indians attacked with long spears fastened to ropes (later called harpoons). After striking a whale, they would tie the rope to a log and follow until they could close in on the injured whale and kill it. Then they towed the carcass back to shore.

Europeans launched the American whaling industry in the 1500s in the fishing grounds off the coasts of NEWFOUNDLAND and Labrador in present-day eastern Canada. These early whalers were primarily from Spain and France. Whaling began in the English colonies in the 1600s at the eastern end of Long Island and Cape Cod in Massachusetts. With iron harpoons and sturdy boats, the colonists soon developed a thriving industry. They hired the Indians of Long Island, known to be skillful whalers. By the end of the 1600s, whaling had spread to Nantucket and other islands off the coast of southern New England.

At first whaling took place only in coastal areas. A few men went out to sea in small boats, hunted and killed whales, and then towed the carcasses back to shore. On land, workers stripped the skin and blubber from the whale, then boiled down the blubber. This thick fat was made into whale oil, which colonists burned in lamps or made into candles. Another valuable product was baleen, or whalebone, found only in certain kinds of whales. The strong but flexible material was sewn into women's clothing to give it shape.

In the early 1700s, colonists began hunting the sperm whale, a large animal prized for its high-quality oil. Because sperm whales lived in warm waters far from North American coasts, whalers began making long voyages on large ships. They would cut up their catch on board and store the blubber until returning to port. Later whalers boiled down the blubber at sea and stored the oil in barrels. By the late 1700s, whaling ships in search of sperm whales often made voyages that would keep them away from their home ports for years at a time.

Indians and colonists valued whales for their thick fat, or blubber, which could be made into high-quality lamp oil. This illustration from Pomet's *A Compleat History of Druggs* (1725) shows a group of men stripping the blubber from a whale carcass.

The colonial whaling industry grew rapidly during the 1700s. By 1774 it employed 4,700 men on 360 ships. Many sailed from the Massachusetts ports of Nantucket and New Bedford, the world's busiest whaling centers. Ships often sailed as far as Africa and Brazil, searching out whales in all parts of the Atlantic Ocean.

The American Revolution caused a setback in the whaling industry because the British captured many American ships. The industry did not recover until after 1800, when large whaling ships began making long journeys into the Pacific Ocean. (*See also* **Fish and Fishing.**)

Wheatley, Phillis

ca. 1753–1784
African American poet

Phillis Wheatley was well known in colonial times not only for her poetry but also because of her race. White colonists who viewed blacks as their inferiors found Wheatley a surprising curiosity. Those who believed slavery unjust pointed to her poetry as proof that African Americans were the intellectual equals of whites.

In 1761 John Wheatley, a wealthy Boston tailor, bought a young African girl from a slave ship. He and his wife, Susanna, named the child Phillis. The Wheatleys treated Phillis more like a member of the family than a slave. Educated by the Wheatley children, she quickly learned to speak and read English. While in her early teens, Phillis began writing poetry modeled on the works of English authors. She composed neat rhymes, using themes and images from mythology, history, and the Bible. Many of her poems dealt with religious subjects.

Wheatley's poetry attracted the attention of educated people throughout the British colonies. In 1773 she visited England, where she was widely

praised and where her book, *Poems on Various Subjects, Religious and Moral,* was published. Liberated by Susanna Wheatley in 1774, Phillis married a free black named John Peters several years later. The marriage was apparently not a happy one, and Wheatley's three children all died at young ages. She spent her last years in poverty, unable to get another book of poems published.

Considered the first important black writer in America, Wheatley spoke out passionately against the evils of slavery, once writing that "in every human breast God has implanted a principle, which we call love of freedom." Among her best-known poems are "On Being Brought from Africa to America" (1773) and "Liberty and Peace" (1784). (*See also* **Literature; Slavery.**)

Wheelock, Eleazar

1711–1779
Congregationalist minister and educator

A minister in Connecticut, Eleazar Wheelock started a school to educate young Indians to become missionaries among their own people. He also founded Dartmouth College in New Hampshire and oversaw the instruction offered at both institutions.

Wheelock was born in Windham, Connecticut. After graduating from Yale College in 1733, he was ordained as a Congregationalist minister and became pastor of a church in Lebanon, Connecticut. A dynamic and emotional preacher, he took part in religious revivals during the period of renewed religious interest known as the GREAT AWAKENING. At the same time, he worked as a teacher, preparing students to enter college.

In 1743 Wheelock took on a new student, Samson OCCOM, a Mohegan Indian. Occom's success encouraged Wheelock to invite more young Native Americans to Lebanon to study. In 1754 he opened Moor's Charity School and began admitting Indian students from tribes in the region. Wheelock's program involved converting the Indians to Christianity, giving them a general education, and then sending them to work as teachers and missionaries among their people.

In 1765 Occom and Nathaniel Whitaker, another minister, went to Great Britain to raise money for Wheelock. The funds were to be used to start a new school in Iroquois territory in New York, but Sir William JOHNSON, the colony's superintendent of Indian Affairs, opposed the project. Instead, Wheelock obtained a charter* from New Hampshire's governor, John Wentworth, to establish a college there. In 1770 he opened Dartmouth College, named for the Earl of Dartmouth—one of the donors—in Hanover, New Hampshire. Wheelock spent the rest of his life serving as president of both Dartmouth and Moor's Charity School. (*See also* **Colleges; Education; Missions and Missionaries; Schools and Schooling.**)

* *charter* document stating the principles of an organization

Whigs

I n both Britain and its colonies in North America, Whigs were people who shared certain ideas about government. Although their thinking changed over time and varied from place to place, Whigs generally saw themselves as champions of individual liberty and opponents of tyranny*. In the years leading up to the AMERICAN REVOLUTION, colonial patriots*

* *tyranny* unjust use of power
* *patriot* American colonist who supported independence from Great Britain

embraced the political views of Whigs. These ideas shaped the colonies' conflicts and institutions as well as the new American nation that emerged after the war.

The term *Whig*—from Whiggamore, the name of a Scottish group—first appeared in English politics in the late 1600s, when two rival groups were struggling to decide the fate of the monarchy and the government. One group, known as Tories, supported the traditional view that kings were chosen by God and had the right to absolute power in their realms. Their opponents, the Whigs, claimed that the people had the right to limit the power of monarchs.

Over time the PARLIAMENT in England became more powerful, while the monarch's authority declined. In the process, most Tories accepted some Whig views, especially the idea of a limited monarchy in which the king's power was restricted by a constitution and elected representatives of the people played a role in government. But the terms *Whig* and *Tory* still referred to opposing beliefs. Tories represented the views of country gentry* and supported the Church of England, the official state church. Whiggism became associated with religious dissent*, the middle class, members of the increasingly powerful commercial community, and the new political ideas of the ENLIGHTENMENT.

* *gentry* people of high social position

* *dissent* opposition to or disagreement with established beliefs

During the 1700s, an assorted group of British journalists and political thinkers developed and published Whig ideas. Some of these people were considered radicals because their views were very different from those held by most people of the time. They believed in the importance of individual liberty, combined with personal virtue, and the need for a government that balanced liberty and power. They argued that people in power always hunger for more power and that citizens have a responsibility to remain alert for abuses of authority and corruption in government. They also believed that if government officials exceeded their legal power, citizens had both a right and a duty to oppose them.

Books, pamphlets, and newspapers carried these Whig ideas from Britain to the American colonies. Some colonists embraced the views because they reflected religious and intellectual freedom. For example, in 1752 three young lawyers in New York City founded a weekly newspaper called *The Independent Reflector* to spread Whig views—especially opposition to plans of colonial Anglicans* to establish an Anglican college in New York. The newspaper argued that the state should favor no particular church, an idea that later found expression in the Constitution of the United States as the separation of CHURCH AND STATE.

* *Anglican* member of the Church of England

Whig ideas also found favor with American colonists who had grown impatient with what they considered unjust rule by the British government. In the 1760s and 1770s, colonists who took part in protests, such as those during the STAMP ACT CRISIS, often claimed that they were following Whig ideals by taking action against tyranny. When the American Revolution broke out, patriots sometimes referred to Loyalists* as Tories, although few Loyalists supported the old Tory belief in the absolute power of kings. Some of the ideals of the Whigs were kept alive after the colonial period with the formation of a new Whig Party in the United States in the 1800s. (*See also* **Independence Movements; Political Thought.**)

* *Loyalist* American colonist who remained faithful to Britain during the American Revolution

White, John

active 1585–1593
Artist and governor of
Roanoke colony

John White's illustrations of Virginia in the 1500s presented Europeans with vivid images of North America. His detailed paintings provided valuable information about the region and helped create interest in colonization.

In 1585 Sir Walter RALEIGH asked White to join an expedition to ROANOKE ISLAND, off the coast of what is now North Carolina. White, an English artist, was to produce pictures of the area to encourage people to migrate there. In Roanoke White created more than 63 watercolor paintings of the region's plants, animals, and Native Americans, illustrating their ceremonies and everyday life. Scholar Thomas Harriot also took part in the expedition, taking careful notes to accompany White's pictures. However, conflicts soon developed between the Indians and the settlers, and most of them, including White, returned to England.

Raleigh still hoped to see the colony succeed. In the summer of 1587, he sent another group of settlers to Roanoke and named John White as their governor. One of the new colonists was White's daughter, Ellinor Dare. Soon after arriving, she gave birth to a daughter named Virginia—the first English child born in America. About one month later, White left for England to obtain supplies for the colony. A war between England and Spain prevented him from sailing back to Roanoke until 1590. When he finally returned, he found the settlement deserted. White believed the colonists had moved to another location farther south and wanted to find them. The ship captain refused to take him any farther, however, and White was forced to return to England.

In 1590 Thomas Harriot's book *America* appeared. It included engravings of 23 paintings and two maps by White—one of the earliest visual records of North America. White's illustrations of the Indians, in particular, influenced European ideas about the original inhabitants of the Americas for many years. (*See also* **Art; Wildlife.**)

Whitefield, George

1714–1770
Traveling preacher

* *evangelical* Christian movement emphasizing the importance of personal faith in leading to salvation
* *Anglican* of the Church of England
* *clergy* ministers, priests, and other church officials
* *denomination* organized group of religious congregations

With passionate faith and a rousing voice, George Whitefield was the best-known evangelical* preacher of the GREAT AWAKENING, a period of intense religious enthusiasm in the 1740s. Through his sermons and his writing, he had a tremendous impact on the religious revivals of that time.

Whitefield was born in Gloucester, England, to parents who kept a tavern. While attending Oxford University, he met John and Charles Wesley, the founders of Methodism—a reform movement within the Anglican* Church that emphasized the importance of faith and personal conversion. Whitefield joined the Methodists and, on the advice of the Wesley brothers, became a minor official in the Church of England.

After leaving Oxford in 1736, Whitefield began preaching in various English cities. His sermons attracted large crowds and earned him a reputation as a dynamic speaker, although some members of the clergy* objected to his practice of welcoming members of other Protestant denominations* to his services. Whitefield turned down a position in a London church because he had decided to join the Wesleys in their missionary work in North America. He visited the colony of GEORGIA in 1738, conducting religious services and

starting several schools. He also became interested in founding an orphanage in SAVANNAH. The following year, he went back to England to be ordained as an Anglican priest and received an appointment as minister of Savannah.

Whitefield returned to Georgia and opened the Bethesda Orphan Asylum outside Savannah. He spent much of his time in North America traveling in New England and the middle colonies, preaching in churches, meeting houses, and the open air. His sermons set in motion many of the local revivals of the Great Awakening. During his travels, he met other leaders of the movement, including Jonathan EDWARDS. However, he offended many people—especially members of the clergy—by criticizing their moral and religious behavior. In 1740 the Anglican Church suspended him from office.

* ***predestination*** doctrine that God alone determines whether a person goes to paradise or hell

While in England the following year, Whitefield became a CALVINIST, a follower of French minister John Calvin, who believed in predestination*. He continued to travel and preach, making several more visits to the colonies, where his sermons drew huge crowds. He died during a speaking tour in Massachusetts.

In addition to his spellbinding sermons, Whitefield spread his ideas through his writing. He published seven volumes of his personal journals, many letters and pamphlets, and two collections of hymns. (*See also* **Protestant Churches; Religious Life in European Colonies.**)

Wildlife

*T*he first Europeans who came to North America found a land rich in wildlife. For thousands of years, the continent's fish, birds, and animals had provided food, skins, and other useful materials for Native Americans. The European settlers soon established their own relationships with the continent's wildlife. Some animals they found very useful—so useful, in fact, that hunters and trappers almost eliminated them. Other wild creatures they regarded as pests but hunted them as well, sometimes to the edge of extinction.

* ***species*** group of plants or animals with similar characteristics

The wildlife of North America included thousands of species*, from the whales of the northern coastal waters and the BUFFALO of the Great Plains to the tiny, jewel-like hummingbirds of the southwestern deserts. Many areas teemed with deer, squirrels, rabbits, birds, fish, and other animals. There were no cows, horses, or sheep until colonial times. All the animals were wild, except for the dogs domesticated* by some Indian tribes.

* ***domesticated*** raised by humans as farm animals or pets

* ***exploit*** to use for selfish reasons without regard to the consequences

To the early European explorers and settlers, this bounty of wildlife was—like the land itself—another resource to be exploited*. North America's wildlife soon fell prey to a combination of elements introduced by the settlers. Among these were firearms and the practice of HUNTING for sport or recreation rather than for survival as the Indians did. Another new element was the colonists' style of agriculture, which involved clearing forests and planting crops in open fields. This practice greatly reduced the natural habitats* that had existed around areas Indians had cleared by fire. As these habitats grew scarce, so did the wildlife that lived in them, including deer, wild turkeys, and quail. The changes brought about by Europeans upset the natural balance between wildlife and the environment so severely that by 1672 a Massachusetts colonist wrote that "'tis very rare to meet with a wild turkie in the woods" where once these birds had flourished.

* ***habitat*** place where an animal or plant normally lives or grows

Wildlife

Populations of many North American animals dropped dramatically as a result of hunting. The beaver, valued for its waterproof fur, disappeared from several parts of the Northeast. This illustration of a beaver pond comes from Lahonton's *New Voyages to North America* (1703).

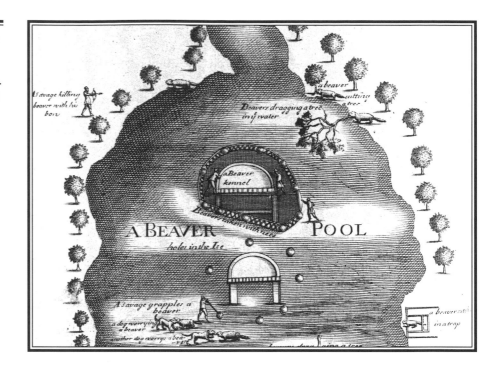

* **pelt** skin and fur of an animal

The FUR TRADE and the ever growing European market for animal pelts* also had a dramatic effect on American wildlife. Hunters and trappers in the northeast almost wiped out the beaver, which European hatters prized for its heavy, waterproof fur. They came close to exterminating other furbearing species such as mink, otter, and wildcat as well. The brisk trade in deerskins in the southern colonies caused such a sharp decline in the deer population that by the late 1700s, Indian hunters could not find enough deer to keep the trade alive.

Long before that time, some colonists began worrying about the decline in wildlife. In 1639 the Rhode Island town of Newport passed the first colonial game law, aimed at protecting deer. Other communities followed with similar legislation. Such laws usually established seasons when the hunting of certain animals was banned and fined those who violated the laws. But game laws were difficult to enforce and had little effect on the size of animal populations.

Wildlife had another meaning for the early colonists, who knew that the forests were home to bears and wolves, animals long extinct or at least very rare in England and many other parts of Europe. These creatures sometimes posed a real danger to settlers or their livestock, and colonists generally regarded them as symbols of the frightening, unknown wilderness. The accounts of European explorers and early settlers are filled with references to savage beasts. In the early 1630s, a colonist named William Wood wrote about wolves: "Late at night and early in the morning they set up their howlings. . . . [T]hey be the greatest inconveniency the country hath, both for the matter of damage to private men in particular, and the whole country in general." Wood doubted that the colonists could ever destroy the wolves, but he was wrong. By the end of the colonial period, wolves had been eliminated from most of the east. In this and many other ways, the spread of European settlement had forever changed the wildlife of North America. (*See also* **Animals; Environmental Impact of Colonization.**)

Williams, Roger

ca. 1603–1683
Founder of Rhode Island

* **Anglican** of the Church of England
* **Separatist** English Protestant who broke away from the official Church of England

* **doctrine** set of principles or beliefs accepted by a religious or political group
* **ritual** ceremony that follows a set pattern

* **charter** written grant from a ruler conferring certain rights and privileges

Roger Williams was an early champion of religious freedom. Forced to leave Massachusetts because of his religious and political views, he founded the colony of RHODE ISLAND. Under Williams's leadership the colony became a haven for groups that faced religious persecution, such as QUAKERS, Baptists, and JEWS.

Born in London, England, Williams graduated from Cambridge University in 1627 and became an Anglican* minister. However, Williams was a Separatist* who disagreed with many Anglican beliefs. He sympathized with the PURITANS, who wanted to reform the church, but he went even further than they did in opposing the established church. In 1630 he emigrated to North America and settled in the Massachusetts Bay colony.

In Massachusetts Williams angered Puritan leaders with his criticisms of their religious policies. He turned down an offer to preach in Boston because the congregation had not fully rejected the authority of the Anglican Church. Instead, he decided to go to the PLYMOUTH COLONY, where his views were more acceptable. Williams stayed in Plymouth for two years but then returned to Massachusetts. Despite the continuing hostility of the colony's leaders, he was offered and accepted a position as minister of the SALEM congregation in 1634.

Williams continued to criticize colonial authorities for their religious policies and for persecuting people because of their beliefs. He called for a complete separation of CHURCH AND STATE, believing that state involvement in religion would damage its purity. He also claimed that colonists had no right to take Indians' land without paying a fair price for it. Such views alarmed Puritan leaders because they threatened both religious and political authority in the colony. In 1635 colonial officials found Williams guilty of "dangerous opinions" and banished him from Massachusetts. He wanted to take some of his followers with him and establish a colony at Narragansett Bay, south of Massachusetts. But Puritan authorities feared a colony based on Williams's ideas and planned to arrest him. Warned by governor John WINTHROP, Williams fled the colony.

The exiled minister took refuge among the NARRAGANSETT INDIANS and bought land from them. Some followers from Salem joined him, and in 1636 they founded PROVIDENCE, the first settlement in Rhode Island. True to his ideals, Williams established a democratic government, religious freedom, and a separation of church and state in the colony. At the same time, he began to question his own religious beliefs. For a short time, he became a Baptist. But in 1639 he declared himself a Seeker—one who accepts basic Christian beliefs but follows no specific doctrine* or religious rituals*.

Williams proved to be a capable leader for Rhode Island. He maintained good relations with the Indians for many years, although he eventually was forced to lead troops against them during KING PHILIP'S WAR (1675–1676). He traveled to England in 1643 to obtain a royal charter* for the colony, and while there he published several pamphlets in favor of religious and political liberty. When a rival politician attempted to split the colony and take control of half of it, Williams returned to England to restore the colony's charter.

Williams served as governor of Rhode Island from 1654 to 1657 and continued to play an important role in political affairs until his death. Through his efforts, the colony became a haven of religious freedom and a model of democratic government. (*See also* **British Colonies; Freedom of Religion; Protestant Churches; Religious Life in European Colonies.**)

Williamsburg, Virginia

*L*ocated in southeastern VIRGINIA, the city of Williamsburg served as the center of the colony's social, cultural, and political life. It also played an important political role immediately before and during the AMERICAN REVOLUTION.

Founded in 1633, Williamsburg—known as Middle Plantation—was originally established to protect the colonial capital of JAMESTOWN from Indian attacks. The settlement grew slowly, remaining a small village for most of the 1600s. On several occasions, however, it served as the colony's temporary capital. It occupied this role during BACON'S REBELLION in 1676 and again in 1677, when a fire devastated Jamestown. In 1693 the colony's first university, the College of William and Mary, was established in Middle Plantation.

At the time, Jamestown served as the capital of Virginia and the site of its colonial assembly. However, the town had two major disadvantages: its location on a swamp-infested, disease-ridden island and its openness to attack. Many colonists who settled there died from malaria and other tropical diseases. In 1698, when the Jamestown state house burned down for the fourth time, Governor Francis Nicholson suggested moving the capital. The VIRGINIA HOUSE OF BURGESSES considered several sites, but it eventually selected Middle Plantation as the location for the new capital.

The House of Burgesses changed the name of the capital to Williamsburg, in honor of England's King William III. Governor Nicholson himself planned much of the city. He had Williamsburg divided into half-acre lots with houses set back six feet from the streets. A later governor, Alexander Spotswood, designed the Governor's Palace and other city buildings. These became models for many of Virginia's grand country houses of the later 1700s.

Williamsburg soon became a center of political and cultural activity. The first permanent theater in the British colonies opened there in 1716. Virginia's

See map in British Colonies (vol. 1).

Once the center of social and political life in the colony of Virginia, Williamsburg has preserved its historic past. Today, visiters to Williamsburg can see rooms like this one, looking as they did in the colonial period.

first newspaper, the weekly *Virginia Gazette,* was published there in 1736. Many other businesses sprang up in Williamsburg to meet the needs of people in government. Taverns served as important social centers, and the Raleigh Tavern became known as a gathering place for political leaders. By 1722 the number of permanent residents in the capital had grown to nearly 2,000, but the population sometimes swelled to more than 5,000 when the courts and the assembly were in session.

As anti-British feeling increased in the 1760s, Williamsburg emerged as a center of revolutionary activity. In 1765 Patrick HENRY gave an important speech in the House of Burgesses against the STAMP ACT, which imposed taxes on paper products and documents sold in the colonies. During the American Revolution, the British captured Williamsburg and used the Governor's Palace as a hospital for British troops. The Americans later recaptured the town, and it served as George Washington's headquarters during the last days of the war. In 1779 the capital of Virginia was moved to the city of Richmond, which was easier to defend and had a better climate. Williamsburg has now been rebuilt to appear as it did in colonial times. (*See also* **Architecture; Cities and Towns.**)

Wills and Inheritance

* *asset* valuable possession

*E*uropean immigrants to North America brought along from their homelands certain traditions concerning wills and inheritance. But because conditions in the new land were so different—in particular, those relating to LIFE EXPECTANCY and economic opportunity—these customs changed in the colonies.

In Great Britain, the wealth and livelihood of most families came from farmwork, and a family's land was its most important asset*. The title to the family property was held by the husband, who could do with it what he pleased. A wife, however, was entitled to a "dower," generally amounting to one-third of the land. Her husband could not mortgage or sell this land without her permission. When the head of the household died, his oldest son usually inherited all the family's land, a practice known as primogeniture. The idea was to prevent dividing up the property into plots of land too small to support their owners.

Younger sons and daughters often received their share of inheritance in the form of payments from income produced by the farm. The wife's dower rights continued after her husband's death. When she died, the dower passed back to the oldest son. If she remarried, it passed to her new husband.

This pattern of inheritance changed considerably in North America. The abundance of cheap land made it easier for a father to divide his property among his children more equally. If a man died without leaving a will, the oldest son usually received a double portion of the estate, with the remaining children receiving single shares. In many cases, sons would be given land while daughters would get personal property, money, or slaves. Because of disease, conflicts with Indians, and the hardships of building a life in the early colonies, men often died while their children were still quite young. As a result, colonial widows frequently received larger inheritances than European widows did and were given considerable power as executors* of their husbands' estates. In the 1700s, however, wills began to favor sons over widows

* *executor* person responsible for carrying out the provisions of a will

179

and daughters. Fewer husbands trusted their widows as sole executors, and many wills stated that a widow's dower would pass back to the eldest son if she remarried.

In the NETHERLANDS, women had more influence within the family than English women had—a fact reflected in Dutch inheritance practices. Joint wills were common methods of providing for more equal distribution of a family's assets in the Netherlands. Spouses often left their share of an estate entirely to the surviving partner, relying on the partner to provide for the children. Moreover, primogeniture was not practiced in the Netherlands. Most wills in NEW NETHERLAND called for equal inheritance by all surviving children, regardless of age or sex.

In FRANCE the husband held complete authority over a family's property. Inheritance laws often led to unequal distribution of property among heirs in order to keep it in the family. For this reason, sons usually received more than daughters. In NEW FRANCE, however, wives shared more equally in property decisions. As in the British colonies, the availability of cheap land and the modest value of a family's possessions also encouraged a more even distribution of inheritances than was the case in France.

SPAIN had a similar tradition of male authority, but its legal code guaranteed some rights to married women. Wives could own property, make wills, and sign contracts. Women in the Spanish Borderlands* retained these rights. Today some areas of the United States that were part of Spanish America have "community property" laws that provide for husbands and wives to share the assets of marriage. (*See also* **Family; Marriage.**)

* ***Spanish Borderlands*** northern part of New Spain, area now occupied by Florida, Texas, New Mexico, Arizona, and California

Winnebago Indians

See second map in Native Americans (vol. 3).

* ***clan*** related families

* ***cede*** to yield or surrender

*T*hroughout the colonial period, the Winnebago Indians lived west of Lake Michigan in the southeastern part of present-day Wisconsin. Known among themselves as the Hotcangara or Ho Chunk, they became allies first of the French and later of the British.

The Winnebago lived in permanent villages and grew MAIZE, beans, squash, and TOBACCO. They also fished, trapped small game, and took part in seasonal BUFFALO hunts on the prairies southwest of their homeland. The tribe maintained generally peaceful relations with neighboring Indians in the Great Lakes region, including the OJIBWA and OTTAWA, and engaged in trade with them. Winnebago society was organized around two main groups called the Air and the Earth. Both groups included various clans*, each with its own customs and special functions within the tribe.

Jean Nicolet, a French explorer, visited the Winnebago in 1634. The Winnebago became allies of the French, joining them in the FUR TRADE and supporting them throughout their struggle with Britain for control of North America. After France lost its North American territory in the FRENCH AND INDIAN WAR, the Winnebago formed an alliance with the British. They supported the British against the Americans during the American Revolution.

After the colonial period, the expansion of white settlement forced the Winnebago to cede* much of their land in Wisconsin. Most members of the tribe eventually moved west of the Mississippi River and settled on reservations set up by the United States government. (*See also* **Native Americans.**)

Winthrop, John

1588–1649
First governor of Massachusetts

* *dissent* opposition to or disagreement with established beliefs
* *heresy* belief that is contrary to church teachings
* *confederacy* alliance or league of peoples or states

John Winthrop, the first governor of Massachusetts, helped guide the colony's development, giving the Puritan church a leading role in government. He envisioned the new colony as a "city upon a hill," a model of virtue for the rest of the world to copy.

As the first governor of MASSACHUSETTS, John Winthrop played an important role in ensuring the early success of that colony. A devout PURITAN, he helped shape both political and religious policy in Massachusetts, creating a society that was unique in colonial North America.

Born in England to a wealthy, upper-class family, Winthrop studied law at Cambridge University. He began working as a lawyer in London in 1613, eventually establishing a successful legal practice. Winthrop had been a deeply religious person since his youth. While in London, he became a prominent Puritan leader and worked to reform the Church of England.

In the late 1620s, Winthrop began to have financial problems, partly a result of economic conditions in England at the time. He became interested in the Massachusetts Bay Company, an organization founded by wealthy Puritans to establish a colony in New England. After joining the company, Winthrop decided to go to North America, despite opposition from family and friends. He took an active role in planning the colony and was chosen to be its governor.

In March 1630, the Puritans set sail for New England. During the voyage Winthrop wrote "A Modell of Christian Charity," an eloquent sermon expressing his hopes for the colony. He saw it as a godly society bound together by Christian ideals that, like a "city upon a hill," would serve as an example to others. Upon arriving in America, Winthrop helped direct the founding of the Massachusetts Bay colony, moving its main settlement from SALEM to BOSTON.

Each year the colonists held elections for governor. Winthrop held the office for most of the years between 1631 and 1649. During the time that he did not serve as governor, he held other positions in the colony's administration. Winthrop helped shape a government in which the Puritan religion played a major role. Suspicious of democracy, he believed that authorities should rule with a firm hand according to their own beliefs. Yet Winthrop governed fairly and earned the respect of the colonists.

Winthrop distrusted new ideas and opposed most religious and political dissent*. Although angry with Roger WILLIAMS for his criticisms of church-state relations in Massachusetts, he liked Williams personally and secretly helped him flee to Rhode Island in 1636. Winthrop was especially opposed to Anne HUTCHINSON's challenge of church authority, which he considered heresy*. He led the attacks that caused her to be banished from Massachusetts and helped pass laws to prevent any of her followers from settling in the colony.

In 1643 Winthrop helped create the United Colonies, a confederacy* of New England colonies formed for the purpose of military defense. He was the first president of the United Colonies and also continued to serve as the governor of Massachusetts until his death in 1649. Winthrop's detailed journal, *History of New England,* has become one of the most valuable sources of information about the early history of Massachusetts. (*See also* **Governors, Colonial; Hutchinson, Anne.**)

Witchcraft

See *Magic and Witchcraft; Salem Witchcraft Trials.*

Witherspoon, John

1723–1794
Presbyterian minister, college president, political activist

Born in Scotland, John Witherspoon came to North America to serve as president of the College of New Jersey (now Princeton University). He was a forceful promoter of Presbyterianism in the colonies, as well as a critic of British policies and a supporter of independence.

Witherspoon became a Presbyterian minister in 1743 and served in Scottish churches for 25 years. In 1768 he assumed the presidency of the College of New Jersey, founded by Presbyterians in New York and New Jersey to train ministers. Witherspoon expanded the college's curriculum, increased student enrollment, and raised money to give the school a firm financial footing. He also played an important role in strengthening the Presbyterian Church and promoting its growth in New Jersey and the surrounding colonies.

In the 1770s, Witherspoon became involved in the American INDEPENDENCE MOVEMENT. He served on a local COMMITTEE OF CORRESPONDENCE and attended various meetings called to discuss the growing crisis with Britain. In June 1776, Witherspoon attended the SECOND CONTINENTAL CONGRESS as a delegate and urged the adoption of the DECLARATION OF INDEPENDENCE, saying the country was "not only ripe for the measure but in danger of rotting for the want of it." He signed the document and remained a member of the congress until 1782. Witherspoon devoted his remaining years to rebuilding the College of New Jersey, which had closed during the American Revolution, and to creating a national organization for the Presbyterian Church. (*See also* **Colleges; Protestant Churches.**)

Wolfe, James

See *French and Indian War; Quebec.*

Women, Roles of

* status social position

* sect religious group

* secular nonreligious; connected with everyday life

Nowhere in colonial North America did men and women have equal status* or fill the same roles in society. Even in the Native American tribes that gave women a voice in tribal government or traced ancestry through them, women performed different functions from men. In general, men hunted, waged war, and engaged in diplomacy and trade. Women gathered plants, harvested crops, prepared food, made clothing, and took care of children.

The Europeans who settled in North America brought with them ideas, beliefs, and traditions that defined the roles of women. The colonists tended to view women as the "weaker" sex—not just weaker in physical strength but also intellectually and emotionally inferior to men. For this reason, the legal status of women was not equal to that of men, and women were denied the right to participate in many important aspects of public life, especially politics and government.

Although Christianity taught that women were individually responsible for their sins and good behavior, only the QUAKERS and a few small Protestant sects* allowed women to preach or serve as church officials. Male figures of authority dominated Christian tradition and controlled Christian churches. This religious tradition served to reinforce the domination of men in the secular* world.

The lives of most colonial women centered around home and family. This anonymous painting, dating from around 1674, shows Boston colonist Elizabeth Freake with her young daughter.

At the same time, however, colonial society was forced to recognize the abilities and strengths of women. The survival of the society, and of families and communities, often depended on them. Women performed an enormous amount of the work involved in settling North America. They helped plant and gather crops, tended livestock, ran households and raised children, delivered each other's babies and cared for the sick, made cloth and clothing, and traded goods and kept shops. When husbands or fathers were ill or absent, women often took on men's responsibilities as well.

Throughout the colonies, the underlying belief in female inferiority was often at odds with the reality of women's abilities and contributions. Time became a force for change, however, and the roles of women changed slightly over the course of the colonial period. By the end of that era, women's status had begun to improve in some ways, especially in British North America.

British Colonies. The basic difference between the roles of men and women in the British colonies was in the realm of work. Public activities such as government, law, and large-scale business belonged to men. By and large, women had responsibility for maintaining the home, either performing household tasks themselves or supervising servants and slaves. But under English law, few women were allowed to own property. Upon marrying, a woman not only transferred all her property to her husband but also gave up her legal identity as an individual. She could no longer conduct business in her own name or appear in a court of law. Her husband had the authority to make all decisions for her.

The boundaries between men's and women's roles grew blurry, however, in such areas as shopkeeping, small businesses, craft workshops, and farm management. Daughters, sisters, and wives often participated in these ventures, either as assistants to their menfolk or by taking charge of activities

See color plate 4, vol. 3.

when their fathers, husbands, or brothers were sick or absent. When a man died, his widow might continue to manage his farm or business. For example, Mary ALEXANDER in New York managed her husband's business after his death, and Anna Zenger, wife of newspaperman John Peter ZENGER, published her husband's *New-York Weekly Journal* while he was in prison. On a few occasions, women such as Margaret BRENT in Maryland even took part in government or military activities, serving as a temporary substitute for a husband or male relative who could not fulfill his duties. While women sometimes did "men's work," men avoided domestic chores, or "women's work," whenever possible.

Most women lived and worked on farms during the colonial period. In the early days of settlement—and on the frontier in later years—they produced most of their household goods. Many women also produced surplus goods, such as butter, yarn, or cloth, and sold or traded them for needed items. By doing so, these women created local trade networks and added to the earnings of their families. By the end of the colonial period, however, many women lived in cities and were buying household goods rather than making them. As a result, they lost their ability to produce marketable goods and became full-time homemakers and caregivers.

Colonial women played a major role in providing education and medical care. They usually served as their children's first teachers. Some women—especially in New England—opened "dame schools" in their homes and taught young girls and boys to read. Women could not study medicine in school and could not be called doctors. Nevertheless, many of them had extensive practical knowledge of herbal medicines and the treatment of illnesses and injuries. Most women dealt primarily with ordinary medical problems within their own families. Some, however, acquired reputations as healers and were called on to care for the sick and injured in the community. Professional midwives helped other women give birth, for it was rare in colonial times for a male doctor to attend a woman in childbirth.

Although churches might say that men and women were equal in the eyes of God, they did not offer women an equal role in church affairs. The PURITANS restricted the behavior of women in church, requiring them to sit apart from the men and to remain silent—except for singing hymns. Women who challenged the Puritan order, such as Anne HUTCHINSON and Mary DYER, met with severe punishment from the authorities. The Quakers came closest to giving women an equal role in their church.

African women in the North American colonies generally enjoyed more economic independence than white women did. They often managed to raise their status above that of men. Physically, they worked as hard as men. In the Chesapeake region and the Carolinas, slave women spent long hours planting, tending, and harvesting TOBACCO, corn, and RICE. Those who were not sent to labor in the fields worked as nurses, cooks, and household servants.

Colonial women did enjoy considerable authority among other women and girls in society. Middle-aged and elderly women supervised the lives and behavior of younger women in the community (or meddled in them, as some younger women probably thought). Older women did not hesitate to advise or scold those whose behavior they considered disorderly or misguided. By law, midwives were required to inform authorities about sexual misbehavior, such

Remember: *Words in small capital letters have separate entries, and the index at the end of Volume 4 will guide you to more information on many topics.*

Women in New Netherland enjoyed greater freedom than those in other European colonies. After the English took over the colony, however, women lost many of their rights. This portrait of New York colonist Magdalena Douw (Mrs. Harmen Gansevoort) was painted sometime around 1740.

as testifying as to whether a child was born early or whether an unmarried mother revealed the name of the baby's father during childbirth. In such ways, women exercised authority while also enforcing the shared values of the community.

Dutch Colony. In the Dutch colony of NEW NETHERLAND, the roles and status of women reflected the customs of the Netherlands and also the realities of life in the colony. Women in the Netherlands enjoyed more freedom and equality than women in most other parts of Europe. To some extent, the same was true in the Dutch colony, where women had a legal right to own and inherit property and to conduct business in their own names.

At the same time, conditions in New Netherland were very different from those in the Netherlands, especially in the early years of the colony. From the 1620s to the 1640s, most Dutch settlers were young men without families. Single men greatly outnumbered women, creating both opportunities and problems for women. One benefit for women was that they were highly valued and could choose from a number of possible husbands. But frontier life also had disadvantages. Women lacked security and comfort in the rowdy, disorderly society, and they often had to deal with unwanted advances from men.

After the mid-1640s, the number of families in New Netherland increased, and society became more stable. Women were primarily housewives and mothers, although many participated in family businesses as well. In many cases, girls went to school along with their brothers. Nearly half of the women and girls in the colony could read and write—a considerably higher percentage than in the English colonies.

Women were widely involved in the economy of New Netherland, working as launderers, farmers, brewers, bakers, and traders. One historian has estimated that by 1650 the colony had nearly 200 women whose role in commerce qualified them as traders. Many of these women were widows carrying on their husbands' businesses, but some were single or married women. When the colony came under English rule (and became New York), English laws restricted the role of women, and their participation in trade and crafts declined. As a result, the Dutch women of colonial New York lost many of the economic and social freedoms they had enjoyed in New Netherland.

French Colonies. Both the customs of Native Americans and the traditions of the French settlers influenced the position of women in the colony of NEW FRANCE. Among the Indian allies of the French, women played a variety of roles—acting as interpreters and traders, helping negotiate alliances, and even choosing chieftains. French men who lived among these tribes, particularly on the western frontiers, tended to adopt Indian customs. In the more settled regions of New France, however, French religion, customs, and laws affected the behavior of local Indians. The Indians began to imitate patterns observed in colonial society, where women had a much more limited role.

As in France, the laws and customs of New France gave men dominance over women, but women could own property independently of their husbands. Men controlled the family and the household—the governor of Montreal reminded colonial men in 1650 that "the law established them as lords of their wives." Men also controlled the institutions of government, the church, and

* *magistrate* official with administrative and often judicial functions

the military. New France was run by male governors, judges, magistrates*, military officers, and church officials.

Pioneering people, however, tend to use whatever talent is available, and conditions in New France created some notable exceptions to male dominance. During the early 1600s, the colony remained small, struggling to survive on the edge of a vast wilderness, neglected by the trading companies responsible for it and by the French crown. In these years, religious orders such as the JESUITS took much of the responsibility for ensuring the colony's survival. Several administrators of women's religious orders made important contributions to the colony during this time. Marie de l'Incarnation, a former businesswoman from France, founded a religious school in Quebec that taught both French and Indian girls. She also wrote thousands of letters to people in France, generating interest in the colony and raising money to help support it. Jeanne Mance obtained money from a wealthy French family to build a hospital in Montreal.

Another aspect of life in New France that affected women's roles was the absence of male family members. Military service or the FUR TRADE drew most men away from their homes for substantial periods of time. As many as one-fourth of all men took part in the fur trade. Wives and daughters had to adjust to the absence of their husbands and fathers. Many took on new responsibilities, overseeing farmwork, buying supplies, keeping accounts, or manufacturing trade goods. Men leaving on fur-trading trips often gave their wives the authority to handle business and legal matters while they were gone.

With so many men busy with military affairs or fur-trading expeditions, women in New France entered quite freely into business. Some of the colony's leading fur traders and merchants were women. Several women ran weaving and sewing shops that became the foundation of the colony's textile industry. Others managed enterprises involved in fishing, seal hunting, canoe making, construction, tile making, and iron forging. Women also worked in most family-owned workshops and businesses. Public life was still seen as a man's world, and women were supposed to confine their activities to private or family life. Yet those roles were less sharply separated in New France than in some other societies of the period.

Spanish Borderlands. The Spanish Borderlands—a region that included Florida, Texas, Arizona, New Mexico, and California—occupied the northern frontier of NEW SPAIN. In these provinces, thinly settled throughout much of their history, the social structure was sometimes less rigid than that in Spain and Mexico. Even so, women in the Borderlands still lived in a society strongly shaped by tradition and custom. Women were expected to be obedient daughters, faithful wives, and good Christians. Those who strayed from such conduct risked fines, public scorn, or even banishment as punishment.

Men controlled the public institutions of the Borderlands—the army, government, courts, and church. But Spanish law also guaranteed certain rights to women. They could own property and keep it after marriage, sign legal documents, and make their own wills. Women often went to court to complain of abandonment or mistreatment by their husbands or to settle property disputes.

One of the few ways in which a Spanish woman could gain some degree of independence from the supervision of fathers, brothers, priests, and other males

A Colonial Businesswoman

Louise de Ramezay, the daughter of a governor of Montreal, had four brothers. Three died and the fourth chose a military career. That may explain why Louise, who never married, was able to manage the family's business interests. After her parents died, Louise ran the sawmill on the Ramezay property. With a business partner, also a woman, she opened more mills and a factory in Montreal to tan animal hides. By the 1750s, she was shipping large loads of lumber and expanding the leather business. Colonial women such as Louise de Ramezay proved that good business sense and the ability to make money were not limited to men.

Wright, Patience

* **convent** residence for members of a women's religious order

was to enter a convent*, as many single women and widows did. Fewer women entered convents in the Borderlands than in Mexico, but many lived near Borderland MISSIONS. The tie between women and the church in Spanish America was very strong. Women undertook many of the tasks that kept the missions and churches functioning, from cleaning priests' robes and dusting the altars to plastering the church walls.

Borderlands women also took on responsibilities that helped keep families and households running smoothly, from doing domestic chores to keeping records of their husbands' finances. Widows often kept ranches operating long after husbands had died. Even on the frontier, however, women's lives were governed largely by men and male institutions. While individual women sometimes struggled to move beyond the limits of traditional female roles, most remained bound by custom. (*See also* **Class Structure in European Colonies; Courtship; Family; Gender Roles; Magic and Witchcraft; Marriage.**)

Woolman, John

See *Antislavery Movement.*

Work

See *Indentured Servants; Labor; Slavery.*

Wright, Patience

1725–1786
Sculptor

A talented sculptor, Patience Lovell Wright became famous for her wax portraits of prominent people. During the American Revolution, she was living in England but managed to help the American rebels by providing information on British plans.

Patience Lovell was born to QUAKER parents in Bordentown, New Jersey. As a child, she became interested in wax and clay modeling. She moved to Philadelphia and married Joseph Wright. The couple had three children.

After her husband's death in 1769, Wright created a traveling wax museum featuring models of important public figures. In 1772 she moved to London, where she continued to exhibit her work. Her subjects included people from both history and her own day, such as Benjamin FRANKLIN and King GEORGE III. Prominent members of London society came to her studio to watch her work. Wright's skill, intelligence, and bold personality won her a wide circle of friends. When the Revolutionary War broke out between Britain and the colonies, Wright learned some of the British military plans from friends. A dedicated supporter of American independence, she passed this information on to Franklin, who was then in France.

After the Revolution, Wright planned to return to America and make a series of portraits of the great American leaders. She wrote to Thomas JEFFERSON proposing the idea, but she died in London before she could carry out the project. Her son, Joseph, also became an artist and produced paintings of George WASHINGTON, among other works. (*See also* **Art; American Revolution.**)

Yamassee Indians

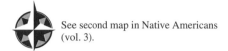

See second map in Native Americans (vol. 3).

he Yamassee, or Guale, Indians were an important southeastern tribe of the colonial period. Mistreated by both the Spanish and the British, the tribe moved several times, settling at various points in Georgia, South Carolina, and Florida.

In the late 1500s, the Spanish established missions among the Yamassee. Mistreatment by the Spanish led many Yamassee to flee to the English colony of South Carolina in the 1680s. There they became trading partners and allies of the English. The Yamassee sometimes worked for the colonists and joined them in fighting the TUSCARORA INDIANS in 1711.

However, the British began to abuse their Yamassee allies. They took their land and often charged the Indians high prices for defective merchandise, then demanded immediate payment for these goods. To settle the debts, British traders captured Yamassee women and children and sold them into slavery.

* **militia** army of citizens who may be called into action in a time of emergency

The Yamassee finally rebelled. On April 15, 1715, they launched a surprise attack in the area of Port Royal, South Carolina, killing 90 colonists and their families. With the help of neighboring tribes, the Indians went on to raid trading posts and plantations throughout the colony in what came to be known as the Yamassee War (1715–1716). To deal with this threat, South Carolina formed a militia* and called for additional troops and supplies from other British colonies. The colonists attacked Yamassee villages and eventually drove the surviving Yamassee southward into Florida, where they settled among other Indians and runaway slaves. From Florida, Yamassee survivors continued to stage raids on South Carolina for the next 15 years. (*See also* **Native Americans; Seminole Indians.**)

Yuma Indians

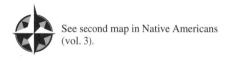

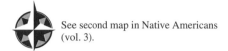

See second map in Native Americans (vol. 3).

he Yuma Indians of southwestern ARIZONA had less contact with Europeans than most tribes. The Spanish did not attempt to settle in Yuma territory until fairly late in the colonial period, and the Indians soon forced them off the land.

Known as the Quechan among themselves, the Yuma lived along the Colorado River not far from the place where the river empties into the Gulf of California. They survived in the area's desert climate by gathering wild foods and planting crops such as corn, beans, and squash, along with some hunting and fishing. They built their homes—wooden frames covered with earth or brush—on high ground to avoid river flooding. Each Yuma village contained several hundred people and had its own leaders and identity. Because of the hot climate, the Yuma put on little clothing. Both men and women generally wore only rawhide sandals and an apron-like cloth around the hips. In cool weather, they added robes of rabbit skin or bark.

The Spanish were the first Europeans to visit the Yuma. In 1540 the explorer Hernando de Alarcón passed through their homeland on his way to meet Francisco Vásques de CORONADO. However, there was little contact between the two peoples for the next 200 years. In 1698 the Jesuit* missionary Eusebio Francisco KINO visited the Indians, but it was not until the 1770s that the Spanish began to establish missions and settlements in Yuma territory.

* **Jesuit** Roman Catholic religious order

The Indians resisted Spanish attempts to convert them to Christianity and to take their land and crops. In 1781 they rebelled, destroying the two Spanish settlements in their region and killing a number of settlers. The Spanish abandoned the area, and the Yuma remained relatively undisturbed until the mid-1800s, when Mexicans and Americans began expanding into the region. (*See also* **Native Americans; Spanish Borderlands.**)

Zenger, John Peter

1697–1746
Colonial printer and journalist

*T*he 1735 trial of newspaper publisher John Peter Zenger—accused of "seditious libel," or criticizing the government—represented an important step toward freedom of the press in America. The Zenger trial also highlighted the special relationship between the press and politics.

Born in Germany, Zenger came to America in 1710 and settled in New York City. After serving an APPRENTICESHIP with a New York printer, he opened his own printing business in 1726. New York was then experiencing political turmoil as two political parties struggled for control of the colonial assembly. In 1732 a new governor, William Cosby, took office. Cosby dismissed Lewis Morris, the leader of one of the parties, from his position as the colony's chief justice. Outraged, Morris and his allies took action.

Backed by Morris and his friends, Zenger published the first issue of the *New-York Weekly Journal* in November 1733. The paper attacked the governor and his policies week after week. In 1734 Cosby had Zenger arrested on the charge of seditious libel, even though he had not written the articles criticizing the governor. Meanwhile, Zenger continued to publish his newspaper from prison in the months before his trial.

Andrew Hamilton, a distinguished lawyer from Philadelphia, defended Zenger in court. The judge in the trial, who supported Cosby, told the jury simply to determine whether Zenger had printed critical statements about the government—it made no difference whether the statements were true or false. Hamilton, however, argued that the jury had the right to decide for themselves whether Zenger had printed truth or lies, and that true statements should not be considered libel. The jury ignored the judge's instructions and found Zenger not guilty.

Although the Zenger trial is regarded as a victory for freedom of the press, the courts did not accept the principle that the press should be free of government censorship for some years. In the meantime, the Zenger case rallied public support for the idea that the press could criticize government authorities and policies, encouraging other printers to do so. Zenger later published his own account of the trial, which circulated widely in the colonies and in Europe. He also served as the official printer for both New York and New Jersey. (*See also* **Press in Colonial America.**)

Zuni Indians

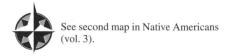

See second map in Native Americans (vol. 3).

*T*he Zuni Indians of western NEW MEXICO were among the first Native Americans in the region to resist Spain's conquering and colonizing forces. They remained in their ancient homeland throughout the colonial period and continued many of their traditions.

The Spanish referred to the villages of the Zuni and related tribes of the Southwest as pueblos. For this reason, these groups became known as the

Zuni Indians

* **clan** related families

PUEBLO INDIANS. Like other Pueblo people, the Zuni were farmers who had mastered the skills needed to grow MAIZE, beans, and squash in the dry climate of the region. Their society was organized in clans*, and clan members traced their ancestry through their mothers. Although the Zuni resembled other Pueblo groups in many ways, they spoke a language unlike any other in North America.

In 1539 a stranger arrived at the Zuni village of Hawikah. He was ESTEBAN, a black man who had survived a long journey through the Southwest with the Spanish explorer Alvar Núñez CABEZA DE VACA and was now serving as guide to a Spanish expedition in search of gold. The Zuni killed Esteban, but his companions returned to Mexico. Their imaginative tales of fabulous cities of gold fueled the legend of the SEVEN CITIES OF CÍBOLA and launched an expedition into New Mexico the following year led by Francisco Vásquez de CORONADO. Coronado and his men raided and pillaged Hawikah and the other Zuni villages, but the Spanish did not establish permanent rule in the region until 1598. In 1680 the Zuni joined the PUEBLO REVOLT against the Spanish. After the Spanish reconquered the region in the 1690s, the Zuni settled in a single village, named Zuni after the tribe. (*See also* **Native Americans.**)

Suggested Sources

Atlases and Encyclopedias

Cappon, Lester J., ed. *Atlas of Early American History: The Revolutionary Era, 1760–1790.* Princeton, N.J.: Princeton University Press, 1976.

Collier, Simon, et al., eds. *The Cambridge Encyclopedia of Latin America and the Caribbean.* Cambridge: Cambridge University Press, 1992.

Cooke, Jacob Ernest, ed. *Encyclopedia of the North American Colonies.* 3 vols. New York: Scribners, 1993.

Delpar, Helen, ed. *Encyclopedia of Latin America.* New York: McGraw-Hill, 1974.

Dictionary of American History. New York: Scribners, 1976.

Farragher, John Mack. *Encyclopedia of Colonial and Revolutionary America.* New York: Facts on File, 1990.

*Garraty, John A., and Jerome L. Sternstein, eds. *Encyclopedia of American Biography.* New York: HarperCollins, 1996.

Harris, R. Cole, and Geoffrey J. Matthews. *Historical Atlas of Canada: The Beginnings to 1800.* Toronto: University of Toronto Press, 1987.

Jackson, Kenneth T., ed. *Atlas of American History.* New York: Scribners, 1984.

———. *Dictionary of American Biography.* New York: Scribners, 1995.

*James, Edward T., and Janet W. James, eds. *Notable American Women, 1607–1950.* Cambridge, Mass.: Belknap, 1973.

Morris, Richard, and Jeffrey Morris, eds. *Encyclopedia of American History.* New York: Harper and Row, 1996.

Trudel, Marcel. *An Atlas of New France.* Quebec: Laval University, 1968.

Voorhees, David W., ed. *Concise Dictionary of American History.* New York: Scribners, 1983.

General Histories

Bannon, John F. *The Spanish Borderlands Frontier, 1513–1821.* Albuquerque: University of New Mexico Press, 1976.

Bethell, Leslie, ed. *Cambridge History of Latin America.* Vol. 1, *Colonial Spanish America.* Cambridge: Cambridge University Press, 1987.

Boxer, C. R. *The Dutch Seaborne Empire, 1600–1800.* New York: Knopf, 1965.

Burkholder, Mark A., and Lyman L. Johnson. *Colonial Latin America.* New York: Oxford University Press, 1990.

* Asterisk denotes book recommended for young readers.

Suggested Sources

*Davis, Kenneth. *Don't Know Much About History.* New York: Avon, 1990.

Eccles, William John. *France in America.* East Lansing: Michigan State University Press, 1990.

Gibson, Charles. *Spain in America.* New York: HarperCollins, 1967.

Haring, Clarence H. *The Spanish Empire in America.* San Diego, Calif.: Harcourt Brace Jovanovich, 1985.

Hawke, David. *The Colonial Experience.* Indianapolis, Ind.: Bobbs-Merrill, 1966.

*Lasky, Kathryn. *A Journey to the New World.* New York: Scholastic, 1996.

MacFarlane, Anthony. *The British in the Americas, 1480–1815.* New York: Longman, 1995.

*Magill, Frank, ed. *Great Events of History: American Series.* Pasadena, Calif.: Salem Press, 1987.

Meinig, Donald W. *The Shaping of America: Atlantic America, 1492–1800.* New Haven, Conn.: Yale University Press, 1986.

Middleton, Richard. *Colonial America, A History, 1607–1760.* Cambridge, Mass.: Blackwell, 1992.

Parry, J. H. *The Spanish Seaborne Empire.* New York: Knopf, 1966.

Reich, Jerome. *Colonial America.* Englewood Cliffs, N.J.: Prentice-Hall, 1994.

*Simmons, Richard C. *The American Colonies from Settlement to Independence.* New York: Norton, 1990.

Ver Steeg, Clarence L. *The Formative Years, 1607–1763.* New York: Hill and Wang, 1964.

Weber, David J. *The Spanish Frontier in North America.* New Haven, Conn.: Yale University Press, 1992.

Primary Sources

*Commager, Henry Steele. *Documents of American History.* Englewood Cliffs, N.J.: Prentice-Hall, 1973.

Demos, John. *Remarkable Providences, 1600–1760.* New York: George Braziller, 1972.

Gibson, Charles, ed. *The Spanish Tradition in America.* New York: Harper and Row, 1968.

Greene, Jack P., ed. *Colonies to Nation, 1763–1789.* New York: Norton, 1975.

———. *Settlements to Society, 1607–1763.* New York: Norton, 1975.

Jameson, Franklin J. *Narratives of New Netherland 1609–1664.* Temecula, Calif.: Reprint Services, 1993.

Jensen, Merrill, ed. *English Historical Documents.* Vol. 9, *American Colonial Documents to 1775.* New York: Oxford University Press, 1955.

Kavenagh, W. Keith, ed. *Foundations of Colonial America: A Documentary History.* 3 vols. New York: Chelsea House, 1973.

Land, Aubrey C., ed. *Bases of the Plantation Society.* New York: Harper and Row, 1969.

*Meltzer, Milton, ed. *The American Revolutionaries: A History in Their Own Words, 1750–1800.* New York: Crowell, 1987.

———. *The Black Americans: A History in Their Own Words.* New York: Crowell, 1984.

*Morris, Richard B., ed. *Voices from America's Past.* Vol. 1, *The Colonies and the New Nation.* New York: Dutton, 1961.

*Nabokov, Peter, ed. *Native American Testimony: An Anthology of Indian and White Relations, First Encounter to Dispossession.* New York: Crowell, 1978.

Schechter, Stephen, ed. *Roots of the Republic: American Founding Documents.* Madison, Wis.: Madison House, 1990.

Thwaites, Reuben G., ed. *The Jesuit Relations and Allied Documents: Travels and Explorations of the Jesuit Missionaries in New France, 1610–1791.* 73 vols. Cleveland, Ohio: Burrows Brothers Company, 1896.

Vaughan, Alden T., ed. *The Puritan Tradition in America, 1620–1730.* Hanover, N.H.: University Press of New England, 1997.

Zoltvany, Yves F., ed. *The French Tradition in America.* Columbia: University of South Carolina Press, 1969.

Biography

Akers, Charles W. *Abigail Adams: An American Woman.* Boston: Little, Brown, 1980.

Alden, John R. *George Washington: A Biography.* Baton Rouge: Louisiana State University Press, 1984.

Beeman, Richard R. *Patrick Henry: A Biography.* New York: McGraw-Hill, 1974.

Cunliffe, Marcus. *George Washington, Man and Monument.* New York: New American Library, 1982.

Cunningham, Noble E., Jr. *In Pursuit of Reason: The Life of Thomas Jefferson.* Baton Rouge: Louisiana State University Press, 1987.

Dunn, Mary M. *William Penn: Politics and Conscience.* Princeton, N.J.: Princeton University Press, 1967.

Dunn, Richard S. *Puritans and Yankees: The Winthrop Dynasty of New England.* Princeton, N.J.: Princeton University Press, 1962.

Eduardo, Paul, ed. *The Life of Olauda Equiano, or Gustavus Vassa, the African.* 2 vols. London: Dawson's, 1969.

*Logan, Rayford W., and Michael R. Winston, eds. *The Dictionary of American Negro Biography.* New York: Norton, 1983.

Martin, James Kirby. *Benedict Arnold, Revolutionary Hero.* New York: New York University Press, 1997.

Middlekauff, Robert. *The Mathers: Three Generations of Puritan Intellectuals, 1596–1721*. New York: Oxford University Press, 1971.

Morgan, Edmund S. *Roger Williams: The Church and the State*. New York: Harcourt Brace World, 1967.

Morison, Samuel Eliot. *Admiral of the Ocean Sea: A Life of Christopher Columbus*. 2 vols. Boston: Little, Brown, 1942.

Rachlis, Eugene, and Henry H. Kessler. *Peter Stuyvesant and His New York*. New York: Random House, 1959.

Smith, Bradford. *Captain John Smith: His Life and Legend*. Philadelphia: Lippincott, 1953.

Wallace, Anthony F. *King of the Delawares: Teedyunscung, 1700–1763*. Syracuse, N.Y.: Syracuse University Press, 1990.

Williams, Selma. *Divine Revel: The Life of Anne Hutchinson*. New York: Holt, Rinehart and Winston, 1981.

Wright, Esmond. *Franklin of Philadelphia*. Cambridge, Mass.: Harvard University Press, 1986.

Exploration and Discovery

Crosby, Alfred W. *The Columbian Exchange: Biological and Cultural Consequences of 1492*. Westport, Conn.: Greenwood, 1972.

Davies, Nigel. *Voyagers to the New World*. New York: William Morrow, 1979.

*Faber, Harold. *The Discoverers of America*. New York: Scribners, 1992.

Fernandez-Armesto, Felipe. *Columbus*. New York: Oxford University Press, 1991.

Innes, Hammond. *The Conquistadors*. New York: Oxford University Press, 1969.

Jennings, Francis. *The Invasion of America: Indians, Colonialism, and the Cant of Conquest*. Chapel Hill: University of North Carolina Press, 1975.

*Lawrence, Bill. *The Early American Wilderness as the Explorers Saw It*. New York: Paragon House, 1991.

Lorant, Stefan, ed. *This New World: The First Pictures of America*. New York: Duell, Sloan, and Pierce, 1965.

Morison, Samuel Eliot. *The European Discovery of America*. 2 vols. New York: Oxford University Press, 1993.

Parry, J. H. *The Age of Reconnaissance*. Berkeley and Los Angeles: University of California Press, 1981.

Sale, Kirkpatrick. *The Conquest of Paradise: Christopher Columbus and the Columbian Legacy*. Cambridge: Cambridge University Press, 1990.

*Smith, Carter C. *The Explorers and Settlers: A Sourcebook on Colonial America*. Brookfield, Conn.: Millbrook, 1991.

Wahlgreen, Erik. *The Vikings and America*. New York: Thames and Hudson, 1986.

Zvi, Dor-Ner. *Columbus and the Age of Discovery*. New York: William Morrow, 1991.

The Settlements

Bailyn, Bernard. *The Peopling of British North America*. New York: Vintage Books, 1988.

Bradford, William. *Bradford's History "Of Plymouth Plantation" from the Original Manuscript*. Bowie, Md.: Heritage Books, 1990.

Crane, Verner. *The Southern Frontier, 1670–1732*. Durham, N.C.: Duke University Press, 1928.

Craven, Wesley Frank. *The Colonies in Transition, 1660–1713*. New York: Harper and Row, 1968.

———. *The Southern Colonies in the Seventeenth Century*. Baton Rouge: Louisiana State University Press, 1946.

*Dougherty, James. *The Landing of the Pilgrims*. New York: Random House, 1987.

Eccles, William J. *The Canadian Frontier, 1534–1760*. Albuquerque: University of New Mexico Press, 1983.

*Faber, Doris, and Harold Faber. *The Birth of a Nation: The Early Years of the United States*. New York: Scribners, 1989.

*Hakim, Joy. *Making Thirteen Colonies*. New York: Oxford University Press, 1993.

Klein, Milton, and Jacob E. Cooke, eds. *A History of the American Colonies*. 13 vols. New York: Scribners; Millwood, N.Y.: KTO Press, 1973–1986.

Lowery, Woodbury. *The Spanish Settlements Within the Present Limits of the United States*. New York: Russell and Russell, 1959.

Miquelon, Dale. *New France, 1701 to 1744*. Toronto: McClelland and Stewart, 1987.

Pomfret, John L., and Floyd M. Shumway. *Founding the American Colonies, 1583–1660*. New York: Harper and Row, 1970.

Rink, Oliver. *Holland on the Hudson: An Economic and Social History of Dutch New York*. Ithaca, N.Y.: Cornell University Press, 1985.

Stanley, George F. *New France: The Last Phase, 1744–1760*. Toronto: McClelland and Stewart, 1968.

Trudel, Marcel. *The Beginnings of New France, 1526–1663*. Toronto: McClelland and Stewart, 1973.

Van der Donck, Adriaen. *A Description of the New Netherlands*. Syracuse, N.Y.: Syracuse University Press, 1968.

Whitaker, Arthur P. *The Spanish-American Frontier, 1783–1795*. Lincoln: University of Nebraska Press, 1969.

Government and Politics

Bailyn, Bernard. *Origins of American Politics*. New York: Random House, 1970.

Dargo, George. *Roots of the Republic: A New Perspective on Early American Constitutionalism*. New York: Praeger, 1974.

Suggested Sources

Dickerson, Oliver M. *American Colonial Government, 1696–1765.* New York: Russell and Russell, 1962.

Dinkin, Robert J. *Voting in Provincial America: A Study of Elections in the Thirteen Colonies, 1680–1776.* Westport, Conn.: Greenwood, 1977.

Greene, Jack P. *The Quest for Power: The Lower Houses of Assembly in the Southern Royal Colonies, 1689–1776.* Chapel Hill: University of North Carolina Press, 1963.

Greene, Jack P., ed. *Great Britain and the American Colonies, 1606–1763.* Columbia: University of South Carolina Press, 1970.

Hoffer, Peter. *Law and People in Colonial America.* Baltimore, Md.: Johns Hopkins University Press, 1992.

Labaree, Leonard W. *Royal Government in America.* New York: F. Ungar, 1958.

Lutz, Donald S. *The Origins of American Constitutionalism.* Baton Rouge: Louisiana State University Press, 1988.

Martin, Cheryl E. *Governance and Society in Colonial Mexico: Chihuahua in the Eighteenth Century.* Stanford, Calif.: Stanford University Press, 1996.

Morgan, Edmund S. *Inventing the People: The Rise of Popular Sovereignty in England and America.* New York: Norton, 1988.

Olson, Alison G. *Anglo-American Politics, 1660–1775.* New York: Oxford University Press, 1973.

Parry, John H. *The Spanish Theory of Empire in the Sixteenth Century.* Cambridge: Cambridge University Press, 1940.

Williamson, Chilton. *American Suffrage: From Property to Democracy, 1760–1860.* Princeton, N.J.: Princeton University Press, 1960.

The Economy

Bailyn, Bernard. *The New England Merchants in the Seventeenth Century.* Cambridge, Mass.: Harvard University Press, 1979.

Barrow, Thomas C. *Trade and Empire: The British Customs Service in Colonial America, 1660–1775.* Cambridge, Mass.: Harvard University Press, 1967.

Bosher, John F. *The Canada Merchants, 1713–1763.* New York: Oxford University Press, 1987.

Bruchey, Stuart. *The Roots of American Economic Growth, 1607–1801.* New York: Harper and Row, 1968.

Condon, Thomas J. *New York Beginnings: The Commercial Origins of New Netherland.* New York: New York University Press, 1968.

Ekirch, A. Roger. *Bound for America: The Transportation of Convicts to the Colonies, 1718–1775.* New York: Oxford University Press, 1987.

Ernst, Joseph H. *Money and Politics in America, 1755–1775.* Chapel Hill: University of North Carolina Press, 1973.

Innes, Stephen, ed. *Work and Labor in Early America.* Chapel Hill: University of North Carolina Press, 1988.

Innis, Harold A. *The Fur Trade in Canada: An Introduction to Canadian Economic History.* New Haven, Conn.: Yale University Press, 1962.

McCusker, John J., and Russel R. Menard. *The Economy of British America, 1607–1789.* Chapel Hill: University of North Carolina Press, 1991.

Perkins, Edwin J. *The Economy of Colonial America.* New York: Columbia University Press, 1988.

Rediker, Marcus. *Between the Devil and the Deep Blue Sea: Merchant Seamen, Pirates, and the Anglo-American World, 1700–1750.* Cambridge: Cambridge University Press, 1987.

Smith, Abbot E. *Colonists in Bondage: White Servitude and Convict Labor in America, 1607–1776.* Magnolia, Mass.: Peter Smith, 1965.

Walker, Geoffrey G. *Spanish Politics and Imperial Trade, 1700–1789.* Bloomington: Indiana University Press, 1979.

Walton, Gary M., and James F. Shepherd. *The Economic Rise of Early America.* Cambridge: Cambridge University Press, 1979.

Daily Life

Andrews, Charles M. *Colonial Folkways: A Chronicle of Everyday Life in Early America.* New York: United States Publishers' Association, 1975.

Carson, Cary, et al., eds. *Of Consuming Interests: The Style of Life in the Eighteenth Century.* Charlottesville: University Press of Virginia, 1979.

Cross, Gary. *A Social History of Leisure Since 1600.* State College: Pennsylvania State University Press, 1990.

Dulles, Foster Rhea. *America Learns to Play: A History of Popular Recreation: 1607–1940.* New York: Appleton Century, 1940.

Durant, John, and Otto Bettman. *Pictorial History of American Sports, From Colonial Times to the Present.* Cranbury, N.J.: A. S. Barnes, 1965.

*Earle, Alice Morse. *Home Life in Colonial Days.* Stockbridge, Mass.: Berkshire Traveller Press, 1992.

Fischer, David Hackett. *Albion's Seed: Four British Folkways in America.* New York: Oxford University Press, 1989.

Franklin, Benjamin. *Poor Richard's Almanack.* Temecula, Calif.: Reprint Services, 1993.

Gilbert, Fabiola Cabeza de Baca. *The Good Life: New Mexico Traditions and Food.* Santa Fe: Museum of New Mexico Press, 1982.

Greer, Allan. *Peasant, Lord, and Merchant: Rural Society in Three Quebec Parishes, 1740–1840.* Toronto: University of Toronto Press, 1985.

*Hawke, David Freeman. *Everyday Life in Early America.* New York: Harper and Row, 1988.

*Hooker, Richard J. *Food and Drink in America: A History.* Indianapolis, Ind.: Bobbs-Merrill, 1981.

Knight, Sarah Kemble. *The Journal of Madam Knight.* Temecula, Calif.: Reprint Services, 1991.

*Langdon, William Chauncy. *Everyday Things in American Life, 1607–1776.* New York: Scribners, 1937.

*————. *Everyday Things in American Life, 1776–1878.* New York: Scribners, 1941.

*Loeper, John J. *Going to School in 1776.* New York: Atheneum, 1975.

*McGovern, Ann. *If You Lived in Colonial Times.* New York: Scholastic, 1992.

Rice, Kym S. *Early American Taverns, for Entertainment of Friends and Strangers.* Chicago, Ill.: Regency Gateway, 1983.

*Smith, Carter C. *Daily Life: A Sourcebook on Colonial America.* Brookfield, Conn.: Millbrook, 1991.

Wolf, Stephanie Grauman. *As Various as Their Land: The Everyday Lives of Eighteenth Century Americans.* New York: HarperCollins, 1993.

Religious Life

Balmer, Randall H. *A Perfect Babel of Confusion: Dutch Religion and English Culture in the Middle Colonies.* New York: Oxford University Press, 1989.

Bonomi, Patricia U. *Under the Cope of Heaven: Religion, Society, and Politics in Colonial America.* New York: Oxford University Press, 1986.

Demos, John. *Entertaining Satan: Witchcraft and the Culture of Early New England.* New York: Oxford University Press, 1982.

Ellis, John T. *Catholics in Colonial America.* Baltimore, Md.: Helicon, 1965.

Gaustad, Edwin S. *Historical Atlas of Religion in America.* New York: Harper and Row, 1976.

*————. *Religion in America.* North Stratford, N.H.: Ayer, 1979.

Heimert, Alan, and Perry Miller, eds. *The Great Awakening.* Indianapolis, Ind.: Bobbs-Merrill, 1967.

Jaenen, Cornelius J. *The Role of the Church in New France.* New York: McGraw-Hill, 1976.

Lippy, Charles H., and Peter W. Williams, eds. *Encyclopedia of the American Religious Experience.* New York: Scribners, 1987.

Marcus, Jacob R. *The Colonial American Jew, 1492–1776.* 3 vols. Detroit, Mich.: Wayne State University Press, 1963.

Mather, Cotton. *The Great Works of Christ in America: Magnalia Christi Americana of the Ecclesiastical History of New England.* Edinburgh: Banner of Truth, 1979.

Morgan, Edmund S. *Visible Saints: The History of a Puritan Idea.* New York: New York University Press, 1963.

O'Neill, Charles E. *Church and State in French Colonial Louisiana.* New Haven, Conn.: Yale University Press, 1966.

Tolles, Frederick B. *Quakers and the Atlantic Culture.* New York: Macmillan, 1960.

Woolverton, John F. *Colonial Anglicanism in North America.* Cambridge, Mass.: Harvard University Press, 1984.

Women, Gender, and the Family

Berkin, Carol. *First Generations: Women in Colonial America.* New York: Hill and Wang, 1996.

Bradstreet, Anne. *The Tenth Muse Lately Sprung Up in America.* Temecula, Calif.: Reprint Services, 1989.

Demos, John. *A Little Commonwealth—Family Life in Plymouth Colony.* Magnolia, Mass.: Peter Smith, 1988.

Dumont-Johnson, Micheline. *Quebec Women—A History.* Toronto: Women's Press, 1987.

Fabend, Firth H. *A Dutch Family in the Middle Colonies, 1660–1800.* New Brunswick, N.J.: Rutgers University Press, 1991.

Frost, J. William. *The Quaker Family in Colonial America.* New York: St. Martin's Press, 1973.

*Glubok, Shirley, ed. *Home and Child Life in Colonial Days.* New York: Macmillan, 1969.

Gunderson, Joan. *To Be Useful to the World: Women in Revolutionary America, 1740–1790.* New York: Twayne Publishers, 1996.

Morgan, Edmund S. *The Puritan Family: Religion and Domestic Relations in Seventeenth-Century New England.* Westport, Conn.: Greenwood, 1980.

————. *Virginians at Home: Family Life in the Eighteenth Century.* Williamsburg, Va.: Colonial Williamsburg Foundation, 1952.

Norton, Mary Beth. *Founding Mothers and Fathers: Gendered Power and the Forming of American Society.* New York: Random House, 1996.

*Salmon, Marylynn. *The Limits of Independence: American Women, 1760–1800.* New York: Oxford University Press, 1994.

Wall, Helena M. *Fierce Communion: Family and Community in Early America.* Cambridge, Mass.: Harvard University Press, 1990.

*Zeinert, Karen. *Those Remarkable Women of the American Revolution.* Brookfield, Conn.: Millbrook, 1996.

African Americans

*Asante, Molefi, and Mark T. Mattson. *Historical and Cultural Atlas of African-Americans.* New York: Macmillan, 1991.

Berlin, Ira, and Ronald Hoffman, eds. *Slavery and Freedom in the Age of the American Revolution.* Urbana: University of Illinois Press, 1986.

Suggested Sources

*Davis, Burke. *Black Heroes of the American Revolution.* San Diego, Calif.: Harcourt Brace Jovanovich, 1991.

Frey, Sylvia R. *Water from the Rock: Black Resistance in a Revolutionary Age.* Princeton, N.J.: Princeton University Press, 1991.

Gomez, Michael A. *The Transformation of African Identities in the Colonial and Antebellum South.* Chapel Hill: University of North Carolina Press, 1998.

Hall, Gwendolyn M. *Africans in Colonial Louisiana: The Development of Afro-Creole Culture in the Eighteenth Century.* Baton Rouge: Louisiana State University Press, 1992.

Higginbotham, A. Leon, Jr. *In the Matter of Color: Race and the American Legal Process, the Colonial Period.* New York: Oxford University Press, 1978.

*Hine, Darlene C., et al., eds. *Black Women in America: An Historical Encyclopedia.* Brooklyn, N.Y.: Carlson, 1993.

Jordan, Winthrop D. *White over Black: American Attitudes toward the Negro, 1550–1812.* Chapel Hill: University of North Carolina Press, 1968.

Kaplan, Sidney. *The Black Presence in the Era of the American Revolution.* Amherst: University of Massachusetts Press, 1989.

*Katz, William Loren. *Proudly Red and Black: Stories of African and Native Americans.* New York: Atheneum, 1993.

*Littlefield, Daniel C. *Revolutionary Citizens: African Americans, 1776–1804.* New York: Oxford University Press, 1997.

*Low, W. A., and Virgil A. Clift, eds. *Encyclopedia of Black America.* New York: Da Capo Press, 1984.

*Mabunda, L. Mpho, ed. *The African-American Almanac.* 7th edition. Detroit, Mich.: Gale, 1996.

Mannix, Daniel P., and Malcolm Cowley. *Black Cargoes: A History of the Atlantic Slave Trade.* New York: Viking, 1962.

McMannus, Edgar J. *Black Bondage in the North.* Syracuse, N.Y.: Syracuse University Press, 1973.

Nash, Gary B. *Red, White, and Black: The Peoples of Early America.* Englewood Cliffs, N.J.: Prentice-Hall, 1991.

*Porter, Dorothy, ed. *Early Negro Writing, 1760–1837.* Boston: Beacon, 1971.

*Salem, Dorothy C., ed. *African American Women.* New York: Garland, 1993.

*Salzman, Jack, ed. *Encyclopedia of African-American Culture and History.* New York: Macmillan, 1996.

Soderlund, Jean R. *Quakers and Slavery: A Divided Spirit.* Princeton, N.J.: Princeton University Press, 1985.

Wheatley, Phillis. *Poems on Various Subjects, Religious and Moral.* New York: AMS Press, 1976.

*Wood, Peter H. *Strange New Land: African Americans, 1617–1776.* New York: Oxford University Press, 1996.

Native Americans

Calloway, Colin. *The American Revolution in Indian Country: Crisis and Diversity in Native American Communities.* New York: Cambridge University Press, 1995.

———. *New Worlds for All: Indians, Europeans, and the Remaking of Early America.* Baltimore, Md.: Johns Hopkins University Press, 1997.

*Capps, Benjamin. *The Indians.* New York: Time-Life, 1973.

Cronon, William. *Changes in the Land: Indians, Colonists, and the Ecology of New England.* New York: Hill and Wang, 1983.

Fagan, Brian. *Ancient North America: The Archaeology of a Continent.* New York: Thames Hudson, 1995.

*Fritz, Jean. *The Double Life of Pocahontas.* New York: Putnam, 1983.

*Griffin-Pierce, Trudy. *The Encyclopedia of Native America.* New York: Penguin, 1995.

Hoxie, Frederick E., ed. *Encyclopedia of North American Indians.* New York: Houghton Mifflin, 1996.

*Jones, Constance. *The European Conquest of North America.* New York: Facts on File, 1995.

*Josephy, Alvin M. *The Indian Heritage of America.* New York: Houghton Mifflin, 1991.

Knaut, Andrew. *The Pueblo Revolt of 1680: Conquest and Resistance in Seventeenth-Century New Mexico.* Norman, Okla.: University of Oklahoma Press, 1995.

*May, Robin. *Indians.* Reading, Pa.: Exeter House, 1983.

Merrell, James. *The Indians' New World: Catawbas and Their Neighbors from European Contact Through the Era of Removal.* Chapel Hill: University of North Carolina Press, 1989.

*Nardo, Don. *The Indian Wars.* San Diego, Calif.: Lucent, 1991.

Richter, Daniel. *The Ordeal of the Longhouse: The Peoples of the Iroquois League in the Era of European Colonization.* Chapel Hill: University of North Carolina Press, 1992.

*Rosenstiel, Annette. *Red and White: Indian Views of the White Man.* New York: Universe, 1983

Rowlandson, Mary. *The Narrative of the Captivity, Suffering, and Removes of Mrs. Mary Rowlandson.* Temecula, Calif.: Reprint Services, 1991.

Salisbury, Neal. *Manitou and Providence: Indians, Europeans, and the Making of New England.* New York: Oxford University Press, 1984.

Steele, Ian. *Warpaths: Invasions of North America, 1513–1765.* New York: Oxford University Press, 1995.

*Stuart, Paul. *Nation Within a Nation: Historical Statistics of American Indians.* Westport, Conn.: Greenwood, 1987.

*Weatherford, Jack. *Native Roots: How the Indians Enriched America.* New York: Fawcett-Columbine, 1991.

Art and Culture

Bailyn, Bernard. *Education in the Forming of American Society.* Chapel Hill: University of North Carolina Press, 1960.

Blackburn, Roderic H. *Remembrance of Patria: Dutch Arts and Culture in Colonial America, 1609–1776.* Albany, N.Y.: Albany Institute of History and Art, 1988.

Bunting, Bainbridge. *Early Architecture in New Mexico.* Albuquerque: University of New Mexico Press, 1976.

Bushman, Richard. *The Refinement of America.* New York: Knopf, 1992.

Copeland, David A. *Colonial American Newspapers: Character and Content.* Newark: University of Delaware Press, 1997.

Cremin, Lawrence A. *American Education: The Colonial Experience, 1607–1783.* New York: Harper and Row, 1970.

*Fitzpatrick, Shanon. *American Artist Volume III: Revolutionary Times.* Cypress, Calif.: Creative Teaching Press, 1994.

Flexner, James Thomas. *American Painting: First Flowers of Our Wilderness.* New York: Riverside Press, 1947.

Grizzard, Mary. *Spanish Colonial Art and Architecture of Mexico and the U.S. Southwest.* Lanham, Md.: University Press of America, 1986.

Kimball, Fiske. *Domestic Architecture of the American Colonies and of the Early Republic.* New York: Dover, 1966.

Rankin, Hugh F. *The Colonial Theater: Its History and Operations.* Chapel Hill: University of North Carolina Press, 1955.

Wright, Louis B. *The Arts in America: The Colonial Period.* New York: Scribners, 1966.

———. *The Cultural Life of the American Colonies, 1607–1763.* New York: Harper and Row, 1957.

Science, Medicine, and Technology

Bedini, Silvo. *Thinkers and Tinkers: Early American Men of Science.* New York: Scribners, 1975.

Bridenbaugh, Carl. *The Colonial Craftsman.* New York: Dover, 1990.

Cohen, Bernard. *Benjamin Franklin's Science.* Cambridge, Mass.: Harvard University Press, 1966.

———. *Science and the Founding Fathers.* New York: Norton, 1997.

Engstrand, Iris H. W. *Spanish Scientists in the New World: The Eighteenth-Century Expeditions.* Seattle: University of Washington Press, 1981.

*Gillispie, Charles C., ed. *Dictionary of Scientific Biography.* New York: Scribners, 1981.

Gordon, Maurice B. *Aesculapius Comes to the Colonies: The Story of the Early Days of Medicine in the Thirteen Original Colonies.* Ventnor, N.J.: Ventnor, 1949.

Hindle, Brooke. *The Pursuit of Science in Revolutionary America, 1735–1789.* New York: Norton, 1974.

Numbers, Ronald L. *Medicine in the New World: New Spain, New France, and New England.* Knoxville: University of Tennessee Press, 1987.

Shryock, Richard H. *Medicine and Society in America, 1660–1860.* Ithaca, N.Y.: Cornell University Press, 1962.

*Smith, Carter, ed. *The Arts and Sciences: A Sourcebook on Colonial America.* Brookfield, Conn.: Millbrook, 1991.

Stearns, Raymond P. *Science in the British Colonies of America.* Urbana: University of Illinois Press, 1970.

From Colonies to Independent States

Alden, John. *The American Revolution, 1775–1783.* New York: Harper and Row, 1954.

Andrews, Charles M. *The Colonial Background of the American Revolution.* New Haven, Conn.: Yale University Press, 1931.

Anna, Timothy E. *The Fall of the Royal Government in Mexico City.* Lincoln: University of Nebraska Press, 1978.

———. *Spain and the Loss of America.* Lincoln: University of Nebraska Press, 1983.

Bailyn, Bernard. *The Ideological Origins of the American Revolution.* Cambridge, Mass.: Harvard University Press, 1967.

Becker, Carl. *The Declaration of Independence.* New York: Knopf, 1942.

*Carter, Alden R. *The American Revolution: War for Independence.* New York: Franklin Watts, 1992.

———. *Birth of the Republic.* New York: Franklin Watts, 1988.

*Coffey, Vincent J. *The Battle of Gettysburg.* Parsippany, N.J.: Silver Burdett, 1985.

Dickerson, Oliver M. *The Navigation Acts and the American Revolution.* New York: Octagon, 1974.

*Dudley, William, ed. *The American Revolution.* San Diego, Calif.: Greenhaven, 1992.

*Fischer, David Hackett. *Paul Revere's Ride.* New York: Oxford University Press, 1994.

*Gay, Kathlyn, and Martin Gay. *Revolutionary War: Voices from the Past.* New York: Twenty-First Century Books, 1995.

Hawke, David. *A Transaction of Free Men: The Birth and Course of the Declaration of Independence.* New York: Scribners, 1964.

*Johnson, Neil. *The Battle of Lexington and Concord.* New York: Simon and Schuster Children's, 1992.

*Kent, Deborah. *The American Revolution: "Give Me Liberty or Give Me Death."* Springfield, N.J.: Enslow, 1994.

Knollenberg, Bernhard. *Origin of the American Revolution, 1759–1766.* New York: Macmillan, 1960.

Suggested Sources

Lanctot, Gustave. *Canada and the American Revolution, 1774–1783.* Cambridge, Mass.: Harvard University Press, 1967.

*Lukes, Bonnie L. *The American Revolution.* San Diego, Calif.: Lucent, 1996.

Lynch, John. *The Spanish American Revolutions, 1808–1826.* New York: Norton, 1986.

Maier, Pauline. *American Scripture: Making the Declaration of Independence.* New York: Knopf, 1997.

*Nardo, Don. *The Revolutionary War.* San Diego, Calif.: Greenhaven Press, 1998.

Neatby, Hilda. *Quebec: The Revolutionary Age, 1760–1791.* Toronto: McClelland and Stewart, 1966.

*Nebenzhal, Kenneth. *Atlas of the American Revolution.* Skokie, Ill.: Rand McNally, 1974.

Paine, Thomas. *Common Sense.* New York: Penguin, 1982.

Ritcheson, Charles R. *British Politics and the American Revolution.* Norman: University of Oklahoma Press, 1954.

Rodriguez, Jaime E., ed. *The Independence of Mexico and the Creation of the New Nation.* Berkeley and Los Angeles: University of California Press, 1989.

Shy, John. *Toward Lexington: The Role of the British Army in the Coming of the American Revolution.* Princeton, N.J.: Princeton University Press, 1965.

*Smith, Carter C. *The Revolutionary War: A Sourcebook on Colonial America.* Brookfield, Conn.: Millbrook, 1991.

*Stokesbury, James L. *A Short History of the American Revolution.* New York: William Morrow, 1991.

*Tebbel, John. *Turning the World Upside Down: Inside the American Revolution.* New York: Crown, 1993.

Ubbelohde, Carl. *The American Colonies and the British Empire, 1607–1763.* Northbrook, Ill.: AHM Publishing, 1975.

———. *The Vice-Admiralty Courts and the American Revolution.* Chapel Hill: University of North Carolina Press, 1960.

Warren, Mercy Otis. *History of the Rise, Progress, and Termination of the American Revolution.* Indianapolis, Ind.: Liberty Fund, 1989.

On-Line Resources

1492: An Ongoing Voyage
http://www.apva.org/history/index.htm

The American Experience: A Midwife's Tale
http://www.pbs.org/wgbh/pages/amex/midwife/transcript.html

Biographies of Colonial Figures
http://odur.let.rug.nl/~usa/B/

A Chronology of Historical Documents
http://www.law.uoknor.edu/ushist.htm

"Cleanse not Your Teeth With the Tablecloth..." and other entries from *Rules of Civility and Decent Behaviour in Company and Conversation: a Book of Etiquette* transcribed by George Washington around 1744
http://www.history.org/life/manners/rules2.htm

Colonial African-American Life
http://www.pbs.org/williamsburg/slavenomore/aalife.html

"Colored Patriots" of the Revolution
http://www.seacostnh.com/blackhistory/patriots.html#nh

Crime, Punishment, and Juvenile Justice in Colonial Virginia
http://www.amberwav.com/cwfeft/justice.html

Cultural Readings: Colonization and Print in the Americas Books, manuscripts, maps, and pictures published in Europe to introduce the New World to Europeans
http://www.library.upenn.edu/special/gallery/kislak/index/intro.html

Declaration of Independence Exhibit
http://lcweb.loc.gov/exhibits/declara/declara1.html

The Early America History Archive
http://earlyamerica.com

The Early America History Archive: The Adventures of Daniel Boone
http://earlyamerica.com/lives/boone/index.htm

The Early America History Archive Interactive Crossword Puzzle
http://earlyamerica.com/crossword/index.htm

The Historical Text Archive
http://www.msstate.edu/Archives/History/USA/colonial/colonial.html

The Illustrating Traveler: Adventure and Illustration in North America and the Caribbean, 1760–1895 (exhibition at Yale's Beinecke Rare Book and Manuscript Library)
http://www.library.yale.edu/beinecke/illus.htm

The Mayflower Web Page
http://members.aol.com/mayflo1620/welcome.htm

Olaudah Equiano's Narrative of the Middle Passage
http://vi.uh.edu/pages/mintz/6.htm

Plymouth, Massachusetts: Its History and People
http://pilgrims.net/plymouth/history/index.htm

Revolution Links
http://revolution.h-net.msu.edu/links/

The Role of African Americans in the American Revolution
http://www.ilt.columbia.edu/k12/history/blacks/blacks.html

Salem Witches
http://www.nationalgeographic.com/features/97/salem/splash.html

Virtual Jamestown
http://www.virtualjamestown.com/courts.html

Witches in Salem and Elsewhere
http://www.salemweb.com/witches.htm

Photo Credits

Volume 1

Color Plates

for *Daily Life* between pages 110 and 111:

1: From the collections of the Henry Ford Museum and Greenfield Village; **2:** K. A. Lamb, *The Departure,* oil on canvas, 32 × 47⅝ inches, 1969.7, partial gift of Patrick Morgan, © Addison Gallery of American Art, Phillips Academy, Andover, MA; **3:** The Granger Collection, New York; **4:** *(detail)* Lester Garland, Dorset County Museum, Dorchester, Dorset, England; **5:** *(detail)* Wesley Chapel Museum at the John Street Methodist Church, New York City; **6:** National Gallery of Canada, Ottawa; **7:** North Wind Picture Archives

Black-and-White Photographs

3: National Archives of Canada; **5:** North Wind Picture Archives; **8:** North Wind Picture Archives; **10:** Library of Congress/Corbis; **14:** Library of Congress; **20:** North Wind Picture Archives; **29:** The Historical Society of Pennsylvania; **35:** The Historical Society of Pennsylvania; **40:** Library of Congress; **43:** North Wind Picture Archives; **46:** Library of Congress; **49:** Library of Congress; **53:** North Carolina Museum of Art/Corbis; **54:** National Gallery of Canada, Ottawa; **57:** North Wind Picture Archives; **62:** *(detail)* Library of Congress; **65:** American Heritage Publishing Company; **70:** North Wind Picture Archives; **73:** North Wind Picture Archives; **75:** I.N. Phelps Stokes Collection, Miriam and Ira D. Wallach Division of Art, Prints, and Photographs, The New York Public Library, Astor, Lenox and Tilden Foundations; **79:** Culver Pictures; **80:** North Wind Picture Archives; **81:** North Wind Picture Archives; **83:** Library of Congress; **89:** Library of Congress; **90:** North Wind Picture Archives; **94:** Library of Congress; **97:** North Wind Picture Archives; **102:** North Wind Picture Archives; **110:** Library of Congress; **112:** Library of Congress; **119:** Peter Harholdt/Corbis; **124:** North Wind Picture Archives; **127:** Library of Congress; **130:** Library of Congress; **134:** Francis G. Mayer/Corbis; **137:** National Archives of Canada; **143:** North Wind Picture Archives; **144:** *(detail)* Wesley Chapel Museum at the John Street Methodist Church, New York City; **146:** Historical Picture Archive/Corbis; **149:** North Wind Picture Archives; **153:** *(detail)* Library of Congress; **154:** North Wind Picture Archives; **162:** North Wind Picture Archives; **167:** North Wind Picture Archives; **174:** The Valley Forge Historical Society; **177:** Library of Congress; **181:** North Wind Picture Archives; **185:** Gift of Joseph W. Revere, William B. Revere, and Edward H. R. Revere, Courtesy of Museum of Fine Arts, Boston; **188:** North Wind Picture Archives; **197:** North Wind Picture Archives; **200:** Library of Congress; **203:** Library of Congress; **206:** The New York Academy of Medicine; **211:** The Colonial Williamsburg Foundation; **216:** Library of Congress; **220:** North Wind Picture Archives

Volume 2

Color Plates

for *Art and Architecture* between pages 118 and 119:

1: © Museum of New Mexico Collections in the Museum of International Folk Art, Santa Fe, photo by Blair Clark; **2:** Rare Books Division, The New York Public Library, Astor, Lenox and Tilden Foundations; **3:** North Wind Picture Archives; **4:** Courtesy of Abby Aldrich Rockefeller Folk Art Center, Williamsburg, VA; **5:** National Archives of Canada; **6:** Museum of Fine Arts, Boston, Gift of a Friend of the Department of American Decorative Arts and Sculpture, A Supporter of the Department of American Decorative Arts and Sculpture, William Francis Warden Fund, Barbara L. and Theodore B. Alfond, Samuel A. Otis, Harriet Otis Craft Fund, Otis Norcross Fund, Susan Cornelia Warren Fund, Arthur Tracy Cabot Fund, Seth K. Sweetser Fund, Edwin E. Jack Fund, Helen B. Sweeney Fund, William E. Nickerson Fund, Arthur Mason Knapp Fund, Samuel Putnam Avery Fund, Benjamin P. Cheney Fund, and Mary L. Smith Fund; **7:** Darryl Kestler

Black-and-White Photographs

3: Library of Congress; **8:** North Wind Picture Archives; **11:** Library of Congress; **20:** *(detail)* Library of Congress; **28:** Library of Congress; **32:** North Carolina Division of Archives and History, Department of Cultural Resources, Raleigh, NC; **38:** Library of Congress; **40:** Library of Congress; **42:** © Collection of the New-York Historical Society; **45:** *(detail)* New York State Historical Association, Cooperstown; **51:** Corbis; **55:** North Wind Picture Archives; **57:** Historic Urban Plans, Inc., Ithaca, NY; **61:** North Wind Picture Archives; **62:** Gibbes Museum of Art/Carolina Art Association; **65:** *(detail)* Library of Congress; **68:** Library of Congress; **71:** North Wind Picture Archives; **76:** *(detail)* Library of Congress; **87:** *(detail)* The Granger Collection, New York; **91:** *(detail)* Library of Congress; **95:** Library of Congress/Corbis; **98:** National Archives of Canada; **101:** Library of Congress; **103:** Library of Congress; **106:** *(detail)* Library of Congress; **111:** The Colonial Williamsburg Foundation; **118:** Library of Congress; **120:** Library of Congress; **123:** North Wind Picture Archives; **131:** *(detail)* Print Collection, Miriam and Ira D. Wallach Division of Art, Prints and Photographs, The New York Public Library, Astor, Lenox and Tilden Foundations; **132:** Library of Congress; **135:** North Wind Picture Archives; **137:** North Wind Picture Archives; **139:** Courtesy of National Museum of the American Indian, Smithsonian Institution, #23/2758; **142:** North Wind Picture Archives; **147:** North Wind Picture Archives; **150:** *(detail)* Library of Congress; **153:** Corbis; **156:** Rare Books Division, The New York Public Library, Astor, Lenox and Tilden Foundations; **160:** Library of Congress; **165:** The Patrick Henry Memorial

Photo Credits

Foundation, Brookneal, VA; **166:** Library of Congress; **171:** Library of Congress; **173:** *(detail)* Arents Collections, The New York Public Library, Astor, Lenox and Tilden Foundations; **176:** Library of Congress; **181:** Courtesy of A. H. Robins Co., Richmond, VA; **185:** Library of Congress; **188:** © Photography by John T. Hopf; **194:** *(detail)* Library of Congress; **198:** *(detail)* Arents Collections, The New York Public Library, Astor, Lenox and Tilden Foundations; **202:** I.N. Phelps Stokes Collection, Miriam and Ira D. Wallach Division of Art, Prints and Photographs, The New York Public Library, Astor, Lenox and Tilden Foundations; **205:** *(detail)* Library of Congress; **215:** *(detail)* North Wind Picture Archives; **216:** Corbis; **222:** *(detail)* National Portrait Gallery, Washington, DC/Art Resource, New York; **224:** North Wind Picture Archives

Volume 3

Color Plates

for *People* between pages 118 and 119:

1: National Portrait Gallery, Smithsonian Institution/Art Resource, New York; **2:** National Portrait Gallery, London/SuperStock; **3:** The Bancroft Library, University of California, Berkeley; **4:** National Portrait Gallery, Smithsonian Institution/Art Resource, New York; **5:** Courtesy of Abby Aldrich Rockefeller Folk Art Center, Williamsburg, VA; **6:** The Granger Collection, New York; **7:** *(detail)* The Historical Society of Pennsylvania

Black-and-White Photographs

2: *(detail)* Library of Congress; **9:** Library of Congress; **11:** *(detail)* Library of Congress; **12:** Library of Congress; **14:** *(detail)* © The Newberry Library/Stock Montage, Inc.; **18:** Library of Congress; **20:** Rare Books Division, The New York Public Library, Astor, Lenox and Tilden Foundations; **23:** Stock Montage, Inc.; **25:** *(detail)* Library of Congress; **30:** Courtesy of American Antiquarian Society; **36:** Child's Gallery; **39:** *(detail)* Library of Congress; **41:** *(detail)* © Ewing Galloway, Inc., Rockville Centre, NY; **42:** Based on a detail, Library of Congress; **45:** Ohio Historical Society, Campus Martius Museum; **51:** *(detail)* © Collection of the New-York Historical Society; **55:** Historic Urban Plans, Inc., Ithaca, NY; **60:** North Wind Picture Archives; **63:** *(detail)* Library of Congress; **67:** *(detail)* Library of Congress; **69:** Library of Congress; **72:** *(detail)* National Gallery of Canada, Ottawa; **80:** North Wind Picture Archives; **84:** *(detail)* Historic Urban Plans, Inc., Ithaca, NY; **88:** National Archives of Canada; **90:** Courtesy of Abby Aldrich Rockefeller Folk Art Center, Williamsburg, VA; **92:** © The Newberry Library/Stock Montage, Inc.; **102:** National Archives of Canada; **105:** Library of Congress; **109:** *(detail)* Library of Congress; **113:** North Wind Picture Archives; **115:** Courtesy of the New-York Historical Society; **123:** Darryl Kestler; **130:** *(detail)* The Metropolitan Museum of Art, Gift of the Society of Iconophiles in memory of William Loring Andrews, 1939; **136:** Library of Congress; **139:** North Wind Picture Archives; **145:** Library of Congress; **148:** Library of Congress; **152:** Culver Pictures; **154:** Courtesy of Museum of New Mexico, Neg. No. 14388; **158:** Library of Congress; **159:** North Wind Picture Archives; **162:** The Historical Society of Pennsylvania; **164:** *(detail)* Library of Congress; **169:** I.N. Phelps Stokes Collection, Miriam and Ira D. Wallach Division of Art, Prints, and Photographs, The New York Public Library, Astor, Lenox and Tilden Foundations; **171:** Library of Congress; **175:** North Wind Picture Archives; **177:** *(detail)* Library of Congress; **181:** North Wind Picture Archives; **187:** *(detail)* Library of Congress; **194:** Courtesy, American Antiquarian Society; **198:** Library of Congress; **200:** *(detail)* Courtesy of the Arizona Historical Society/Tucson, AH#58,945; **202:** North Wind Picture Archives; **213:** *(detail)* Library of Congress; **217:** *(detail)* Library of Congress; **221:** Library of Congress; **223:** Bequest of Maxim Karolik, Courtesy of Museum of Fine Arts, Boston; **227:** North Wind Picture Archives

Volume 4

Color Plates

for *Conflict* between pages 118 and 119:

1: Private Collection/ET Archive, London/SuperStock; **2:** The Granger Collection, New York; **3:** Courtesy of Peabody Essex Museum, Salem, MA; **4:** Museum of Art, Rhode Island School of Design, Gift of Mr. Robert Winthrop, photography by Del Bogart; **5:** The Granger Collection, New York; **6:** Library of Congress; **7:** The Granger Collection, New York

Black-and-White Photographs

1: Library of Congress; **8:** Library of Congress; **10:** Courtesy of National Gallery of Art, Washington, DC; **15:** North Wind Picture Archives; **18:** Library of Congress; **26:** *(detail)* Gibbes Museum of Art/Carolina Art Association; **34:** © Collection of the New-York Historical Society; **38:** Historic Urban Plans, Inc., Ithaca, NY; **42:** Corbis; **45:** The Granger Collection, New York; **46:** The Connecticut Historical Society, Hartford, CT; **50:** *(detail)* Corbis; **57:** Library of Congress; **59:** Brown Brothers; **66:** Library of Congress; **69:** Corbis; **75:** Library of Congress; **77:** North Wind Picture Archives; **84:** Corbis; **88:** Gibbes Museum of Art/Carolina Art Association; **91:** Corbis; **96:** Darryl Kestler; **98:** Library of Congress; **101:** Arizona State Museum, University of Arizona; **106:** Rare Books Division, The New York Public Library, Astor, Lenox and Tilden Foundations; **108:** Corbis; **115:** Hudson's Bay Company Archives, Provincial Archives of Manitoba; **117:** Corbis; **123:** North Wind Picture Archives; **125:** *(detail)* Library of Congress; **130:** *(detail)* Corbis; **134:** Cliché Bibliothèque nationale de France, Paris; **139:** Library of Congress; **144:** North Wind Picture Archives; **150:** Library of Congress; **157:** *(detail)* Cliché Bibliothèque nationale de France, Paris; **160:** Brown Brothers; **165:** *(detail)* Library of Congress; **168:** Cliché Bibliothèque nationale de France, Paris; **171:** *(detail)* Library of Congress; **176:** *(detail)* Library of Congress; **178:** Corbis; **181:** Corbis; **183:** *(detail)* Worcester Art Museum, Worcester, MA, Gift of Mr. and Mrs. Albert W. Rice; **185:** Courtesy of Winterthur Museum

Index

Index

Index

Index

Index

Index

Index

Index

Index

Index

Index

Index

Index

Index

Index